By Joseph D. Bates, Jr.

SPINNING FOR AMERICAN GAME FISH

TROUT WATERS AND HOW TO FISH THEM

Trout Waters and How to Fish Them

Painting of Third Musquacook Dam Pool by Milton C. Weiler

TROUT
WATERS
and
How to Fish Them

By JOSEPH D. BATES, Jr.

Illustrated with drawings
by
ROBERT BALL *and* SAMUEL BRYANT
and with photographs

LITTLE, BROWN AND COMPANY · BOSTON

1949

*Published simultaneously
in Canada by McClelland and Stewart Limited*

PRINTED IN THE UNITED STATES OF AMERICA

Introduction

FOR YEARS I was one of those so-called "unlucky" fishermen who traveled many miles to supposedly good trout water, usually to come home with a creel that was empty or nearly so and without even the satisfaction of having battled a respectable trout and returned him to his native pool. To make it even more embarrassing, I owned an ample selection of the best of equipment. My wife would meet me at the door, quickly surmise the situation, and inquire with malicious feminine solicitude, "What was the matter this time, dear? Was the water too high or too low? Was it too muddy or too clear; too warm or too cold? Or just didn't you take along the right flies?" Then she would try to make me feel better by saying that Mrs. Smith reported that Bill Smith brought home half a dozen big "brookies" from the Farmington while John Jones hooked a three-pound brown trout on the Middle Branch and put several smaller ones back. She would stress the point that all this happened while I, with my expensive tackle, was out admiring the scenery.

Of course, a man can't stand this sort of thing for very long. Entirely too late in my lifetime, I began to ask myself why others habitually brought home big fish when the best I normally could do was to catch a few little ones which anyone with a suggestion of sportsmanship in his blood would leave alone to grow up.

It was scant consolation for me to realize that many other fishermen had no better luck than I. Of the fifteen million or so people who have taken out fishing licenses this year, it is safe to assume that more than fourteen million nine hundred thousand of them have little more than the slightest idea why they can't catch trout when they fish waters where they hope there are trout to catch.

All this added up to the fact that there was a great deal I didn't know about trout fishing. There still is, but it is fortunately in a relative sense. After many years of exerting an inquiring mind upon the vagaries of the art I have had it forcibly impressed upon me that trout are not quite as unpredictable as the uninitiated might assume. In fact, they are surprisingly human in their behavior.

They like to live in safe and comfortable surroundings, even as you and I. Their urge to travel follows such a predictable pattern that they almost surely may be found in certain places at certain times of year and elsewhere in others. When it is too cold or too hot, they go to pleasanter locations if they can get there, much as humans do. Like ourselves, trout eat little when it is too warm to enjoy food and under such conditions the angler had best fish for them where water conditions exert a more favorable effect upon their appetites. They have the human characteristic of seeking sheltered surroundings near where there is an ample food supply. The temperatures must be within their range of comfort. They eat when they are hungry and they ignore good food when they are not. For an angler to understand something of the foibles and fancies of the several families of the trouts and charrs is to open wider the door of success to him in his ability to catch fish.

Many of the reasons why trout behave as they do are highly technical and are found only in scientific books wherein it would take months to separate the wheat from the chaff, even if such books were well known and easily available. Few anglers will bother to delve into such works in an effort to improve their knowledge. It is hoped that *Trout Waters* will make it unnecessary for them to do so. If this book aids the angler in his ability to separate trout waters from non-trout waters; if it shows him how he can tell where trout live and when and why they live there, it will have served its purpose. If it indicates the wealth of detailed knowledge available in the sciences of limnology, ichthyology, aquatic biology, entomology and the many other 'ologies that are associated with fishing for trout, it will have done more than that. As an angler, it is surprising to me that no author previously has translated and abridged into the anglers' language the vast store of fishing lore contained in these books and scientific papers, adding to it pertinent actual experiences which will serve to illustrate the subjects under discussion, at the same time leavening what might otherwise be somewhat dry reading.

Trout Waters does not attempt to tell anglers *how* to catch trout. Many eminent experts have covered this field thoroughly in a wealth of excellent books on the subject. It does, however, attempt to reveal *where* to fish for them under the changing conditions of season, location and weather.

In this book I have attempted to explode several theories or beliefs, based on natural phenomena, which have been accepted without question by countless fishermen for ages past. Perhaps "superstitions" is a more pertinent word than "theories" or "beliefs" because if they have any scientific basis it is at present unknown. In place of these superstitions I have attempted to show that the seasonal locations and feeding propensities of trout are dictated largely by water temperatures, influenced by certain other related factors. I am unaware of any other nontechnical book which utilizes the firm scientific proof of this fact. Yet it is of vital importance to all anglers and a wealth of research is available to support it conclusively.

After reading *Trout Waters,* it is hoped that anglers will agree that trout are not as unpredictable as they usually are reputed to be. The fact that they always will be unpredictable to a degree is what makes trout fishing the fascinating sport that it is. I hope that no book ever is published which entirely removes the element of chance from trout fishing, even if such a book ever could be. I have fished in places where the catching of a limit of large trout is a foregone conclusion and I must say that it is much less fun than angling for them when their taking is more difficult.

No one man, regardless of his experience, is qualified to write a book such as this. No man, were he to spend a long lifetime in fishing, could ever glean for himself even a part of the information it contains. With all my heart I thank the brotherhood of

anglers and their closely related body of scientists for so greatly
enhancing the small amount of knowledge which I have acquired over the years. It is only due to them that this book could
be written and to them should go much of the credit for whatever success *Trout Waters* may achieve. Trout fishing is a noble
and an absorbing sport, but the friendships it develops and fosters
put it beyond price.

My good friend Don Harger of Salem, Oregon, sent me many
pages of carefully prepared information on Western trout streams
before I ever had met him or fished his Western waters with him.
Ted Trueblood, the eminent angling writer, took time from his
books and magazine articles to answer questions and to help
prepare material. So did Al McClane, Fishing Editor of *Field
and Stream* and Joe Brooks, Jr., author of *Bass Bug Fishing* and
other angling works. Milton Weiler, who so beautifully illustrates
angling books, contributed amply from his years of stream-side
experience. So did Peter J. Schwab, Reginald Ellis, Walter Dette,
Harry Byrnes, Jim Deren, Dana McNally, Jim Parsons, Harold
Traver, Gerry Wade and a long list of others.

I am fortunate that members of my publishing firm are also
excellent and sympathetic anglers. To Arthur Williams, noted
book designer for Little, Brown and Company, go my thanks for
his artistic care in preparing this book. Their editor, Angus Cam-
eron, gave me the original idea for the subject matter and has
improved the book greatly with his pertinent advice. Little did I
know what I was getting into when he suggested it!

The scientists whose lifetimes of study have contributed to
these pages are almost beyond count. The American Fisheries
Society has allowed me to quote from the published papers of
the eminent authors of its Transactions. Dr. Paul Needham, Dr.
George Hunter and Lyle Thorpe have been kind enough to read
parts of the manuscript and to offer valuable suggestions. Dr.
C. McC. Mottley, Dr. Dwight A. Webster and other experts also
have contributed much to its pages. To all these and to many
others I am deeply grateful.

The photographs in this book were taken by the author with

the exception of the following, for which he expresses his appreciation to Maine Development Commission, for the photograph facing page 129; Ross Hall, Sandpoint, Idaho, page 201 and page 249; Lake Pend Oreille (Idaho) Club, page 200; Don C. Harger, Salem, Oregon, page 216; and Oregon State Game Commission, page 217.

I have added greatly to my store of fishing knowledge in writing this book. If it contributes in a like degree to the pleasure and the angling success of those who read it, the labor of its preparation will have been more than amply repaid.

J. D. B., J<small>R</small>.

Contents

PART II

Characteristics of Trout Waters

Line — Positions Near Logs — Shelving Riffles — How
to Fish Riffles — Split Riffles — Where to Find Trout
in Pools — Limestone Streams

Winter and Summer Steelhead Runs — Size and Speed
of Fish — Time of Runs — Migratory Influences —
Changes in Appearance — Spawning Grounds — Steelhead Streams — Holding Positions — Unusual Methods
— Use of Salmon Roe — Attaching Lead to Line —
Steelhead Tackle — Methods of Casting — Steelhead
Flies — Favorite Locations — Unusual Water Conditions — Sea-Run Cutthroat Trout — Habits and Fishing Methods — Sea-Run Brook and Brown Trout

PART III

Fishing Famous Trout Waters

Wilderness Flying — Tiny Flies — Big Trout and Fly-
ing Ants — Feast of the Red Buds — Dry Conditions
— Deep Trolling — Old Log Dams — Landing Trout
without a Net — Seasonal Variations — Fishing the
Spring Holes — Stream Angling — Brooks and the Dry
Fly — Old Dave and the Bear — Fall Fishing — High
Water Conditions — Bars and Islands

The Split Bamboo Rod — Birth of the American Dry
Fly — Golden Days of Angling — Historic Flies — Early
Season Fishing — Naturals and Imitations — Water
Temperatures — Locations of Trout in Pools — Warm
Water Migrations — Fall Fishing — Recommended Fly
Patterns — Favorite Stretches — Decline of a Famous
Trout Water

Illustrations, Maps and Charts

PART I

Getting Acquainted with Trout

CHAPTER ONE

Family Traits

To Know Trout Waters, First Know Trout

IN LOOKING BACK over more than a score of years of trout fishing I dislike to remember the countless days when I hopefully fished trout streams and lakes in places where I now know that no trout possibly could be. Even today, in my years of more mature understanding of trout waters I often find myself fishing a promising spot and wondering at the same time whether trout are in it even though an intuition born of knowledge assures me that they surely must be there.

To differentiate trout waters from non-trout waters, it seems highly important that the angler first should possess a basic understanding of the family characteristics of the trouts and their first cousins, the charrs. This will become apparent when we realize that these various species of fish each have a liking for certain types of waters, thus basically establishing where they can live and where they can not live. Some varieties enjoy warmer water than others. All of them shun waters which are above temperatures in which many unsuspecting fishermen attempt to fish for them. Some are partial to fast water and others to slow. Oftentimes the same species will enjoy either type under conditions which can be predetermined. Water temperature is but one restriction to their choice of abode. The oxygen content of the water is another. While few anglers will bother to determine how much oxygen there is in the waters they choose to fish, it can be estimated roughly with absurd ease and with sufficient accuracy to assure the fisherman whether trout should or should not be in a certain place on account of it. Since oxygen content may vary widely in parts of a single mile of stream and even in the same pool or riffle from time to time, this bit of knowledge also is important in knowing where to go to catch trout.

Quite obviously, fish congregate where they can find a satisfactory supply of food in a media of suitable temperature. Yet certain waters may be barren of suitable food, or nearly so, while near-by spots on the same stream can furnish a sumptuous repast. The ability of a piece of water to provide food will vary with the weather, the season and the type of soil or rock near by. For this reason we should find trout in certain places at certain times and not there in others. The diet of trout varies depending upon the ability of the stream or lake to provide food which is to their liking. Thus, if the seasonal changes in diet of the trout are known and if the angler can determine what parts of trout waters provide such food, he then knows where to fish for them and has an idea of what type of lure he can present most successfully.

I sat on the bank of the White River in Vermont on a day in early June when the caddis fly larvae were emerging from their cases in the riffles above a likely looking pool. While both bait fishermen and fly-fishermen were fishing the pool without result an angler of greater knowledge or intuition fished the riffles with a nymph and took large trout in rapid succession. Here was an instance where an understanding of trout waters enabled one angler to take trout while all the others were fishing spots temporarily barren. The angler knew that the caddis flies should be hatching at that time of year. He knew that they emerge in greatest quantities from their resting places on the stones and gravel of the fast water. He knew that the surface temperature in the pool was too warm to induce trout to rise to a fly. He also knew that while the riffles were about the same temperature the turbulence of the water there gave it a greater degree of dissolved oxygen, more to the liking of trout under such conditions. His knowledge of trout waters told him all these things and furthermore suggested the type of lure to use. He was catching fish when even the worm and streamer fishermen were unsuccessful.

Trout, then, enjoy best waters which have a range of temperatures which is to their liking, combined with a percentage of dissolved oxygen which must be greater in warm waters and which need not be so high in cooler places. They require an abundance of food and are most usually found where food to their liking is most readily available. They also need peace and security and this may be found in the sanctuaries of deep water, under shady banks or near rocks and logs which offer them protection. They may emerge from such havens to feed, as did the trout in the instance just related, but they rarely will be located in stretches of stream which offer them no protection unless shelter be near by.

Trout demand all of these things, and others of less consequence, and yet the various species and subspecies of trout require some of them only in a relative degree, a knowledge of which also is important to the angler. We know that there are many species of trout. We are told that the brook trout is not a trout at all, but rather a charr. What are the differences in these various families of trouts and charrs and what do these differences have to do with finding them in trout waters?

In this book, simplicity seems best served by eliminating the difference between trouts and charrs and terming them all "trout," an appellation which is adequate for all but the truly scientific angler. For all normal purposes, the two types are the same. It is true that they possess certain structural differences, but these are of little or no value in helping us to find them or to catch them. Perhaps the difference most worth-while remembering is that the trouts have rather pronounced scales while the charrs have scales so tiny and so well hidden that a superficial examination of them would indicate that they have no scales at all.

In these two basic types of fish some authorities tell us that there are a score or more of species. To attempt to segregate all of these species and subspecies would complicate matters needlessly. In an effort to keep this volume nontechnical and thus attempt to put it within my capabilities to write it, and perhaps for anglers to read it with some degree of pleasure, let us immediately combine these many species into the six which seem most important. If we do so, the family trees will look like the table on page 7.

There are anglers who will be quick to insist that this attempt at simplification has caused the species to be combined to too great an extent. They may cite as an example their belief that the rainbow trout and the steelhead are quite different types of fish and that the Kamloops trout is yet another. The studies of eminent ichthyologists seem to establish that if any of these three trouts were transplanted to other localities they would revert gradually to the type of rainbow which inhabits the waters into which they were transplanted. This is true even of certain structural differences that have led to the isolation of the so-called subspecies in the first place. It is true that certain strains of rainbow trout mature in the sea and make their spawning runs up the coastal rivers after two or three years spent there; their silvery sides and oceanic upbringing earning for them the appellation of "steelhead." It is also true that certain types of rainbows do not choose to go to sea, even if they are free to do so. In the long run, however, if a few generations of these rainbows of varied habits were reared together under the same conditions, they eventually would be found to be one and the same species of fish, even if the types did not interbreed.

Another example of this is the Eastern brook trout. In small streams he rarely attains great size, yet in the lakes of northern Maine many have been caught weighing four pounds or better. Like the famous Kamloops trout of Lake Pend Oreille, which has established several world's records for these fish of late, the difference in size is due to the type and abundance of feed rather than to a difference in the species. Brook trout are caught whose flesh is tinged various degrees of pink or even a bright red while in other places the flesh of the trout is white. The red-fleshed fish have been thought by some to be a different species, their flesh color so closely resembling that of the salmon that they are often

CHARRS[1]

BROOK TROUT (*Salvelinus fontinalis*)	LAKE TROUT (*Cristivomer Namaycush*) also called	DOLLY VARDEN (*Salvelinus malma*)
Squaretail Speckled Trout	Togue Mackinaw Trout Great Lakes Trout Forktail Trout	Salmon Trout Western Charr Bull Trout Sea Trout

TROUT

CUTTHROAT or BLACK SPOTTED TROUT (*Salmo clarkii*)	RAINBOW or STEELHEAD (when sea-run) (*Salmo gairdnerii*) also called	BROWN TROUT or LOCH LEVEN (*Salmo trutta*)
Salmon Trout Harvest Trout Mountain Trout Blueback Trout	Kamloops Trout (in special cases) Shasta Rainbow, etc.	

[1] Either spelling, char or chars, charr or charrs, is correct. The derivation of the word is from the Gaelic, meaning "red or blood-colored," with reference to the reddish color of the belly noted on many fish of this species.

called "salmon trout." It now seems agreed that the flesh color is caused by the food which the trout eat[2] rather than by any difference in their family tree.

The matter of protective coloration is more pronounced in the trouts than in most other fishes. If a trout inhabits a stream where the stones and pebbles are light in color, his back will be such a pale green that he is scarcely discernible from the bottom of the stream itself. The same trout, transplanted to waters with a darker bottom, will take on the color tones of his new habitat and his other bodily markings will be brighter. I have caught trout in bogs and beaver ponds whose bottoms consisted of black muck. The backs of these trout were as black as the pond bottom from which they came. The speckles on their sides were as brilliant in color as those on any trout I have ever seen.

If these superficial differences in type are so unimportant, why is it that in certain trout waters the fish are so much larger than in others, particularly in ponds and lakes where migration from one pond to another is impossible? I have fished a pond in Maine where the trout are all short and fat but all very close to a pound in weight, with never one much larger or smaller. In another pond the trout may be long and lean, but all of nearly the same length. For many years I have been a guest at a seigniory in Canada possessed of a large private lake wherein one catches many brook trout but never one of over four pounds and rarely under two. In this relatively unfished lake why are not a few five- and six-

---

[2] On this subject, Dr. Dwight A. Webster, Assistant Professor of Limnology and Fisheries of Cornell University writes: "Various carotenoids contain the pigments which are responsible for flesh color in trout, in particular, astacin and astaxanthin have been shown to be responsible in many species of fish. These red lipochromes are present in crustacea such as copepods, daphnids, the so-called fresh water "shrimp" or scuds, probably crayfish as well as many aquatic insects and other invertebrates. It is also present in certain species of fish. The pigment is apparently retained and colors the muscular tissue of some fish, of which the salmon family contain well known examples, but produces no visible effect on others. For example, trout feeding on crayfish have intensely pigmented flesh, whereas smallmouth bass never exhibit any flesh color despite the fact that crayfish bulk large in their food in most waters."

pound fish caught occasionally? Where are all the little ones? In my explorations I have found the smaller trout thriving in the brooks and backwaters, safe from the cannibalistic tendencies of the bigger fish. As they grow larger, they move nearer to the main body of water until, large enough to compete with the big trout, they roam the wide expanses of the lake itself. As for the ultra-large fish, I believe that the inbreeding of the squaretails has caused their growth to be arrested at approximately four pounds and that none become larger due to the limitations which this inbreeding and the food supply have placed upon them. This is also true in the case of the short, fat trout which rarely exceeded a pound in weight. (Those of us who served in the South Pacific during the war have noticed a similar condition of arrested growth among certain tribes of natives in the islands.) The situation can not be ascribed to the size of the waters because I have seen trout in very small lakes which exceed four pounds in size. Trout in the Chase Lakes in Maine's Aroostook County are an example of this.

It is not usually inbreeding which causes trout to be long and thin. Lack of food in proportion to the number of fish in the lake is more often the cause of this. A lake can support adequately no more poundage of fish than its size and food supply permits. When a greater number of trout is in the lake, competition for food becomes more intense and each individual fish, having less, becomes slimmer or remains smaller in consequence. Even with an adequate food supply, this situation often is noticed in the early spring while the water is still too cold for the trout to overcome their winter lethargy and browse actively in search of food. Due to their near hibernation in the winter months they are thin and scrawny, with ungainly big heads and narrow bodies. I have taken such trout weighing two pounds which would have weighed more than four, were they fattened up. Such fish only deserve to be returned to the water so that they may become a better prize for someone else later in the season.

Water temperatures are a vital factor in determining whether lakes, ponds and streams are trout waters or not. Each of the species of trout will tolerate somewhat different temperatures. When waters exceed these temperatures, the trout will move to cooler waters which are more to their liking or, lacking the means to do this, they may die. Water temperatures have an important effect upon feeding, since the desire of trout to take food diminishes as the water temperatures increase or decrease beyond the optimum point. I have known people to stock ponds with trout when temperatures were too warm for trout to live in such places. These lines will explain why they should not do so. The fishing in a near-by river is good in the spring because of stocking and because large fish return to these waters for the winter. In the summer and early fall, fishing falls off to nothing. Water temperatures are the answer. And yet anglers consistently fish this stream all summer through, catch nothing save for a few small bass, and then wonder what has happened to the trout!

It seems agreed by aquatic biologists and trout breeding experts that the following should be considered the optimum temperatures within which trout will thrive and the maximum in which they can exist:

	Optimum	Maximum
Brook Trout	60° — 70° F.	76° F.
Brown Trout	65° — 75° F.	81° F.
Rainbow Trout	60° — 75° F.	83° F.

While the above temperatures are those most commonly agreed upon, certain latitude must be allowed to them due, for example, to the greater or lesser oxygen content of the water involved. Experiments indicate that brook trout will die at temperatures approximating 83°. Thus, while trout may live through necessity in waters slightly warmer than the maximum temperatures given here, they are not apt to be found commonly in such waters. At the other extreme, trout will tolerate near freezing temperatures, but they are most active and feed best in the optimum temperature range given.

During warm weather the surface water of a pond, lake or pool is always warmer than the water farther down. If all of the water

in a stream or pool is too warm for trout, they will have moved to
spring holes, up the brooks or down into the lakes where temperatures are within their range of comfort. If the surface water
is too warm but the water in the depths of a pool is to their liking,
they may be lying in the coolness of the waters at the bottom. In
this case, they may come up through the warmer layer to take
a fly, but usually they will not, except perhaps in the early morning, late evening or at night. Surface waters may vary as much
as ten degrees or more during the day. This fact has a great deal
to do with their interest in taking food. It explains why fishermen
prefer early morning or late evening fishing in warm weather. On
summer evenings, hatches of flies are more abundant and furnish
an added incentive for the trout to feed.

It always has seemed to me that anglers feel, because trout
are prone to feed in the early morning in warm weather, that they
must also do so in the early spring. Thus, they get up long before
the break of day, tolerate freezing lines and frozen fingers and
catch very little until the sun comes up, warming the waters and
giving the trout the temperatures in which they like to feed. In
early spring, when crusts of ice are on the brooks, I prefer to
stay in bed until a reasonable hour. I have noted that those who
do so usually catch as many trout as those who get on the streams
several hours earlier. Water temperatures are a vital factor in determining where trout are and when they will feed. They feed
most voraciously during optimum temperatures, very little when
it is colder and when it is warmer perhaps not at all. This is especially true of brown trout. When the surface waters are too
warm, they lie on the bottom and usually are indifferent to food.

I hate to think of the many years I have spent in learning fishing the hard way. Some years ago a companion and I fished the
White River in Vermont on a June day when the stream was too
low and too clear; the day too bright and too hot. I took a large
brown trout in the early morning but nothing else during the
rest of the day. We fished wet flies, dry flies, streamers and with
spinning tackle. We fished fine and far off. We could not interest
a fair trout in anything we had.

After thoroughly working a favorite pool, I found a high spot, sat there quietly for a half hour or so and tried to see what was in the water. It was most surprising. Partially hidden under rocks here and there were several large trout. On the gravel bottom of the deepest part of the pool, the very spot where I had been fishing my flies, were several others of respectable size, plus a few chubs. The trout lay motionless for as long as I was there. I directed my partner in how and where to fish for them. His expertly handled flies and lures were within their vision so many times that we could be firm in the conclusion that these brown trout would touch nothing. We returned to the pool just before dark. Knowing exactly where the trout had been, it was easy to put our lures in the same places. When flies again were unsuccessful, I tried small spinning lures, fished as near the bottom as possible. Although we worked the pool until dark, we did not get a strike from a trout. Without doubt, if we had returned to that pool late at night or in the early dawn, we would have caught some of those fish. Undoubtedly it was the warm water temperatures which made them disinterested in feeding during the day.

The next morning a friend telephoned to report that he had spent the week end ten miles away from where we had been. He and his party had fished a small woodland tributary where the pools were sheltered from the sun and fed by many springs. They had caught large trout all day long, especially during the morning and evening hours.

This occurrence should have taught me a valuable lesson at the time, had my powers of analysis been acute enough to understand it. It should have been obvious that there was little logic in fishing such waters under the bright, warm conditions which prevailed. Better would it have been had we observed the high water temperatures and immediately forsaken that stretch of water in favor of the cooler, shaded sections farther upstream, as my more intuitive friends had done.

Brook trout were natives of the Northeastern United States when this country first was settled by our Pilgrim forefathers.

At that time many of them were of prodigious size, often reaching weights of ten pounds and over in some of our larger lake and stream systems such as the Moosehead and Rangeley lakes of Maine. Today, a ten-pound squaretail is an almost unheard-of rarity in the East. In fact, a brook trout of five or six pounds can be considered a trophy fish well worthy of a place of honor on the library wall.

I have often been asked where one may go and be most apt to take a trophy brook trout. In the Eastern United States, the place most certainly is in the sequestered lakes of northwestern Maine. In company with Dana McNally, who lives in Portage, Maine, and who owns fishing camps in that unfrequented territory, I have fished those waters many times. Before knowing him, I had fished them with others, season after season, during the past twenty years. There I have caught some of the largest squaretails I have ever seen, but I have never landed one of over six pounds. If there still remain any true wilderness trout waters in the East, they are here, deep in the spruce forests with the moose, the bear and the deer.

In recent years, the brook trout has been transplanted to other waters farther west, just as the Western rainbow has been planted in the fast running streams of the East. The brook trout loves cold, clear water, whether it be in large lakes, little spring fed ponds or in mountain streams. It has been noted that he can not tolerate waters as warm as those suitable for other trouts. For this reason, we do not find him often in relatively warm lakes and river systems where the brown trout and the rainbow can exist. When little, he prefers the cold, tiny brooks of his birth, gradually working downstream when his parr marks disappear and he is able to fend for himself despite the cannibalistic tendencies of other large fish. Baby brook trout will winter on the bottom of the deep pools of their native brooks. Larger fish will move downstream, after their spawning urge has been satisfied and just before freezing weather, to winter in the larger pools of the rivers or in the depths of the lakes. There they will be found in the spring and early summer. As the waters become warm they seek the spring holes or the mouths of brooks, gradually migrating up the brooks as their desire to reproduce gradually overtakes them.

Neither the brown trout nor the Loch Leven are natives of the United States. The brown trout was introduced from Germany. His close relation, the Loch Leven, came to us from Scotland. These two fish, when first brought here, had certain minor differences in characteristics. Due to interbreeding, the two types in the main have lost those differences to such an extent that today, in most localities at least, they can be regarded as one and the same fish. Any differences today are largely in name, those in the East being called "brown trout" while those in our Western states are known also as "Loch Levens."

The brown trout is by no means as pretty as the brook trout, but many anglers consider him more difficult to take on a fly especially toward the end of the season when streams are low and clear. When he is large, he often is sluggish and puts up a battle less worthy than does the squaretail, but, unlike the brook trout, he is inclined to jump to a moderate extent and is favored also for this reason.

We have noted that the brown trout can tolerate water at least five degrees warmer than can the brook trout. This opens up to him a vast range of borderline waters in which the brook trout can not exist. He thus is becoming well established in many river systems formerly the domain of the brook trout, but which, due to deforestation, are suitable to the brook trout no longer. Because of this propensity for warmer waters, the brown trout does not migrate as far up the little streams to lay eggs as the brook trout does. He (or she) prefers streams less swift running and often can be found in flat meadow stretches not unlike the chalk streams so loved by his English cousins. Oftentimes, both brook trout and brown trout inhabit the same waters. When this is so, the "brownie" is more often in the deep, slow running pools, while the brook trout is in the faster, colder stretches. I have seen large brown trout run up small brooks in the fall, but this seems to be from necessity rather than from choice and is done only when mounting temperatures drive them from waters which have become too warm.

Large brown trout especially are notorious cannibals. They feed voraciously on smaller fish of every description, including other trouts. A few of them can clean a pool of every small trout in a relatively short time. For this reason, it seems unwise to plant them in river systems which are suitable for brook trout. When waters are too warm for brook trout, the brown trout often does well and offers good fishing when otherwise good fishing could not be had. Because of the voracity of the brown trout it is a satisfaction to me to catch them when they reach a size of two pounds or better and to remove them from the water. In so doing I feel that I am preserving the lives of many baby trout, enabling them to be fair game for the fly in seasons to come.

Much is being said currently about the ability of the new angling method of spinning to take large trout. Uninformed anglers use this as an argument to discourage use of spinning tackle on trout streams. Spinning, properly used, demands such light tackle that the fish has a better chance of getting away than the angler has of landing him. The matter of sportsmanship is not the point. Tackle of the spinning enthusiast can be just as sporting as that of the fly fisher, or more so. To me, trout are a crop to be harvested, but only by true sporting means. When a trout reaches a weight of two pounds or better he should be fairly taken and killed to make way for the smaller fish which have less rapacious appetites than he. If spinning tackle, properly used, takes the larger fish, more power to it. Let the fly man try spinning and use it as an auxiliary method to his fly rod. Both types of tackle have distinct places in modern angling. Let the fly rod man direct his attentions to his brother who uses this tackle to take baby trout with live bait. Such a man kills countless fish which should be left alone to grow up. Yet I dare say that that same man would not shoot a fawn when deer hunting. If he would not do the one thing, why does he do the other?

The rainbow is chiefly a fast water trout. He indulges in aerial acrobatics to a greater extent than do any of the other trouts, never giving up the fight until he lies exhausted on his side ready for the net. As such, he is to me the favorite of all the trouts. He is a native of our Western mountain streams but his exceptional adaptability to relatively warm waters has influenced his transplanting to Mid-western and Eastern streams where he is now prominent in numbers and in popularity among all fresh-water game fishes. He can be happy in waters much warmer than the brook trout will stand and even warmer than the brown trout enjoys. Give him a stream free of impassable dams and pollution, filled with turbulent white water, deep pools and rocks and he will multiply and prosper, delighting the heart of any angler who will try for him with a fly.

This tolerance of warm water makes the rainbow very adaptable to lakes and reservoirs which are too warm for the brook trout. Like his anadromous brothers, the rainbows which go to sea, the landlocked rainbow prefers a river system up which he can migrate when the streams are free of ice. Where there are rainbows in lakes, fishing for them should be good on the surface in the early spring. Soon thereafter they will seek the mouths of the tributaries, awaiting a storm and heavy water to begin the upstream migration in safety. Far up the streams their young are born, remaining there until they are large enough to compete with the adult fish in the lakes. When the spawning run is over, the majority of large rainbows return to the lakes for the summer. During this period, one rarely can take them except by deep trolling. They sink to the depths when the surface waters grow warm and remain there until cool fall weather again makes the upper stratum cold so that they may roam the surface once more to pursue their food and take the fly.

The spring upstream migration of large rainbows is a sight to behold. They will collect by the scores and hundreds in the great pools below negotiable dams. There they will rest for a day or two, finally leaping into the torrent of downcoming water, perhaps to be forced back and made to try again. One by one, dozen by dozen, they flash into the seemingly impassable current, forcing their colorful bodies upward with prodigious sweeps of

fins and tail, eventually to surmount the obstacle and sweep vic-
toriously into the relative calm of the river beyond.

Why some rainbows which can do so do not go to sea does not
seem known. The fact remains that in many of our coastal rivers
there are rainbows which remain there for their entire lifetimes.
No generic distinction is drawn between the rainbows which mature in the sea and those which do not. Those which go to sea do
so when two or three years old or at an age when they should be
able to defend themselves. They remain there for from two to four
years, eventually returning to migrate up their native streams
to propagate their kind. The urge to go to sea perhaps is an
hereditary one, present in certain fish and not in others.

In the sea the rainbow trout grow large and fat on a diet of
shrimp and forage fish. They take on the dark backs and silvery
sides of sea-run trout and return far different in appearance and
much larger in size than the rainbows which have spent their
entire lives in the rivers and lakes. Upon their return from the
ocean their bright color merits for them the designation of "steelhead," a noble fighting fish to test the skill of any angler and his
tackle. In the rivers, this bright color gradually leaves them to
the extent that, if they do not return to the sea upon completion
of spawning, they will revert to the brilliantly red striped coloration of the nonmigratory rainbow, from which they will then
differ in no respect save possibly in size.[3] While the steelhead may
reach a weight of over forty pounds, I believe that none of over
thirty have yet been taken on a rod and reel. In the coastal rivers
a steelhead of fifteen pounds is considered large and can be compared to a nonmigratory rainbow of half that size.

Steelhead return to the Western coastal rivers in small numbers during every month in the year. The large runs are in
winter and summer, the winter run beginning in November and
lasting until mid-March, with a peak during the month of January. The summer run brings in somewhat smaller fish, starting
in June and lasting until late in September, usually with a lull

---

[3] The Kamloops rainbow trout is an exception to this, as will be noted in
Chapter Eleven.

during August if low water conditions prevail on the streams.

The cutthroat trout, so called because of a bright red streak running under his lower jaws, is, like the rainbow, landlocked in inland waters and sea-run when he has an outlet to the ocean. His habits are very similar to the rainbow, in whose western waters he often is found. Unlike the steelhead, the sea-run cutthroat does not migrate far up the river systems. Neither does he go far into the sea, preferring to feed in or not far from the estuaries on the food of the sea and in a few months to return up the rivers with the tide. Thus, the sea-run cutthroat may be taken on flies or lures where the fresh water combines with the salt during changes of the tide, as well as in fresh-water pools. Many cutthroats have run up the Western river systems in generations past, subsequently to become landlocked. Interbreeding among these has given rise to many varieties, considered by some authorities to be distinct species, such as the Greenback trout, the Utah, Colorado River and Rio Grande cutthroats and the Piute trout, to mention a few. These are spring spawners, making their pilgrimages as do the rainbows, from which their habits differ very little from the anglers' point of view.

The Dolly Varden is a distinctly Western charr, less attractive in habits and appearance than its name might imply. Its range is from northern California to Alaska, where frequently it attains great size. A voracious and highly cannibalistic fish, whose manners are even more uncompromising than the Loch Leven, it feeds ravenously on or near the bottom upon fry of all descriptions and takes flies and lures with complete disregard for their lifelike appearance and action. As these fish grow larger they become less interested in flies and tiny lures and are more often taken on deeply trolled baits. When access to the sea is possible, the Dolly Varden may or may not be anadromous, making its migratory run in the fall. Landlocked fish are very similar to the brook trout in habits and resemble them to a considerable degree.

The Great Lakes trout, or togue, is lake-bound through choice, spawning on the gravel beds of the lake itself and rarely, if ever, leaving it. Unlike other trouts and charrs, he has a forked tail. His gray-green lightly speckled coloration is much less attractive than that of his more brilliantly colored cousins. Essentially a deep water fish, he most often is taken by deep trolling with spinners or live bait near rocks, or along the slopes of deep reefs, ledges or gravel bars. When the surface of the lakes is cold in the early spring or late fall, the togue may be taken with a surface lure or fly; notably with a streamer fly or bucktail. This is true especially of the smaller togue of fifteen pounds and under, the larger ones being more prone to seek deep water at all times of the year. When taken on or near the surface, the lake trout offers an excellent battle on light tackle. Upon being hooked he runs to his usual sanctuary in the depths of the lake, rather than carrying on his fight upon the surface. Upon reaching deep water, he has an annoying habit of sulking there, making it difficult for the angler using light gear to move him. Often this may be done by strumming the tight line, the vibrations thus caused usually being sufficient to urge him into action.

The lake trout prefers water between 40° and 50° and normally will not tolerate a temperature in excess of 65°. When lake surfaces warm up, he seeks the coolness of the depths, remaining there until fall. At such times, dredging with heavy trolling gear and live bait with spinners attached is the only way to reach him. He usually is lazy and a dull battler at such times, the ability to bring him to boat depending more upon strength of tackle than upon skill.

These are the six species of trouts and charrs most widely prevalent in the United States. That there are others of considerable local importance many readers will be quick to insist. However, the varieties mentioned here are known to comprise more than ninety-five per cent of the trouts and charrs taken by anglers in America. Others, such as the beautiful *Salmo aureolus*,[4] which is the Golden or Sunapee trout of Lake Sunapee, New Hampshire, and the *Salmo agua-bonita*,[5] the Golden trout of California's high Sierra Nevada mountains, are thought to be descendants of one

---

[4] This is considered to be a subspecies of the Eastern brook trout.

[5] Scientists consider this fish to be of the rainbow ancestry.

of the more prevalent species of trout discussed above, their distinctive characteristics being the result of years of isolation.

Knowing these brief facts about the backgrounds of these game fish should be of general interest to the serious angler. To understand where they live and why, when they make their migratory runs and where they go to do so; how, when and where they feed, plus the countless other bits and pieces of information pertaining to them all should combine to the credit of the anglers' success in understanding trout waters and thus of locating trout in them. Many of the points mentioned in this chapter are spoken of here only because they seem necessary in assisting the fisherman to get acquainted with trout. Those which have not been covered with sufficient thoroughness will be dealt with in greater detail in the chapters to come.

CHAPTER TWO

The Travels of Trout

How Migratory Habits Influence Angling

A N ANGLER who had devoted many years to fishing New
England streams excitedly told of the large brook trout he
had taken from a tributary to one of our large reservoirs just before the trout season closed in the early fall. "Beautiful big ones;
two and three pound squaretails," he said, "and the peculiar part
of it is that every year I fish this brook all season through, but
only can catch the big ones in the fall!"

The gentleman seemed most surprised to learn that his success
at that time of year, and his lack of success at others, was due
directly to the "facts of life" as they pertain to the several species
of trouts and charrs. Their basic reproductive instincts have a
direct relation to migratory tendencies and thus to a better understanding of where trout may be found at certain seasons of the
year. Usually, their locations may be determined with timetable
predictability. To know and understand this timetable is to add
greatly to the fascination of fishing and to the ability to find the
big ones. There is no doubt that "luck" is a contributing factor to
success in fishing. It seems to me, however, that luck is more the
result of knowledge than most anglers realize. One of my angling
friends quite regularly returns home from his expeditions with
three or four large trout, much to the amazement of his friends,
because our part of New England is not noted for its large trout.
Once I asked him how he knew where to go in order always to
return home so successfully.

"Son," he said, "I've fished these brooks and streams for more
than sixty years. I began with a willow switch, a hook and a piece

of string when your daddy was a baby. Then, getting the big ones wasn't much trouble, but it is now. I just think of what time of year it is and something tells me that there will be trout in Smith Brook, but there won't be any at the spring hole in the river. Next week I'll think again and my mind will tell me to go some other place. It never is the same spot for more than a week or two and I only can fish Saturdays."

The old gentleman had spent sixty years in learning where to fish for trout. And yet I dare say that if he had been forced to move to another part of our country his great local knowledge would have served him nearly as a total loss. He knew where to find trout from experience, but his years of experience had never told him why they were there.

Those who say that trout are unpredictable tell only a partial truth. Trout are far more predictable than most anglers seem to realize. There are many reasons which govern their predictability. The migratory urge to spawn is one of them. Others will be discussed in the chapters to come. To know the reasons why trout behave as they do, why they seek various living conditions at various times of the year, why they will be in one place at one time and not there at another, is to insure to a reasonable degree that the angler will fish over trout rather than over barren water. To know where to go to enjoy the best chance of fishing over trout is the major half of the problem. To catch them when one knows where they are is quite another thing. Fortunately, there are answers to that problem also, but the answers are not so conclusive as to make success in trout fishing certain.

The urge to spawn influences the locations of all trouts and charrs everywhere at certain times of year. It varies little with a single species regardless of location, but its timetable does vary somewhat between certain of the species. Thus, let us begin with the Eastern brook trout (*Salvelinus fontinalis*) and later discuss the differences which apply to other species. Since I have observed the spawning of the brook trout and have seen something of the actions of the lake trout during his reproductive period, part of the information herein contained is from personal observa-

tion. The rest of it is the result of experiences of competent ob-
servers. While knowledge of the act of reproduction is of no
value in helping the angler to catch fish, it is included here because of its great general interest and because it does not seem
that this chapter would be complete without a description of it.
Reproduction is the culmination of several weeks of migration.
Knowing where trout should be found during these weeks of
migration is of primary importance in knowing where to go to
catch them.

During the warmth of the summer, roe is developing in the
females and milt is accumulating in the males. Thus, as the coolness of fall gradually arrives, the urge becomes ever more increasingly pronounced for brook trout to lay and fertilize their
eggs. This they do, whenever possible, where the clear, cold water
of upwelling springs flows over the gravel beds of tiny tributary
brooks and streams far up river from the lakes, spring holes and
pools which they inhabit in the summer. If there are no tributary
streams, the trout may spawn in the lakes themselves, as we later
shall see. This annual pilgrimage may begin as soon as late July or
early August, or it may not start until much later, depending
somewhat upon the tendencies of the strain of trout involved and
considerably upon the increasing degree of coolness of the water.
While I can find no information to justify the statement, it would
seem logical from what I have read and observed to believe that
the spawning migrations of trout are timed by the decreasing
temperatures of the water as much as they are by the gradual
swelling of the eggs and milt within the fish.[1]

Thus it happens that trout fishing should be successful near the

---

[1] Experiences in hatcheries indicate that water temperatures are not a
factor there. In hatcheries it has been observed that the time of spawning
is the same, almost to a week, in certain strains of trout, but varies to a
degree in others. Waters in hatcheries are usually from springs and are at
nearly constant temperatures, so that this factor must be eliminated in determining what stimulates the spawning urge in artificially reared trout. Quite
obviously, the degree of readiness to spawn is the dominant motive here,
while in the case of wild trout the seasonal cooling of water temperatures
seems to be an equally impelling reason.

mouths of tributary streams and brooks for several weeks beginning soon after the first few crisp days of early fall have begun to cool down the temperature of the water. The influence of these cool days is more pronounced upon the tributary streams than it is upon the larger waters. Gradually, the little streams become refreshingly cold, awaking the adult trout in the big waters from their summer lethargy, signaling to them that it is time to collect and feed at the brook mouths for a week or two, preparatory to ascending the smaller streams.

In many northeastern states this start of the migratory run coincides with the closing of the trout season. Usually there are a few weeks of late fishing between the start of the run and the closed season; weeks when the urge of the fish to take the fly are as pronounced as at any other time of year.

At this early state of the spawning run, the fish may not be in the visible mouths of the tributary streams as much as they may be in the influence of the cooler current farther out in the major stream or lake. The incoming water dissipates itself in the delta far out from the tributary mouth, its extent depending of course on the swiftness of the current. Thus, the fish may be found in the larger body of water, where the cool current of the smaller stream mixes with the warmer water of the larger. This location is usually a good place to find trout, particularly when rainstorms have raised the level of the tributary, bringing cooler water and an abundance of feed downstream.

At such a place the fish which are getting ready to spawn first collect. They rest here for several days to feed and gain strength preparatory to continuing the upstream run. As these fish slowly move upstream, others take their places, until finally all of the fish which select that particular stream for their migration have begun the ascent of the water.

On the upstream run they may not tarry in the riffles and fast water for long. They will not remain in the haven of slack water behind logs or boulders. They will steadily work upstream, feeding as they go, and will stay in the larger pools for a night or for several days, depending upon their strength, the temperature and

volume of the water and the intensity of the spawning urge which
is upon them.

Many years ago, Joe Stickney and I spent a week or two in
late September on Cupsuptic Brook in the Rangeley section of
Maine. Fly-fishing in the big pools was so good that we soon grew

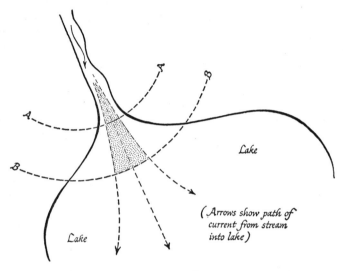

FIGURE 1.

LOCATIONS OF TROUT AT BROOK MOUTHS

*Trout may be found where cool water of the tributary
stream mixes with the warmer water of the lake, rather
than in the visible stream mouth itself. Best trout fishing should be in stream bed, denoted by shaded area.
Usual fishing locations are upstream of line A–A. Better
locations may be in shaded area between lines A–A
and B–B.*

tired of it and devoted several days to exploration. We walked
up what was then an old corduroy logging road, its timber base
long since rotted with disuse. This road, which goes in the direction of Canada, follows the brook and I am sorry to say that it
has since been replaced by a motor road, making what was once

a wilderness territory into a picnic area with less attraction to the angler who enjoys fishing in remote places.

As we walked upstream toward the falls, we occasionally would walk down to the brook to poke our heads through the alders in order to observe the trout. At this time, the spawning run was in active progress. The few days we spent in watching it always will stand out in my memory as being among the most interesting of my fishing career.

Cupsuptic Brook averages about ten feet in width. Composed of the accumulated waters of many tumbling brooks and bubbling springs in the spruce bordered coolness of the hills, it meanders through miles of relatively level ground which must have been at one time the bed of a lake. During this part of its length, before it empties into the famous Rangeley Lakes, its bottom is flat, composed of gravel and sand, which, with its clear, cold, steadily flowing current makes it an ideal spawning ground for the vast numbers of great trout which run up its sequestered and winding length from the backwaters of the lakes below.

We sat for an hour or two on the grassy bank of a tributary brook where it flows into the main body. Trout were everywhere, nearly uniform in size and averaging between two and three pounds. Here was one of nature's hatcheries at the height of its operation. As befits brook trout in spawning time, the males were bright in coloration, instantly distinguishable from the relative drabness of the females. Of the two sexes, the males were much in the majority and seemed to be the more anxious to get about the business at hand. Some of them felt the urge to travel up the smaller brook rather than to ascend the main body of Cupsuptic Brook. In this desire, the few females did not always share. Thus, an intrepid male would brush by a supposedly demure female and rush from the stream into the brook. If she did not follow him, he would pause for a moment and presumably with great disappointment would drop back to repeat the maneuver. In this the larger trout took the initiative. If a smaller male showed too much attention to a female, the larger fish would rush at him and drive him away. When the big trout resumed his attempts at seducement, the smaller males again would approach, always careful to remain at a respectful distance from the larger fish, yet near enough to take over his pleasant duties if he perchance should give up his efforts and go away.

Migration upstream seemed to take place slowly. We observed a brilliant and determined four-pound male make repeated attempts to coerce a big female up the smaller brook. As befits the female, she seemed to have difficulty in making up her mind, remaining purposefully where the waters met, rarely indicating the extent of her interest except by moving aimlessly for a few feet or so when the stronger of the sexes seemed to nudge her too roughly. Whether she could not decide which of these two wilderness waters to use for a nursery or whether she was undecided upon accepting the advances of the big male in case a larger and more beautiful trout should come along, I do not know. In any event, after half an hour or so of this sort of goings on, she made her decision and, with a final defiant flip of her tail, swept majestically up the little brook convoyed by the joyful spouse and followed by several smaller males who evidently had decided to accept their secondary roles as supernumeraries.

Next day, Joe and I went to observe activities farther upstream. In some places there were no trout at all, but in others they were so numerous that their numbers could be estimated but roughly. We looked between the tall grasses of the overhung bank into the stream below. In one place the bottom was level and sandy, scarcely shaded by the few alders which grew along the bank. The bottom here was solidly covered with trout which could have been counted well into the thousands. Seemingly callous to danger, they lay facing upstream, rank upon rank, row upon row. So many were there in the crystal-clear water that the bottom scarcely could be seen. They hung in the current virtually motionless, their pectoral fins gently moving and their tails slowly working to hold their positions in the water.

We sat and watched them for an hour or so. From what I have been told, the sandy bottom here was not suitable for spawning and we could observe no attempts of the fish to dig beds in which to lay their eggs. I doubt if there would have been room for them to do so. The gravel spawning bottom was farther upstream. Evidently these fish were not yet ready to deposit their eggs and were waiting patiently until the urge compelled them to do so.

Joe crawled back through the grass and returned with a fistful of grasshoppers. He tossed these in the water, one by one, but not a single trout made any effort to take them. I went back and dug in the sod for a few worms. Returning with these and a few other odds and ends of live food, I threw the handful over the trout. The worms drifted downstream, gradually falling to the bottom. One of them touched a trout's nose and he merely moved an inch or two away to give it room to wash by.

Upstream on the gravel beds the activity was much more pronounced. Here, the trout were fewer in numbers. Here, a half mile or so below the falls, was the end of their long nuptial pilgrimage, fifteen or twenty miles from their usual habitat in the lakes. We picked a vantage spot on a grass covered part of the bank and lay there for hours watching such a scene as I have never before witnessed and may never see again. Few anglers have had the opportunity of observing the spawning of trout under such ideal circumstances. Our stealthy arrival did not seem to have interrupted the trout. We remained motionless, lest they be disturbed.

Several trout were in the act of building nests in which to lay their eggs. These, as I later have been assured, were females. The males remained near by, occasionally causing a flurry of excitement by driving away other smaller males who ventured too close. Even though they chased the unwelcome fish for a considerable distance, they would return swiftly to resume their guard while construction of the nest was under way.

In building the nest, the female rooted about in the gravel to dislodge it with her nose and allow it to be washed downstream. This plowing of gravel was accompanied by a brushing of the gravel with her tail and by rubbing her body around in order to make the nest somewhat circular in shape. In doing this she would seem occasionally to lie on her side in an effort to use her tail as a spade. While we neglected to time this operation, it would seem that construction of the nest took an hour or more to complete. The nests seemed to be somewhat more than a foot in diameter and several inches deep.

We could see the male fish, who had been an inactive observer and guardian up to this time, join the female on the nest shortly after it was completed. Because of the turbidity of the water, occasioned by the motion of the fish, I am not sure that we saw the actual act of spawning. If so, it was with such incompleteness of clarity that I cannot relate it with any degree of accuracy. For this part of the story I must draw upon the observations of Dr. Paul R. Needham, who describes the occurrence most completely in his valuable book *Trout Streams* (Comstock Publishing Co., Inc., 1938).

Dr. Needham relates that when the male trout joins the female on the nest or redd, he forces her upon her side, the bodies of both fish being parallel and their vents close together. The depositing of the eggs and milt takes but a few seconds to the accompaniment of quivering by both fish. Eggs and milt are deposited in the nest at the same instant, with the result that the majority of the eggs are fertilized on contact. Nature has a way of preventing the eggs from washing downstream where they would fall prey to predatory fish. Each egg is coated with a glutinous substance which causes it to adhere to the gravel which it touches.

Immediately upon laying her eggs, the female again turns sideways and covers them with gravel by digging with her nose and tail on the upstream edges of the nest so that gravel will wash into the excavation and bury the eggs. As soon as the female feels that her nest is protected properly, she moves upstream to a point several feet above the first nest and starts to dig another. Whether by chance or intent, this second excavation serves additionally to cover the first one even more thoroughly. In this second nest, the spawning act is repeated; usually again in a third or fourth and occasionally in more, until all of her eggs are eliminated and the fish is spent. The male fish seems to consider it beneath his dignity to join in the act of nest building or covering. He remains in the immediate vicinity for the purposes of driving away other males who may attempt to usurp his duties and of dealing with smaller fish who may attempt to devour the eggs before they are covered safely. After the egg laying is completed, the female feels that her mission is ended and she soon moves downstream to spend the winter in deep water. The male may remain on guard over the redds for a period of two or three weeks before he also returns downstream to his winter residence in the deep pools of the river or in the lake.

Late September, even in Maine, is rather early for trout to spawn, but under conditions of cold weather they may do so, rather than during the more usual months of October and November. In any event, it may be considered that the spawning urge starts the upstream migration just after the first cold nights of fall bring an added coolness to the water. The end of spawning coincides with the gradual freezing of the brooks just before winter weather sets in.

Even if the laws of some states allow anglers to do so (and most of them do not) it seems very unsportsmanlike to attempt to catch trout in any manner when they have progressed to the spawning areas of the tributary streams. As a matter of fact, it would suit many farsighted and conservation-minded anglers if it were made unlawful to fish the tributary brooks at any season of the year. Small tributaries are nurseries for baby trout. They hatch from their eggs far up in the little brooks and remain there for a year or so, when they reach a length of six or seven inches. Then, better able to defend themselves, they work downstream as their size increases, until as adult fish they reach the deep pools of the rivers and the depths of the lakes, fair game for the angler and his fly.

Many ponds and lakes do not have tributary streams in which trout may spawn. In this case, they are compelled to lay their eggs in the lakes or not at all. I have noticed such spawning beds on several of the lakes of northern Maine. They usually have a gravel bottom and border the shore in a foot or two of water. As in the streams, it is preferable for spawning locations to have an upward seepage of water due to springs since such locations provide an excellent flow of pure water at an even temperature, and the gravel is less densely packed, making it easier for the fish to dig their nests.

When brook trout spawn in lakes, they frequent the spawning beds for a period of several weeks, usually arriving two or three weeks before the actual act of spawning begins. During this waiting time they remain relatively motionless in the water, occasionally moving about to clean the area of sticks, weeds and other debris so that all will be in readiness when the urge to lay and fertilize their eggs overtakes them.

I shall remember always one of these spawning beds on Island Pond in the Fish River section of northern Maine. Local residents from a settlement several miles away from this beautiful wilderness lake had built a platform of logs over the spawning beds in order to fish for the ripe trout with worms. Since trout frequent spawning beds for many weeks prior to the actual act of spawning, I wonder how many large fish these selfish people must have killed. Without doubt it is so many that the productivity of the pond will be impaired for years to come. To make matters worse, they built a fire on shore and departed without wetting it down, with the result that when the blaze was extinguished by the fire wardens one could have parked a large truck in the spot and walked around it in the ashes. Papers, refuse and tin cans were strewn everywhere. Such is the damage that a few thoughtless people can do!

The ethics of fishing on or near spawning beds would seem to demand that these places be left alone during the late fall weeks when spawning is taking place. If they are fished at other times, perhaps little harm will be done, especially if the female trout are liberated. I have never been very pleased with myself when I have killed a trout and found her to be full of roe. Since the dull coloring of the female trout during and just before spawning season distinguishes them so readily from the males, it is a simple matter for the sportsman to return them to the water, rewarded by the knowledge that in so doing he has made it possible for hundreds of baby trout to be born to provide better fishing in seasons to come.

While brook trout are apt to spawn far up in very tiny brooks, brown trout or Loch Levens (*Salmo trutta*) habitually choose somewhat larger waters. The act of spawning in all trouts and charrs is so similar to that of the brook trout that no useful purpose will be served by discussing this occurrence further. Brown trout are happy in waters which are five to ten degrees warmer than brook trout enjoy. Thus, the brown trout are not so apt to seek the cold headwaters, but rather to spawn much farther downstream on the gravel bottoms of pools and riffles of the larger streams. The time of the spawning runs of the brown trout coincides almost exactly with that of the brook trout, beginning with the first cold crisp days of late summer or early fall and lasting until the trout return to their havens in the deep pools and the lakes just prior to freezing weather.

It should be apparent that the basic fact to be derived from this chapter to assist the angler in catching fish is that careful attention must be paid to the timing of the spawning runs to make it most possible to locate brown and brook trout during the last few weeks of the fishing season and rainbow trout in the spring. During the spring and summer, the brown trout should be found in their accustomed places in the pools and riffles of the larger streams. Late in the season, the reproductive urge impels them to leave these places to work upstream to the spawning grounds. In some streams, these spawning grounds may not be far from their usual home. In fact, it is noted that brown trout may go downstream for short distances to spawn, but this is rarely the case.

Thus it has been observed that in the fall there are pronounced runs of large brown trout in small streams (usually not brooks) where no brown trout can be found in the spring and summer save perhaps for a few of the little ones. In New England the stocking of small streams in populated areas provides fair fishing for a few weeks after the season opens in the spring. Later, this fishing falls off to the extent that anglers ignore these heavily fished streams for the remainder of the season. One of the most successful fishermen I know of makes it a habit to return to such places just before the season closes. From one stream which comes to my mind he returns invariably with two or three large brown trout and tells stories of the others he has released. He is the same old gentleman who has fished these places for sixty years. He knows when the fish are there, but he does not know why.

Unlike the brook and the brown trout, the rainbow predominantly is a spring spawner. There are, to be sure, strains of rainbow trout which make their spawning run in the late summer, but this is not usually the case. The rainbow trout (*Salmo gairdnerii*) comprises both the sea-run rainbow or steelhead and the landlocked rainbow which either cannot or does not choose to go to sea. Both of these two types of rainbows make their migratory run in late winter or early spring, depending upon temperatures, water conditions, the locality in which they live, and upon the strain of fish which is involved. In this chapter, we have so far ignored the sea-running tendencies of the brook trout and the brown trout, certain strains of which spend part of their lives in the sea if they inhabit waters which allow them to do so. The sea-running habits of anadromous trouts are of sufficient importance to merit a chapter by themselves and are therefore described later in this book.

Rainbow trout which are landlocked, either by circumstance or by desire, are happy under the relatively warm water conditions which satisfy the brown trout. Where they can obtain sufficient oxygen they thrive in waters which may become as warm as 83°. This characteristic makes them ideal for stocking in large lakes and reservoirs where the waters may become too warm for brook trout.

If the angler knows that certain lakes or reservoirs contain rainbow trout, the streams and brooks which are tributaries to them should afford excellent fly-fishing directly after the season opens in the spring. It seems to me that the average fisherman relies far too much on the dubious knowledge of others rather than on the more successful methods of locating trout, a few of which it is hoped that this book will provide. For example, in the early spring someone telephones the information that a brook or river recently has been stocked with trout. We get in our car and go there, parking near a convenient pool where many other anglers possessed of the same information have collected. Whether or not we catch a few fish is beside the point. We have fallen into the rut of following others to less desirable, heavily fished waters rather than finding something better for ourselves. The fact is that if we had considered a few of the basic facts of local knowledge and trout lore we would have gone somewhere else and would have been much more successful.

Not far from my home there is a lake well stocked with rainbow trout. The boats which fish it in the late spring make passable catches, usually of small fish. While they are doing this, a very few anglers fish a rather unimpressive tributary brook and have the time of their lives battling migrating rainbows of three or four pounds in size. By the time this information gets around, the spring run is over and fortunately there are few who remember it from year to year. This is but one of numerous instances in a single locality where lack of knowledge and foresight forces anglers to be content with modest catches or with nothing at all, rather than to return with two or three trout of respectable size in their creels and the satisfying memory of the several others they have fought and returned to the water.

Rainbow trout love fast water. It is chiefly for this reason that migratory runs from lakes and reservoirs up the tributary streams occur in times of freshet after heavy spring rains. Thus it may be that even during the proper time for the migratory run there will be few rainbows in a tributary stream except under high water conditions. It is usually the case that when the waters are not heavy enough to allow rainbows to migrate upstream in comfort and safety, they may be caught near the mouths of such streams, where they are waiting for high water to enable them to make the trip.

Rainbows spawn wherever possible on gravel bars up the tributary streams in much the same manner as do brown trout. When there are no inlets to the body of water in which they live, or when passage up the tributary streams is prevented by falls or dams, the fish may spawn in the outlets to the lakes. I believe that under ideal conditions they may spawn in the lakes themselves, although I can locate no information to establish the fact.[2] Conversely, there are many instances of rainbows having been caught when they have passed by their spawning time and are in the process of absorbing their eggs. This is often the case when insurmountable dams have been built preventing the fish from reaching their natural spawning grounds. The fish, finding no satisfactory place to reproduce themselves, do not do so and the productivity of the waters suffers in consequence.

The lake trout (*Cristivomer namaycush*), which is also called the gray trout, Mackinaw trout or togue, is native to large, cold water lakes, and rarely, if ever, ascends tributary streams. Thus, the entire spawning operations of the lake trout are carried out in the lakes in which they live. This is done in the late fall, just before winter freezes the lakes, and for this reason the reproductive activities of the lake trout are merely of general interest and of no particular value in assisting the angler to catch them.

I remember vividly an occasion when we crossed a Maine lake late at night during a deer hunting expedition. The air was so cold that we bent hard against our paddles in an effort to keep warm. Northern lights shimmered overhead painting the entire sky with wavering shafts of violet and green. Ahead, the silence of the wilderness was broken by violent motions in the water. Drifting our canoe with the faint breeze, we came upon an area where great fish were rolling in the dim light. There seemed to be hundreds of them, since several were visible at a time, breaking the surface with their tails and dorsal fins. With their great size and their forked tails they could have been nothing else but lake trout.

---

[2] The Oregon State Game Commission states that rainbow trout will not spawn in quiet lake waters, but will do so when there are fresh running inlets or when wind action causes currents in lakes.

"There is a gravel bar here," said my companion casually. "The togue always roll this way when they spawn."

Next day I returned to the spot. There was not more than three or four feet of water on the bar, with a bottom of clean gravel, which could be observed but indistinctly in the slick made by the canoe, because the waves prevented vision into the water in other directions. Lake trout frequent such places for several days or weeks when the spawning urge is upon them, reproducing their kind in much the same manner as do the other species of trout.

I have heard it said that lake trout spawn in deeper water than this. Most anglers consider the lake trout to be far inferior to the brook trout or "squaretail" in whose waters he oftentimes lives, usually to the detriment of the brook trout. To get rid of him, some ichthyologists recommend introduction of smelt into these waters. The smelt feed on the spawn of the lake trout and are themselves excellent food for the squaretails. Therefore they do a double service to the brook trout whose spawning is less apt to be interfered with than that of the lake trout, since the brook trout habitually spawns in tributary streams beyond the range of migration of the smelt.

There are some who maintain that beaver dams develop ponds which are excellent breeding places for trout. Usually, I do not believe this to be so. Beaver dams are seepage dams whose crest is built up and repaired continually by the beavers, and if such dams are placed on migratory streams there is no possible way for the trout to get over them in order to reach the spawning waters beyond. I have observed many such dams whose presence is a definite menace to the propagation of fish. Despite this, in many states the Fish and Game Departments draw no distinction between a harmless dam and a harmful one.

At present, there is a large beaver dam on Fish River, in Maine, between Portage Lake and Fish Lake. This stream is an important waterway for the migration of fish, yet I doubt that a single trout can get over the dam. Many have tried to get through. They are caught in the maze of sticks as effectively as if in a gill net, their decaying bodies bearing mute testimony to the thoughtlessness of conservation officials. If families of beavers in locations such as this were trapped or moved elsewhere, it is safe to say that the free passage of fish would affect most favorably the productivity of the lakes and streams. The furs from a family of beaver can at best bring profit to but a few people. The improvement of sport fishing is of vital general interest. The revenue from it is one of the chief means of support of many of our states.

The comments in this chapter should in no way be construed as an encouragement for anglers to fish for trout in the vicinity of their spawning areas. The important thing to be remembered is that the migratory runs take place with clocklike regularity at definite times of the year. These runs last for several weeks, during which time the places frequented by trout can be predicted. During the earlier parts of the run and in the legal season trout are not yet ready to spawn and no more harm is done in fishing for them than at other times of year.

It is an often debated question as to how much food, if any, trout take during the migratory run. In its early stages it is known that they feed as avidly as at any other time. As the run progresses and the fish draw nearer to their spawning grounds they feed less and less. When the urge to reproduce is upon them in full force they feed very little. Analyses of stomachs during this period indicate an extremely small amount of food in them. Thus, fishing near spawning beds should not be as productive to the angler as fishing for the late arrivals farther down stream, regardless of the ethics involved. It can be reasoned that when spawning is imminent trout have things on their minds which are more important to them than food. Even at this time, however, trout may strike at a lure, not so much because they desire to eat as because it is a disturbing object in the water which they desire to kill in order to get it out of the way.

CHAPTER THREE

Weather and Water Conditions

Where Trout Live and How to Locate Them

NO TWO FISHERMEN I have ever known agree completely on the ideal conditions under which to catch trout. Most certainly, then, most of them will not agree with me. One man with whom I fish insists that a rising barometer is most productive while another is equally vehement in favor of a falling one. There are people who go fishing at times dictated by published tables based on the pull of the tide and others who think these are not worth the paper on which they are printed. Some will not wet a line when the wind is in a certain direction; the phase of the moon may or may not be an inducement; both bright and dark days have their advocates and so do the before or after rain theories. We could go on and on listing the diverse conditions which anglers think affect fishing, but it doesn't seem necessary. Perhaps it is a shame to attempt to explode some of these beliefs, or should I call them superstitions? The scientific research which has hidden for years behind words of many syllables seems to prove beyond reasonable doubt that many of these beliefs are more superstition than fact. So many fishermen have meekly acceded to staying home and beating the carpets when the moon seemed to be in the wrong phase, rather than roaming their favorite trout stream, that it might be well to bring some of these "conditions" into the open and see which of them make sense.

In taking this dangerous step, I shall try to eliminate personal opinions because I realize that those of one man are no better than another's. Where research fails to provide a definite solution I have polled the experiences of expert anglers until the

The barometer, and a knowledge of wind direction, is most important in determining what type of fishing weather lies ahead. This table, prepared by the United States Weather Bureau, is used throughout the world for this purpose.

Wind direction	Barometer reduced to sea level	Character of weather indicated
SW. to NW.	30.10 to 30.20 and steady.	Fair, with slight temperature changes, for 1 to 2 days.
SW. to NW.	30.10 to 30.20 and rising rapidly.	Fair, followed within 2 days by rain.
SW. to NW.	30.20 and above and stationary.	Continued fair, with no decided temperature change.
SW. to NW.	30.20 and above and falling slowly.	Slowly rising temperature and fair for 2 days.
S. to SE....	30.10 to 30.20 and falling slowly.	Rain within 24 hours.
S. to SE....	30.10 to 30.20 and falling rapidly.	Wind increasing in force, with rain within 12 to 24 hours.
SE. to NE..	30.10 to 30.20 and falling slowly.	Rain in 12 to 18 hours.
SE. to NE..	30.10 to 30.20 and falling rapidly.	Increasing wind, and rain within 12 hours.
E. to NE...	30.10 and above and falling slowly.	In summer, with light winds, rain may not fall for several days. In winter, rain within 24 hours.
E. to NE...	30.10 and above and falling rapidly.	In summer, rain probable within 12 to 24 hours. In winter, rain or snow, with increasing winds, will often set in, when the barometer begins to fall and the wind sets in from the NE.
SE. to NE.	30.00 or below and falling slowly.	Rain will continue 1 to 2 days.
SE. to NE.	30.00 or below and falling rapidly.	Rain, with high wind, followed, within 36 hours, by clearing, and in winter by colder.
S. to SW...	30.00 or below and rising slowly.	Clearing within a few hours, and fair for several days.
S. to E.....	29.80 or below and falling rapidly.	Severe storm imminent, followed, within 24 hours by clearing, and in winter by colder.
E. to N.....	29.80 or below and falling rapidly.	Severe northeast gale and heavy precipitation; in winter, heavy snow, followed by a cold wave.
Going to W.	29.80 or below and rising rapidly.	Clearing and colder.

WIND CONDITIONS

As a rule, wind from the east quadrants and falling barometer indicate foul weather; and winds shifting to the west quadrants indicate clearing and fair weather. The rapidity of the storm's approach and its intensity are indicated by the rate and the amount in the fall of the barometer.

The indications afforded by the wind and the barometer are the best guides we now have for determining future weather conditions. As low barometer readings usually attend stormy weather and high barometer readings are generally associated with clearing or fair weather, it follows that falling barometer indicates precipitation and wind, and rising barometer, fair weather or the approach of fair weather.

The wind directions thus produced give rise to, and are responsible for, all local weather signs. The south winds bring warmth, the north winds cold, the east winds, in the middle latitudes, indicate the approach from the westward of an area of low pressure, or storm area, and the west winds show that the storm area has passed to the eastward. The indications of the barometer generally precede the shifts of the wind. This much is shown by local observations.

During the colder months, when the land temperatures are below the water temperatures of the ocean, precipitation will begin along the seaboards when the wind shifts and blows steadily from the water over the land without regard to the height of the barometer. In such cases the moisture in the warm ocean winds is condensed by the cold of the continental area. In the summer months, on the contrary.

FIGURE 2.

HOW TO FORECAST WEATHER

net results of their observations seem to support the information here offered beyond any reasonable doubt.

When speaking of the effect of wind direction upon fishing success, our old friend Izaak Walton remarked, "He that busies his head too much about the winds, if the weather be not made extremely cold by an east wind, shall be a little superstitious: for as it is observed by some, there is no good horse of a bad color. So I have observed that if it be a cloudy day, and not extreme cold, let the wind set in what corner it will, and do its worst, I heed it not."

On the same subject, this patron saint of anglers says, "You are to take notice that of the winds the south wind is said to be best. One observes that

> When the wind is in the south,
> It blows your bait into a fish's mouth.

Next to that, the west wind is believed to be the best: and having told you that the east wind is the worst, I need not tell you which wind is the best in the third degree."

There are many anglers today who will agree with these seventeenth-century observations of the renowned Izaak. While he feels that wind direction is unimportant in deciding when to go fishing, he also believes that certain winds stimulate the productivity of trout waters more than others. This most certainly is because some winds are weather breeders bringing rainy or clear conditions and temperature changes which affect fishing. Modern meteorology offers solutions which are too complex and varied to be worthy of note by the average angler. It can be said that south and west winds bring warm and clear weather while north and east winds bring cold and rain, but latitude, altitude and barometric pressures influence these broad statements to such an extent that such observations become of questionable value.

On stream and lake I have taken fish when heavy winds were blowing and I have done so in calm weather as well. So have we all. We have noted that the windward shore of a lake should

offer better fishing than the leeward side because winds blow
surface food with them and drift it to the windward shore.
Usually fishing in a glassy calm offers poorer results than when
the surface is rippled by a breeze because the angler and his
equipment is less noticeable to the fish. Unless one is a student of
meteorology and can unravel the complexities of the science,
further comments regarding the effects of winds upon fishing
would make it necessary to present so many exceptions that the
observations would be ineffectual. I agree with anglers of many
years' experience who feel that wind direction generally should
be disregarded in determining when to go fishing. If it blows so
hard that handling the line and lure becomes difficult, let us
try our luck in more protected places.

If we wish to attempt to forecast what kind of weather is in
store for tomorrow's fishing, I prefer to trust the barometer and
the appearance of the sun and moon rather than to rely too
much on wind direction. Even if there has been bad weather
during the day, a red sunset usually assures fine weather tomorrow. A red sunrise should result in wind and rain. When the
moon is dull, rain can not be far away. A ring around the moon
foretells a coming storm and a double ring may be taken to indicate prolonged stormy weather.

For several years I have carried a small barometer with me
in an attempt to determine for myself what effect barometric
pressures have on fishing, without regard for their obvious advantages in forecasting weather. Printed on it is the statement that
when the barometer is falling or low, fishing is poor; while
when it is rising or high, fishing should be good. It also says
that a pressure change usually finds fish active but it makes the
obviously erroneous suggestion that bait should be fished deep
when the reading remains constant. This little barometer has
accompanied me on more than a hundred fishing trips. When I
had an unusually successful or unsuccessful period of fishing I
would return to our base of operations and note whether the
pointer indicated rising, falling or steady conditions. Because
of this bit of research I took a good deal of ribbing from my

friends, particularly since my investigations offered no conclusive information whatsoever. I caught fish at certain times when the glass was rising, when it was falling and when it was steady. At other times I did not catch any. This research with the barometer proved nothing, one way or the other, as far as fishing success was concerned. I have never met an angler who had sufficient information available to induce me to change this statement, and I have discussed the matter with a great many.

In an effort to check the lack of conclusions from my barometric experiences, so that this point could be settled beyond reasonable doubt, I wrote to several of the most eminent fisheries research experts in this country and posed the question to them. Their answers may be summed up accurately by the statement of one of these gentlemen who said, "There is no scientific evidence to support the claims often made that barometric pressure, phases of the moon, or other natural phenomena affect the feeding of trout." The eminence and experience of this scientist satisfies me that, in view of the conclusiveness of his statement, my barometric research need be carried on no further.

From this it should not be assumed that a barometer is useless to anglers. A steadily falling barometer leads us to expect a storm. As long as the needle ceases to fluctuate after a gradual rise, good weather will continue. A fast rising or fast falling barometer will bring high winds, frequently accompanied by rain. A glass falling very slowly from a high reading will bring a period of steady rain and little or no wind. Since the barometer forecasts weather for approximately a day ahead, this information is of value in helping us to decide whether we want to go fishing or not and if so whether to take our rain clothes with us or to leave them at home. It may influence our decision as to whether we will fish the lake or go to the more protected waters of a stream. It will not tell us, once we get there, whether we are apt to find the trout feeding or not, although it will predict stormy weather which should result in rising waters which often stimulate trout to feed.

The statement made by the expert quoted above may lead

us to doubt the efficiency of the sun and moon tables which have been published for several years. These purport to indicate the feeding periods of fish as a result of the inland influence upon them caused by the pull of ocean tides. I should like to support this theory because I have the greatest respect for its author. But disagreement is inherent among anglers and I am forced to list myself among those who have found that these tables prove nothing of value. I have purchased them every year and keep one of them in my fishing kit on my travels. When there is a good period of fishing I often record the time and then satisfy my curiosity by noting whether or not the tables say that I enjoyed my success during a feeding period. I have not noticed that the results are conclusive. Since this is merely a personal observation, I have asked several highly experienced anglers what their conclusions have been. There is a wide difference of opinion. Several nationally known hunters and fishermen depend upon them implicitly; so much so, in fact, that I am led to believe that their faith is built on something more than superstition.

Of late years various fishing tackle companies and other organizations have been offering calendars telling fishermen the days of the month when fishing should be best. Each day is indicated by the outline of a fish, some partly or wholly filled in with black. "The blacker the fish, the better the day for fishing" these calendars say. They are compiled on the basis of the phases of the moon and therefore are pertinent to the subject under discussion. To my mind, the gentleman who invented them was far more clever than the superstitious fishermen who use them. Scientists and angling experts seem agreed that there is no logical basis for them whatsoever.

The phases of the moon, as they pertain to night fishing, have their proponents also. The difficulty is that some of them believe that the nights which influence best fishing success are when the moon is full, or nearly so, while others maintain that one should go only when the moon is dark. Even the believers disagree! As an infidel regarding this theory and as a subscriber to the scientific

opinion that such tenets founded on natural phenomena are without basis, I have enjoyed good fishing and bad regardless of the
phases of the moon.[1] Being as busy as most people, it would be
difficult for me to select the day when the moon calendar ad-
vises me to go fishing, and then to be on the stream at the time
of that day when someone else maintains a feeding period should
be coming up. With everything narrowed down to that auspicious
few minutes, I am sure that a telegram would arrive demanding
my presence in Bridgeport. To my mind, the best time to go fishing is when the desire and the opportunity present themselves. I
refuse to clutter my mind with apparently baseless theories which
tell me when I should go fishing and when I should not go fishing. *Where* I go seems to be the important thing. A knowledge of
the habits of trout is of the greatest value in guiding me there.

The extent of darkness desirable in night fishing seems to be a
matter of choice. When it has been too dark to see, I have heard
big trout rising but, if the law allows, I prefer to fish for them
when the moon lights the beauty of the night and lets me see more
clearly what I am doing. In lakes at night large trout come into
the cooling shallows of the shore line to feed. Big brown trout,
whose feeding periods are more limited than those of most other
species, often feed only at night. As an example of this, a friend
of mine complained that he had stocked a private trout pool, made
by damming part of his brook, but that a few very large brown
trout were eating all of his small fish. We tried many times to
catch them during daylight hours and met with no success. One
method after another was attempted until our entire bag of tricks
became exhausted, save for one. During the day, we caught a few

---

[1] Partial creel census records of Fish Lake, Utah, for the season of 1941–
1943, were analyzed for evidence of a relationship between moonlight and
fishing success. For both trolling and fly fishing, the difference in the catch
at times of new and full moon was not significant. Further studies were made
over five years' time during the periods of the full moon and the dark of the
moon when over twenty-seven thousand rainbow trout were caught at Paul
Lake, British Columbia. After removing all factors of chance the scientists
agreed that "the difference in the catch between the two periods is not
significant."

small field mice. Late that evening we went to the head of the pool, hooked one of the mice through the back fur and placed him on a piece of shingle, allowing the slow current to carry him out into the pool. Spinning tackle was used because we felt that the smooth flow of the line from this type of reel would not pull the mouse from his tiny raft.

In the darkness of the night, we barely could see the piece of shingle and its occupant as it drifted slowly downstream, but as it began to disappear from sight it seemed that we could detect a swirl in the water near by. Could one of those big brown trout have seen the mouse and, if so, was he waiting for him to fall from the piece of wood? We snubbed the reel and twitched the mouse into the water. The big brownie had him in an instant and soon afterwards we landed the fish. The method may have been unorthodox but it proved to be effective. Later on, my host reported that he had rid his pond of the big trout by this means and said that their stomachs proved that they had been feasting on a diet of his stocked trout.

Whether or not the phase of the moon has an effect on fishing in trout waters, the intensity of sunlight certainly does. Trout may be in brightly lighted waters or they may be in the shadows, depending upon water temperatures, feeding facilities, hiding places and other less important variable factors. In the glare of bright light, they do not see as well as when illumination is dimmer. The brighter the light the less sensitive they are to the color and size of the fly. This will become apparent when we hold a fly against the bright sun and try to determine its size and color scheme. It is much easier to do so when we can inspect it with a minimum of glare. So it is with the trout. Since they can not evaluate its color and shape in brilliant light, they may rise to it when they would refuse it in less well illuminated waters where their vision is keener.

I have sat on streamside banks and watched the effect of sunlight on the positions of trout in pools. Invariably they would remain in the shadows. When the light reached their shady position they would move from it into a darker spot. In moving around, they would move leisurely in the shadow but would dart through brightly lighted water, when they had to cross it, in an effort to do so as swiftly as possible. Therefore, while trout may be less selective in sunlight, I believe that one is more apt to find them in the shade.

Rains seem to have little or no effect upon fishing success except as they influence the conditions of the waters in which the trout live. There are anglers who prefer to fish just before a rain; others who maintain their luck is best while it is raining; and some who think that the period immediately following a rain is the ideal time. Some like to fish during thundershowers and some do not. Warm summer rains always have seemed to be stimulating both to the angler and to the trout, whether they be thundershowers or not. Before the storm the stream may be a bit warm for good fishing. The trout are deep in the coolness of the pools, hidden under the overhung banks of brooks, or they may be lying on the gravel beds of spring holes where the water is cooler and more comfortable for them than it is in the body of the stream. The warmth of the water makes them lazy and disinclined to leave their cool little sanctuaries in search of food until the night air lowers water temperatures and stimulates their desire to feed.

Then, along come black clouds which hide the brightness of the sun. The rain falls and a bit of wind comes up. The gently lashing branches of streamside trees and bushes drop flies and bugs into the water. The stream gradually rises and cools down. The fish in their havens awake from their lethargy and look about. They see stream-borne food in the water and rush out to take it. A feeding period begins and the wetter the angler becomes, the more fish he may take.

Getting wet under such circumstances can be pleasant rather than otherwise. Attired in cotton clothes and sneakers, unencumbered by unnecessary creel and net, the angler can wade the stream and absorb all the dampness which nature provides. Soon the warm sun will reappear and thin clothes will dry like magic. A trout properly played can be lifted from the water without a

net and no creel is necessary if one has a towel to wrap his prizes
in and a game pocket in his fishing vest in which to store them
away. While being out in a heavy deluge quickly can cease to be
pleasant, gentle summer rains are to me a stimulating and productive time for catching trout, whether they be accompanied
by thunder and lightning or not.

During summer rains, either wet or dry fly-fishing is the ideal
method while the stream is rising. If the storm is a mild one,
the waters should not discolor to any great extent and the fly
may be employed productively all day. When discoloration starts,
little flies become increasingly useless because in the cloudy
stream the trout can not see them easily. Stream discoloration
usually marks the end of surface feeding and causes the trout to
go deep. Thus, at the start of pronounced cloudiness it may be
better to change to larger flies, such as streamers and bucktails,
and to fish them deeper. When the body of the stream becomes
badly discolored the alternative presents itself of fishing below the
surface with live bait or of trying our luck in the less muddy
waters near shore. Trout do not like turbid water. While the
body of the stream may be highly colored in the current, little
nooks and corners along the banks will be found which are
relatively clear. Trout go to these under such conditions to see
more easily the food which the storm and rising water provides
for them.

If the rain be prolonged, the waters will rise steadily and become swifter in volume. The trout will not fight the muddy
current but rather will choose to be in the deep holes where they
are more protected and where the water is clearer. There we
must go for them, using spinning lures or live bait fished near the
bottom, because surface lures will avail us little or nothing
at all.

Rains stimulate lake and pond fishing in a somewhat similar
way except that the muddying of the waters is less pronounced
and the water temperatures are less affected. Rains may induce
trout to feed, but where they will feed will depend largely upon
temperatures, as will be discussed in detail in the chapters to

come. During and after downpours it is most logical to expect that the rising waters of incoming streams will cause the trout to seek the stream deltas to take the food the water brings down to them. In such cases, where the muddy waters dissipate and become clear as they enter the lake should be the most productive places to fish for feeding trout.

Earlier in this chapter I have attempted to explode several superstitions connected with the influence of natural phenomena on fishing for trout. The anglers who read this book may agree with me or they may not. There is a wealth of scientific research and angling experience available to warrant relegating such beliefs to the field of angling nonsense which includes the suggestion that results will be better if we spit upon our hook for luck. I have tried not to go into such detail in disproving these superstitions as to make for dry and tedious reading. Each of us can accept or reject the evidence as he sees fit.

To compensate for removing these old wives' tales from the category of what some fishermen may have thought were surefire formulas for being at the right place at the right time to catch fish, I should like to present a radically different and scientifically proven concept which will assist anglers to select productive trout waters whenever they wish to fish for trout. The scientific evidence to support it fills many technical books and has been the subject of countless papers and theses written by eminent aquatic biologists. Since it immediately separates trout waters from non-trout waters, it is the underlying theme of this book and will be enlarged and elaborated upon in succeeding chapters.

Trout demand comfortable water temperatures in which to live. They must also have an available food supply, adequate protection and sufficient oxygen to allow them to breathe easily. Their temperature requirements are best served in an optimum range in which they feed voraciously, are lusty, healthy and active and furnish maximum sport for the angler and his tackle. Adjoining this optimum range are tolerant ranges of borderline temperatures, both warmer and colder, in which trout will live indefinitely but wherein they become lazy and semidormant; in which they feed and grow very little and thus provide increasingly inferior attraction for the angler as the water temperatures deviate farther and farther from the optimum range. Above the borderline range are temperatures too warm for trout to tolerate, which therefore can not be classed as trout waters at all. These temperatures are listed in Figure 3 and should be committed to memory.[2] In doing so, it must be remembered that they are approximate, varying slightly with species, altitudes, oxygen and other factors. Most biologists do not agree on the exact temperature ranges suitable for the trouts. All biologists agree upon an approximation of the figures as given here. While the use of a thermometer is helpful to the angler in checking surface temperatures, a bit of practice will allow anyone to judge them with sufficient accuracy by putting the hand into the water. Subsurface temperatures can be taken with the thermometer as explained on page 83 but, since this usually is a good deal of trouble, most anglers will prefer to estimate them on the basis of information given in succeeding chapters.

Before discussing further how to differentiate trout waters from non-trout waters by the additional requirements of oxygen, shelter and food, let us enlarge upon the interesting effects of fishing for trout in the borderline tolerant temperature ranges where trout can live but where it is too cold or too warm to induce them to take a lure with satisfactory frequency and vigor.

On a trip to Maine a few years ago we found that the season was fully a month behind normal and that the waters were too cold for the trout to respond well to the fly. Surface water temperatures were below 50°. In the pools where we were accustomed to catch large trout, the big ones would not respond to small flies at all. Those which took streamer flies or bladed lures were few and far between. They were thin, emaciated and with-

[2] The Temperature-Activity Table in Figure 3 is primarily for resident fish, as differentiated from trout which are used to the colder and more constant temperatures of the sea. Steelhead and other sea-run trout are very active in water temperatures varying between 45° and 55° or 60°.

out fight. Their large heads and slim bodies indicated that they
had not fed to any extent since the preceding fall. In another
month of higher temperatures, they would have weighed nearly
twice as much as when we caught them. Little trout seemed fat
and active. Quite obviously they are not as susceptible to low
temperatures as the larger fish. Occasionally a large trout would
lazily swim up to inspect and refuse the lure. Their actions were
not characterized by the smashing strikes of which they would
have been capable if the water had been from ten to twenty
degrees warmer.

This is a typical instance of the behavior of trout when water
is too cold for their comfort. During the winter they seek the
depths of large pools or lakes and are relatively dormant, eating
little because the cold temperatures have slowed down their
metabolism to such an extent that they are no longer hungry. I
have seen similar cases repeatedly early in the season and I am
sure that many readers can relate additional instances. The only
solution to the problem is to fish the bays, bars and shore lines of
lakes and the riffles of streams where the sun has made surface
waters relatively warm and thus has stimulated to greater activity
the trout that are there.

Experiments in aquaria confirm these facts. Trout will feed all
winter when the water temperature is above 50° but they become
dormant and feed very little when it is lower. As water temperature rises, the digestive and bodybuilding processes are speeded
up and the fish become hungry and active in foraging for food. I
have fished icy streams early in the season and have caught little
or nothing at all. This is the major reason why. Under such conditions it seems logical to wait for a few warm, sunny days and
then fish in shallow water where the heat of the sun has had its
effect.

Going to the opposite extreme, what is the effect upon trout
of water that is too warm? Basically, it is the same effect that
extremely hot days have upon human beings. Under such circumstances we eat very little save at night when it is cooler. It is the
same with the trout. We seek a cool porch or lazily rest under

AT WATER SURFACE TEMPERATURE	WATER IS	FISH ARE	FISHING SHOULD BE	FISH ARE FOUND	SUGGESTED LURES
FREEZING TO 40°F	MUCH TOO COLD	INACTIVE	VERY POOR	VERY DEEP (in lakes or pools)	BAIT FISHED DEEP
40°–50°F	TOO COLD	PASSIVE	FAIR	DEEP (or along shore lines or riffles where water is warmer)	LIVE BAIT / SPOONS OR SPINNERS / NYMPHS / STREAMER FLIES
50°–60°F	JUST RIGHT	ACTIVE	GOOD	NEAR SURFACE	WET FLIES / STREAMER FLIES / NYMPHS / SPOONS OR SPINNERS
60°–70°F	JUST RIGHT	VERY ACTIVE	EXCELLENT	NEAR SURFACE	DRY OR WET FLIES / STREAMER FLIES / NYMPHS / SPOONS OR SPINNERS
70°–80°F	TOO WARM*	ACTIVE TO PASSIVE*	FAIR	DEEP (or in spring holes, brook mouth, shaded streams)	LIVE BAIT / STREAMER FLIES / NYMPHS / SPOONS OR SPINNERS
80°F and up	MUCH TOO WARM	INACTIVE	VERY POOR	VERY DEEP (or in spring holes and cold water brooks)	BAIT FISHED DEEP

OPTIMUM TEMPERATURES

TOLERANT TEMPERATURES

* These ranges are more accurate for brook trout than for rainbow or brown trout, which are active at temperatures about 5° higher than shown here. While all anglers and scientists will not agree completely with these ranges, they are most generally accepted.

FIGURE 3.

TEMPERATURE–ACTIVITY TABLE FOR TROUT

the shade of a tree. The trout seek cool spring holes or the depths of pools or brook mouths. When I have known that trout are in streams which are too warm I occasionally have fished for them all day without result. In the evening or early morning I have taken trout from the same pools with the same lures.

Experiments have been made to find out the maximum warmth of water which trout can stand. This temperature varies with the strain or species of trout involved and also with the quantity of oxygen dissolved in the water. There have been instances where temperatures of over 75° have been fatal to brook trout. Aquarium experiments show that they become distressed at temperatures bordering 80° and die when the thermometer reaches 83°. Yet, in many cases, well-meaning sportsmen stock pools where summer temperatures reach this dangerous maximum and then wonder why the trout do not survive. Anglers fish such waters and seem surprised that there are no trout in them to catch.

Trout need oxygen to breathe, even as you and I. Under usual circumstances, sufficient oxygen is dissolved in the water to keep them comfortable. This comes partly from the photosynthesis of aquatic plants in the presence of sunlight. Occasionally we see oxygen rising from underwater leaves in minute bubbles which often dissolve before reaching the surface. These bubbles are not to be confused with the larger ones of carbon dioxide which rise from pool bottoms where vegetation is rotting. Since the chemical action which produces oxygen in underwater plants requires sunlight to complete the reaction, it can not take place deep down in lakes containing so much microscopic plant life that it clouds the water and prevents penetration of light. Thus it is that deep in some lakes which are not sufficiently clear plants can not grow, oxygen can not be manufactured and trout can not live. The depths of these lakes are barren of game fish.

The second source of oxygen in water is from the air, from which it becomes dissolved due to wind and wave action and aeration as the water tumbles over rocks and ledges. The warmer water gets, the less oxygen it can absorb. Even warm water, however, can absorb a great deal of oxygen as it mixes with the air. Trout may not come up through the warm layer of surface water in a pool to take a fly, but they may take the same fly in the same water temperature in riffles which churn oxygen into the water and thus make it more comfortable. This is one reason why trout often feed in riffles. The fact that there is a great deal of food there is another.

Quite obviously it is impractical for an angler to attempt to estimate the oxygen content of water. Where trout streams or lakes are at satisfactory temperatures, we may as well forget it. If we think stream temperatures are at a dangerous high, yet we know that the waters contain trout, we had best look for them in the riffles or below waterfalls where aeration of the water provides extra oxygen to compensate in part for the high temperatures. Lakes and ponds may be assumed to contain enough oxygen for trout if their waters are within the proper temperature range and provided there is not an excess of decomposing organic matter on the bottom, such as is found occasionally in waters which have been flooded by man or by the work of beavers.

Shelter is another primary requisite of trout waters. This is perhaps too obvious to experienced anglers to warrant that much space be devoted to it. Since there is reason for discussing it in chapters to come, it will be passed over lightly here. Shelter for trout in streams is provided by undercut banks, overhanging trees and bushes, rocks, logs and other underwater obstructions, dams and deep pools. In lakes, the depth of the water is in itself suitable shelter but many of the just mentioned factors should be included also. Shelter from what? Trout demand shelter from swift water and therefore they may rest behind rocks or in other places where the strength of the current is lessened. They demand hiding places from man, from fish-eating birds and animals, and from larger fish. They may leave these shelters for short periods to travel or to feed, but in such sequestered spots they usually will be found and there the angler should fish for them most frequently.

The feeding habits of trout is a subject so admirably covered

by so many excellent angling books that any detailed discussion
of it here would seem to be needless duplication. Charlie Wetzel
has written an indispensable treatise on it in his *Practical Fly
Fishing.* So has Art Flick in his *Streamside Guide to Naturals
and their Imitations,* wherein he pays particular attention to the
use of dry flies. Where the feeding of trout has a close relationship to their location in trout waters, I later shall touch upon the
subject. This book is concerned with where trout live, why they
live there and how to locate them. What they eat is a matter
which shall be left for the most part to other writers who are far
more capable than I on the subject. Where they find their food
under the constantly changing conditions of season and weather
is of vital concern to the angler in his study of trout waters and
it therefore will be referred to frequently in chapters to come.

The riffles of a stream are the meadows and the pools are the
pastures for trout. Trout are inclined to pass their days in the
sanctuary of deep pools and to travel to the riffles in the cool of
the evening to feed. In the riffles a rich abundance of trout foods
clings to the rocks, buries itself in the gravel and is dislodged by
high water to be borne downstream. Shallow, swift riffles produce
more food than deep ones, and to these places hungry trout go to
feast on the wealth of nymphs of the May fly and stone fly and
on caddis fly larvae, beetles, midges and other water-borne delica-
cies. Large trout prefer the more stomach-filling meals of minnows, crayfish and shrimp, but they will not pass by the tinier
tidbits to be found in the riffles. Their feeding chiefly is near and
after dark, when they leave their daytime shelters of stumps,
stones or logs or beneath undercut banks to forage in the shallow
riffles or backwaters of pools where they know that, regardless of
season, they can locate an abundant meal.

It is quite obvious that anglers who choose to study the habits
and habitats of trout in trout waters will hook more fish than
those who do not. In their efforts to do so, it seems that fishermen
who prefer to use artificial lures immediately divide themselves
into two categories: those who, from their knowledge of trout
waters, can select the type of artificial lure the fish are most likely

to desire and present it properly and those who, without reason, select something pretty from their fly box and hope the trout will take it. This latter type of fisherman is prone to fish a bucktail or streamer in places where natural minnows are not usually found. Whether or not he fishes it properly is still another matter. The bucktail may be badly overdressed; its bulk in the water bearing no relation to the slim, streamlined shape of a forage fish. These same anglers fish May flies when no May fly hatch exists. The fly may be of the wrong size or have a dangerous excess of hackle, yet this fisherman will blithely proceed with his efforts and be greatly perplexed because he usually does not catch fish. Knowing how to find trout in trout waters is of vital importance. Knowing how to catch them is equally so.

Pollution has turned many excellent trout waters into non-trout waters. Its presence normally is apparent to the angler, who can judge whether or not it is of sufficient seriousness to remove that part of the stream from the category of trout waters. If there is any doubt, it is better to fish somewhere else. Pollution may poison fish. Its presence may reduce the oxygen content of the water, because of chemical action, below the percentage which will be tolerated by trout. Sawmills are often disregarded as a source of pollution. An excess of sawdust in the water is most distasteful to trout, which will go elsewhere if it is present in large quantities.

In this narrowing-down process to determine where trout feed and how to locate them there are, then, five factors to consider. These are: optimum temperatures (or nearly so), adequate oxygen, freedom from pollution, an abundance of food and safety of shelter. Let us see how these requirements can be most easily estimated, so that we can determine quickly and without effort which waters are trout waters and which are not.

As far as natural, unpolluted, swift flowing streams are concerned, the amount of oxygen in them seldom falls below the minimum required by trout. Only under conditions of high temperatures and little or no current, such as might be found in quiet backwaters heated by the sun, will the stream's oxygen content drop to dangerous limits. In lakes or ponds with an excess of rotting vegetation or a superabundance of oxygen-consuming organisms, or in the depths of lakes where sunlight does not penetrate, there may be found too little oxygen for trout to exist. Thus, it should be simple for the observant angler to decide upon the matter of oxygen content and that of pollution by a quick inspection of the waters and to fish them or to pass them by in accordance with his judgment.

The three remaining requirements of temperature, food and shelter are similarly easy to decide by observant glances at the stream or lake. We can familiarize ourselves with desirable water temperatures and accept or reject the waters by feeling of them, so far as surface temperatures are concerned. Temperatures in the depths will be colder and may support hungry trout even if the surface waters will not, as will be discussed in the chapters on lakes and streams. These usually must be estimated, but this is not as difficult of accomplishment as it might seem. Surface and near surface temperatures will vary seasonally and even hour by hour, so locations which will be ideal at certain seasons and times of day will not be satisfactory at others. Many lakes and streams will be eliminated completely as trout waters for thermal reasons. Many parts of suitable lakes and streams will be eliminated for months, for weeks or even for hours for the same reasons.

Let us first then segregate our fishing spots for reasons of temperature alone and eliminate all other waters, either temporarily or permanently. Let us reinforce our decisions by a consideration of the abundance of oxygen and freedom of pollution. Then let us satisfy ourselves that the selected waters fill the needs of trout for food and shelter. Having done so with our applied knowledge of seasonal variations, we shall be fishing in trout waters indeed.

Since shelter means hiding places, we generally will approve of deep waters and ignore the shallows unless they be rocky riffles to which trout journey for food. Sandy or muddy bottoms normally will be passed by in favor of rocky places. In streams, the current will be fished to the exclusion of slack water, although there may be exceptions to this such as the deep eddies and backwaters of pools where cruising trout go to find minnows and other bits of food. Usually we will give up the bright sun-lit stretches and do our fishing in the shade. We will suspect that trout lie in the protection of large rocks in the current and under submerged logs and undercut banks. Overhanging trees and bushes always mean shade and a possible source of food and there too we should find trout, particularly if additional shelter be near by.

In rocky, swift flowing brooks or woodland streams an abundance of food can be taken for granted. In the deep pools of rivers, incoming waters of lakes and around their islands, bars and ledges, food usually is abundant. Riffles so shallow that it would seem they could hardly float a trout may contain fish of surprising size, particularly during the hours when the sun is down or on dark, cloudy days.

Following a great many years of angling it is my firm conviction that good anglers realize the importance of fishing for trout where there is protection for them. Such places are the spots they seek out first. Pollution is another factor which they immediately take into account. Oxygen and a food supply usually are present in fishable waters to a reasonable degree and, even if these factors are ignored, the travels of a fisherman are destined to reward him with a few fish. The one requirement, of the five which have been discussed, which anglers are most prone to ignore is the basic and vital factor of water temperature. While there is a range of only forty degrees in which trout will live in satisfactory comfort it has been noted that, of this, there is a range of but about twenty degrees in which trout may be expected to feed voraciously and to give anglers good sport with either artificial lures or live bait. Air and water temperatures vary so much from season to season and even from hour to hour that this vital twenty degrees becomes of paramount importance. Whether we are fishing over trout or not, if the water temperature is not in this optimum or near-optimum range, we will find the fishing either poor or nonexistent.

If this favorable temperature range lasts for a week or more, the angler can expect good fishing all day long during this period.

If it exists but for an hour or two, he will take fish consistently during that time only. When this range deviates more and more above or below its limits the trout will become increasingly inactive and less interested in the lure. The exceptions to this are very few, if any. Some may say that trout will rise through warm water to take a lure on the surface when the surface water is far above the optimum range. This is most assuredly true, but they have come from the cooler waters beneath where the optimum range stimulated their activity, and they will return to it as soon as they have taken the food they desire. If the subsurface range had not been within these prescribed limits, it is very doubtful if the trout would have risen at all.

I submit this direct relationship between water temperatures and the activity of trout not as a theory but as a fact. The vast amount of evidence to support it is only in an infinitesimal part my own. It is information compiled by noted scientists and fisheries experts over a long period of years and it has been reported in a wealth of scientific books and in the papers read before ichthyological societies. Since this is so, it seems amazing to me that it has been so inadequately stressed in angling books and articles of a nontechnical nature. I hope that by stressing it here this important temperature-activity range will guide anglers to the places where they can catch trout. Fortunately, the rule does not restrict the fisherman as to when he should or should not go fishing. It serves merely as a guide to where to go for best results.

Perhaps its happiest reaction upon me is when I think of the many times I have torn myself from bed long before dawn on freezing mornings to be among the first of those present on the April opening day of my favorite stream. Now, I leave it to the others to combat freezing lines and fingers. I have an excuse to stay in bed until a reasonable hour, after which I find a sun-warmed spot where the trout should be reasonably co-operative. More usually, though, I ignore the opening days entirely. Our New England streams are so cold that the trout are lazy and inactive in the very early days of the season. Even the worm fishers have little success and less sport. Now I know the reason why.

PART II

Characteristics of Trout Waters

CHAPTER FOUR

Why Lakes Turn Over

Water Temperatures, and How They Affect Fishing

THE FAMOUS AUTHOR and hermit-naturalist, Henry
Thoreau, was the first to observe the peculiar phenomenon
of "thermal stratification" which exists in certain types of lakes;
such as Walden Pond, near Concord, Massachusetts, on which
he lived a part of his sequestered life. Noting the warm surface
waters and the coldness of the depths of Walden, he observed,
"How much this varied temperature must have to do with the
distribution of fishes in it! The few trout must oftenest go down
in summer."

This comment preceded the birth of the science of limnology,
or the study of lakes and other inland waters. Little was known
of this subject prior to 1850, but since then a vast store of information has been accumulated. Much of this has a decided influence in assisting the angler to fish in the right places and
depths at the right time, and thus to catch more fish.

An annual red-letter day in the fisherman's calendar happens
in early spring in our northern states when the ice leaves the
lakes. One day their surfaces are great expanses of ice which
have gradually thinned and become porous and rotten due to the
increasing heat of the sun as the new year advances. The next
day, seemingly without warning, the ice has completely disappeared and the clear, cold water dimples and boils with the
action of trout and salmon newly freed from winter confinement
and anxious to fatten themselves at the expense of smelt, shiners
and other forage fish in the oxygen-saturated waters near the
surface.

It is then that the northern sporting camp owners send "ice is out" cards and telegrams to their impatient clientele of sportsmen throughout the country. Fishing gear and duffel are hastily collected and the anglers descend upon the reborn fishing grounds by plane, train and automobile, anxious to enjoy the superb surface fishing for which these lakes are so famous at this time of year.

Now, the leaping landlocked salmon, the swirling squaretail and the tugging, boring lake trout are on the surface, insatiably hungry and avid for the artificial fly or the properly trolled bait. Where there is the landlocked salmon, there is usually the smelt for his food. The smelt in vast schools assemble their ranks and begin their annual pilgrimage to the inlets and up the feeder streams to spawn. Here and there, the placid lake suddenly breaks into a shower of spray as the salmon lash into the smelt from below, driving their terrified prey to the surface, where they whip the water into a semblance of falling rain as they seek to escape the raids of the feeding fish beneath.

Daily, the salmon follow the smelt and the anglers follow the salmon. A fortunate boat locates a school and others collect in the vicinity as if by magic. Often trolling is unnecessary. The fly rod and the streamer fly is the favorite tackle. Many are the arguments around the cabin fireplaces each night over the relative merits of the Edson Tiger, the Supervisor, the Nine-three, the Black or Gray Ghost and other famous streamer flies. When the salmon follow the smelt into the rivers, fly-fishing from their banks is at its best, and few are the anglers who fail to return home with photographic evidence of the "big one that didn't get away."

While the salmon are on the surface, their leaping activity causes the angling interest to be centered chiefly on them. The fly which is cast for salmon frequently brings in trout, because the big squaretails share the abundance of food with the salmon and they enjoy the clear, cold surface waters nearly as much. Most northern lakes, of course, contain no landlocked salmon. When both species are in existence, their feeding habits are so similar during this mutual surface feeding period that it seems proper to discuss them both together.

One does not need to be an angling expert to take salmon and trout on the fly at this time of year. In fact, the element of luck frequently is on the side of the novice. For many years I have hoped to take a squaretail of over six pounds to replace the five-pounder which rests on a bark slab on my library wall. Every year makes it look less desirable as repeated dustings by unappreciative cleaning women mar the beauty of its fins. Late May or early June, therefore, usually finds me in Maine in search of a big tackle-buster to supplant the rather moth-eaten relic which still retains the family championship. To the readers of these lines who have had the same desire, the following story will prove that luck does not always follow the angler possessed of expensive tackle and better than average knowledge of the habits and desires of trout.

One year before the war there arrived at a small hotel on Lake Mooselookmeguntic, in the famous Rangeley section of Maine, a portly gentleman and his wife who both confessed their ignorance of the art of angling and their desire to learn.

"We're going to catch a six-pound trout," the confident lady announced, as we chatted together around the fireplace that night. "It's for Harry's new den. Harry just loves fishing!"

Harry, with pardonable pride, brought down their new Thomas rods to show to us. He brought their virgin tapered lines (which did not fit the rods), the expensive, if ill-chosen assortment of flies, and the leaders they had purchased, which were marked "heavy trout." Those leaders would have better served to moor their canoe! Bill Edson, who was my fishing companion and who was at that time a well-known distance fly casting champion, attempted to bring this collection of angling paraphernalia into a semblance of order by matching the rods, reels and lines as best he could. He presented them with a few of his Edson Tiger flies, which are always favorites for trout and salmon. He hired for them a good guide and spent the evening answering their many questions and in trying to convince them that while there *were*

six-pound trout in the lakes, one should not count on catching
them as frequently as the hotel advertising folders might indicate.

In the morning, long after Bill and I had started out, the canoes
bearing Harry and his wife drifted into sight. Harry's wife was
of the jolly, over-talkative type, who wore slacks with complete
disregard for the ample proportions of her figure. She fished too
close to our boat and her comments and requests for advice were
without end. As we tactfully drifted away, her canoe relentlessly
pursued us.

"Let's get nearer to that nice Mr. Edson," she instructed her
guide from time to time, and wherever Bill would put his fly,
there would Harry's wife attempt to put hers, unmindful of the
coils of line and leader which accompanied her inexpert, but over-
enthusiastic casting.

Bill and I took trout and salmon frequently. We had pinched
the barbs from our hooks and were releasing the fish without
taking them from the water, because not one of them was of
trophy size. Finally we stopped to light our pipes and to answer
the inexhaustible questions of Mrs. Harry, who was, of course,
fishing near by. She had laid down her rod, with the fly trailing in
the water, and when the inevitable happened, she was busily in
the process of inspecting her face for sunburn, with a little pocket
mirror that is the indispensable accouterment of every female.

The trout was big and hungry, and he hit her fly with a splash
like that of a brick thrown into the water. Fortunately, the reel
caught against the thwart of the canoe and kept the rod from
going overboard. I must say that she handled things well after
the first frenzy of excitement was over. The trout was well hooked
and nothing could have broken that leader! It was a battle between brute force and feminine determination from start to
finish. No ordinary rod possibly could have withstood it. The
lady's screams for help and advice, greater when the outgoing
line pulled her fingers from the reel handle during a long run,
were beyond comprehension. No engagement of such proportions
can last for long, and soon the exhausted trout was hauled in beside the canoe and then was safely flopping his great bulk in

the net for the well-merited admiration of the exhausted lady and the many onlookers who by then had collected.

Anything else that morning would have been an anticlimax, so we took the lady and her fish to Herbie Welch's taxidermist shop near by to weigh it and to have it mounted. It weighed six and three-eighths pounds and I think it was the largest square-tail taken from Mooselookmeguntic that season!

Whenever an angler comes home to brag of a big fish he has caught, the ample expanse of Mrs. Harry rushes to my mind. Frankly, my thoughts frequently are tinged with jealousy, because I could have reached that trout myself. I'm glad she caught it and I should like to meet Harry and his wife again to hear the latest version of the battle. I imagine that it differs somewhat from this one and therefore, in deference to the right the Red Gods give anglers to doctor their stories a bit, I hasten to remark that Mrs. Harry's husband was not named Harry at all. As a matter of fact, I have forgotten his name, but I shall never forget that fish or the way in which it was caught. I relate it in part to bring out the point that big trout roam the surface of lakes in the early spring before the water warms up. Later on, they seek out the cooler depths or the spring holes and they are found in the fast water of inlet streams where the flow into the lakes brings food, comfortable water temperatures and oxygen down to them.

Every angler who has caught trout, togue and salmon in lakes in the spring knows that there is a great difference in the ways in which these species of fish act after they have taken the fly. The tugging, boring, depth-seeking bulldog actions of the togue make it quickly apparent what type of fish he is before the angler can see him. The salmon is frequently in the air immediately he is hooked and usually he will jump several times before being brought to net. Rainbows (and brown trout to a smaller degree) are jumpers too, but rarely to the extent that the salmon is. The brook trout, or squaretail, is a top-water fighter and intersperses his runs with swirls on the surface, rather than with jumps. His rushes have a wavering motion to them that is easily transmitted to the rod tip to indicate the type of fish which has taken the lure.

During these few weeks after the ice goes out, the ascending sun warms the surface water more and more. Gradually, the salmon and the lake trout no longer come to the fly. Quite obviously something has happened to change their habits. Simply expressed, the lakes have "turned over"! What actually happens is less simple to describe, but the phenomenon is of utmost importance to fish life and therefore a knowledge of it is of corresponding value to the angler in determining when, how and where to fish most logically.

While lakes are covered with ice, the water just below the ice is slightly above 32° F. becoming gradually warmer toward the

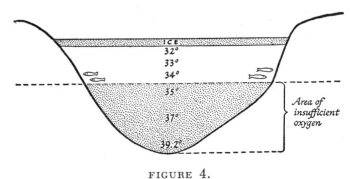

FIGURE 4.

WINTER STAGNATION PERIOD

Water is heaviest (at maximum density) at 39.2° F. Thus, water at this temperature settles to the bottom and both warmer and colder waters rise and mix. During this period trout go to warmest level containing sufficient oxygen.

bottom, until it reaches its maximum weight or density at a temperature of 39.2° F. *If the water is either warmer or colder than its maximum density temperature, it becomes lighter in weight and therefore will tend to rise toward the surface.*

This is called the winter stagnation period. At this time there is relatively little movement in the water. After the ice has left the lakes, the sun heats up the surface, which day by day be-

comes warmer; the warm layer sinking and extending deeper as
the heating process goes on. The action of wind and currents
mixes the warmed surface water with the colder water underneath until the entire lake reaches a uniform temperature of
39.2°. At this stage in the turnover process, all of the water in
the lake is at its maximum density. Therefore, since there is no
difference in weight between the surface water and that which
lies below, the winds can roll and mix the water thoroughly from
top to bottom.

The spring turnover stage begins almost immediately after
the ice has left the lakes. The time taken for the mixing process

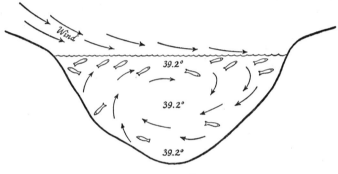

FIGURE 5.

SPRING TURNOVER STAGE

*As the sun warms the icy surface waters, they mix with
the colder waters below until the entire lake is at its
maximum density of 39.2° F. During this period, trout
roam the surface.*

depends upon the temperature of the air and is hastened by the
force of the wind. Thus, with a warm spring and steady winds,
it may take but a few days, while a cold spring and the relative
absence of storms may cause this period to last for two weeks
or more.

Trout are constantly in search of aerated cold water and food.
During the spring turnover period, there is little or no choice,

insofar as the water temperature is concerned, between the surface water and the depths of the lakes. Hungry from the relatively dormant winter period and bored with months-long diet of nymph-creepers, shrimp and other bottom feed, they roam the surface for top-water minnows and early hatches of flies. There, they also enjoy the abundance of oxygen which wind and wave dissolves into the surface water.

From the time the ice goes out to and through the spring turnover period is, then, one of the active surface feeding times for big trout in lakes. It is then that the giant Kamloops rainbows and cutthroat trout of Lake Pend Oreille seek and devour the smaller sockeye salmon and whitefish on or near the surface. It is then that the biggest squaretails and lake trout of Maine feed on smelt and shiners and are avid for the trolled or cast streamer fly. And so it goes throughout the tens of thousands of lakes in our northern latitudes, wherever lakes freeze over in the winter and clear themselves of ice in the spring. While the surface water is cold, the "big ones" come up to feed, and they furnish thrilling sport for the surface angler as long as the cold top-water lasts.

It has always seemed to me that the best trout fishing in the spring is a week or two *after* the ice leaves the lakes, when the sun has warmed the surface waters to higher than their winter temperature of nearly 32°. Landlocked salmon seem more active in near freezing temperatures than do trout, and the best fishing for them is usually immediately after the ice goes out. From my experiences, this is not so with squaretail trout, even if it be so with lake trout and landlocked salmon.

For many years, I have fished the waters of Maine and Canada as soon as their freedom from ice permits me to do so. In many places on the lakes there, I know that there are trout as well as salmon. Yet very early in the season the salmon come to the fly and the trout, for the most part, do not. Those trout that are taken usually have seemed thin and without life, while the salmon, caught at the same time, were fat and full of fight.

As the days go by and the sun warms the surface water, I

believe that the warmer temperatures induce the trout to feed.
The more they feed, the more active they become. So long as the
surface water is cold, but somewhat less than its winter temperature, both trout and salmon are fair game for the fly. As the surface water warms, the salmon drop down to the colder depths.

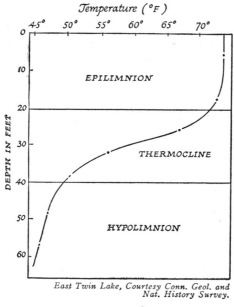

East Twin Lake, Courtesy Conn. Geol. and
Nat. History Survey.

FIGURE 6.

TYPICAL TEMPERATURE CURVE FOR
THERMAL STRATIFICATION

Thus, while a certain spot in a lake may be excellent for salmon
when the ice leaves, and trout at that time seldom may be caught
there, a few warm days will bring the trout to the fly, and both
species of fish may be taken on the same type of lure in the same
spot at the same time. When the salmon seek the colder water, the
trout remain near the surface and furnish good top-water sport
long after the salmon are gone.

Salmon, then, seem to come to the fly from "ice-out" time to
and through the spring turnover stage. Trout fishing is excellent

during the turnover stage and into the summer stagnation period, but it is not at its best until the spring turnover stage commences.

The summer stagnation period begins immediately after the ending of the spring turnover stage and it lasts as long as warm weather continues. As the air temperature rises, the surface

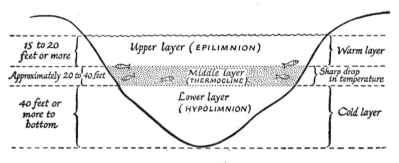

FIGURE 7.

SUMMER STAGNATION PERIOD

After the spring turnover, further surface heating causes warm water to remain on top while the heavier cold water stays at the bottom. A transitional layer separates the two. Trout are in or near the middle layer.

waters become gradually warmer. As they become warmer, they become lighter. The density of the water and its temperature are so related that complete circulation of water can not take place when warm water (above 39.2°) is on the top and colder water is beneath, in lakes so deep that the action of the winds cannot mix it. Thus, when the surface waters become increasingly warmer a period of thermal stratification sets in, known as the summer stagnation period, in which the lake divides itself into three definite temperature layers. The warm water remains on the surface, the cold water stays on the bottom, and, between the two, there is a transitional layer in which the water temperature takes a very decided drop between the upper and lower layers.

Herein lies one of the most important reasons why fishing may be good in parts of a lake at certain times and poor at others. It clears up many of the so-called mysteries of the changes which take place in fishing conditions throughout the season. It helps anglers to know where the various species of fish may be expected to be and it gives at least a partial reason why. It also influences the choice of lures and fishing methods which should be most successful and it immediately discourages methods which, once lake conditions are understood, are quite obviously of no value at all.

The upper thermal layer has the rather imposing technical name of "epilimnion." In it, the water is almost uniformly warm, varying only a few degrees between the surface temperature and that of the upper side of the middle layer. This upper layer normally has a depth of from fifteen to twenty-five feet or more, depending largely upon the size and shape of the lake, the surface temperatures and the extent and direction of the prevailing winds which cause the surface waters to mix. In ponds and shallow types of lakes, with a depth of twenty-five feet or less, all of the water may be regarded as the epilimnion, since these lakes usually are too shallow to permit thermal stratification.

The middle layer, dividing the upper and lower layers, is the transitional area for the vastly divergent temperatures between the two. It is called the "thermocline," and is usually between twenty and forty feet in depth. The thermocline stratum is defined as the zone where the drop in temperature is at least one degree Centigrade per meter in depth. To those of us who are not used to thinking in terms of the decimal system, it may be roughly considered that waters in the thermocline vary at least one half a degree Fahrenheit per foot of depth. Since the thermocline separates the warm upper layer and the cold lower layer, it has a very sharp drop in temperature; perhaps, for example, as high as 76° in its upper part and 45° at its lower level. The lower level, known as the "hypolimnion" is, like the upper layer, fairly constant in temperature, rarely varying more than five or six degrees between its top and bottom. It is usually the deepest of the three layers, its thickness depending, of course, upon the depth of the lake and weather conditions.

Summer water currents and the action of wind and wave on the surface tend to make the warm surface water mix with the colder water below the thermocline. The colder water is heavier and resists this mixing. This results in layers nearly as well defined as oil or gasoline on water, with the cushioning effect of the thermocline in between.

When we stop to think that trout are cold water fish which do not prefer high temperatures, this matter of thermal stratification takes on considerable importance to anglers, yet the tendency of

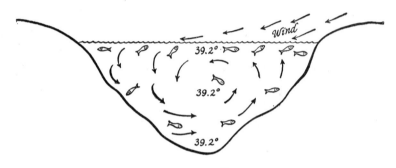

FIGURE 8.

FALL TURNOVER STAGE

Cold fall weather reduces surface water temperatures, allowing the lake to again reach uniform maximum density. The waters mix again, as in the spring turn- over stage. Trout again come to the surface.

trout to seek cold water is only one of several reasons why it is valuable in understanding fishing conditions and what to do about them.

With the coming of cold fall weather, the period of thermal stratification reaches its end, and the reverse of the spring turn- over stage takes place. The cold days and nights gradually reduce the temperature of the surface water until it is colder than the water immediately below. As this water becomes colder, it be- comes heavier, sinking gradually to displace the warmer water

underneath. This fall stage continues until all of the water has
again reached a. temperature approaching that of maximum
density, or 39.2°.

It is at this time, with the breaking up of thermal stratification
and the cooling of surface waters, that fall fishing is at its best,
for the same reasons that it is good in the spring. Big squaretails
forsake the spring holes and the depths to roam the lakes whose
surface waters had been too warm during the summer. Togue
and salmon return to the surface and will take the fly. Even in the
lower altitudes, nights are crisp and cold, days are bright and
sunny and the woods are dry and brilliant with fall colors.

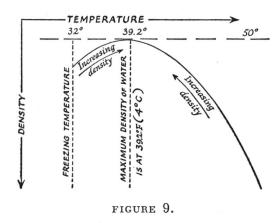

FIGURE 9.

WATER IS HEAVIEST AT ITS MAXIMUM
DENSITY OF 39.2°

*Thus, water at this temperature seeks the bottom and
water at both higher and lower temperatures rises
toward the surface.*

With the advent of freezing weather, the winter stagnation
period begins again, and the cycle has been completed. As the
surface waters approach the freezing point, they become lighter,
and therefore stay on top. Ice forms on the northern lakes often
to a depth of three feet or more and the anglers who live in this
area have put away their gear or have journeyed west for steel-

head and salmon or south to continue their sport in warmer waters.

As we reflect upon this phenomenon of the thermal stratification of lakes, we realize that it explains why lakes do not freeze solidly from top to bottom during cold weather. If water at temperatures lower than 39.2° were heavier, rather than lighter, lakes might freeze at the bottom as well as at the top!

To understand fishing during these periods, one must study the requirements of trout as well as the peculiarities of the waters in which they live. Brook trout prefer water colder than 70°, although some strains can do well in shallow ponds where the water temperature is 75° or even higher, provided that warm-water game fishes, such as bass, perch and pickerel do not exist to compete with them for food. Brown trout, rainbows and most other species can tolerate even warmer temperatures, running as high as 81° for brownies and 83° for rainbows.

There is danger in making arbitrary statements concerning maximum, minimum and optimum temperatures for trout. Various strains of fish vary in their ability to exist under high temperature conditions. Authorities seem to agree, however, that trout prefer temperatures in the vicinity of 60°, and that water between 50° and 70° is entirely satisfactory for their existence. Oxygen and the presence of adequate food supply are even more important than temperature. The higher the water temperature, the less dissolved oxygen it will hold. Thus, in warm water, trout frequently are to be found in riffs and fast water where surface action increases its oxygen content.

In many lakes, in Maine and other far northern states, during the summer the water surface temperature does not go above 70°. Therefore, regardless of water stratification, it would seem that trout should take the fly on the surface. In many cases this is true, especially in the early morning when surface waters are cool and in the evening when the trout move into the warmer waters to feed. Large trout seem to prefer optimum temperatures even more than the smaller trout do. Thus, even if the surface water is of a temperature which is tolerable, the larger fish may prefer the cooler spring holes or the mouths of brooks, and they usually do.

One of the important reasons for understanding water stratification is that it partially explains why trout may be on or near the surface at certain times of year and why they may be at different levels at other times. Since the upper layer varies little in temperature, the fish may find it too warm for comfort and will thus be in or near the thermocline or even in the bottom layer. The bodies of fish adjust their temperatures to that of the water in which they live. If we catch a fish on the surface, when the water is warm, the body of the fish will be similarly warm. If, however, we should troll deep with a copper line and catch a fish in the cold water near the thermocline, the fish will be as cold to the touch as is the water from which he has just been taken.

The water temperature has a decided effect upon his activity and his feeding habits. Fish grow more slowly at lower temperatures. They eat more slowly and digest less readily. Their metabolism, like that of other cold-blooded animals, is dictated by environment. For this reason anglers have noted, when fishing in very cold water, that trout are apt to be sluggish and to come less readily to a lure. In fact, under such cold water conditions, it frequently is true that they will not come to the fly at all.

The depth from which a fish is taken may not affect his desire to feed, but it has a definite relationship to his activity. One need only bring up a trout, salmon or togue from the depths of a lake to find out how true this is. When togue (lake trout, or gray trout as they are variously termed) are taken on the surface in the spring or fall, they are as lively fighters as one could desire. Pulled up from the depths, they are so lacking in activity as to have their action likened to the hackneyed expression "pulling in an old boot." This is also true because, taken from the bottom, the lighter surface pressure, to which they have not been accustomed, is so exhausting that the fight is over almost before it has begun. Deep in the lake, the pressure upon them is that of a column of water bounded by their length, width, and the distance to the surface, plus the pressure of the atmosphere. Deprived of the crushing effect of the 64 pound per cubic foot weight of water above them, their bodies expand and their bodily functions are so greatly disturbed that they may be virtually dead when they reach the surface. Both humans and fish can gradually accustom themselves to changing altitudes and pressures, but they cannot maintain vigor when the change is too sudden. This is as true of fish as it is of humans when mountain climbing or when brought to high altitudes in an airplane.

In lake fishing, in the early spring just after the ice leaves, we have noted that the surface water may be too cold for trout to be active. Under such conditions, it may be well to fish for them farther below the surface, but it might be better to look for active fishing in shallower places where the surface waters have warmed up a bit. A shallow stream on a warm day may have its water heated by the sun to such an extent that trout will be feeding at the mouth of such a stream, enjoying the relative warmth of the oxygen-filled water and the food which the stream brings down to them. Shallow bays in lakes are frequently worth trying, although in some cases the waters in them may be colder than the lake itself. Many anglers look for gravel bars and points of land, and they find feeding trout where the water shelves off deeply. The shore line is always worth investigating, since trout frequently are in the warm shallows at this time of year, looking for small forage fish. In the very early spring, I have caught landlocked salmon, and trout too, on the streamer fly by fishing so close to shore that it would not seem logical for large game fish to be there. I well remember a trip to the Rangeley Lakes when the early spring mornings were freezing cold and ice formed along the shore at night. We caught no fish far off shore, but when we cast our flies to the very shore itself, and fished them in water less than a foot deep, the results were amazing. I would not have thought that any angler in his right mind would have fished such locations, but that was where the trout and salmon were at the time!

It is not always well to "follow the crowd" or to adopt the advice of guides. To be sure, when other anglers are catching fish, it may be good strategy to use their methods. Guides are supposed to know their business, and many of them do, but too many are hidebound in their opinions and make a pretense of greater fishing knowledge than they possess. I have been blessed with the opportunities of fishing with many well-known and highly experienced anglers and from them I have learned a great deal. I have noticed that many of these experts completely ignore the methods of others. They may ask for the advice of their guides, but they don't always adopt it. Invariably, they have better results because they know the "when, where and why" of angling. As a case in point, remember the shore line fishing episode just related. People who saw us fishing so close to shore that day may have thought that we were out of our minds! If so, they must have changed their opinion when they saw us catching big fish. How often have I been at lakes where the "experts" say "The Parmachene Belle and the Montreal are the only flies which take fish here," or some such similar innocent advice! And yet my obstinate mind deliberately prompts me to use something else. Often the "something else" works better than the locally preferred methods.

Bearing in mind what has been said about the spring turnover period, we know that during this time big fish come up from the depths and may be taken on the surface. Where on the surface? I have taken large ones on flies in the middle of lakes, and in other unlikely spots. Better results should be enjoyed, however, by fishing in the places where trout congregate to feed. The mouths of streams and brooks have the highest priority at this time of year and most other times, for that matter. Shore lines, bays, coves, narrows and ledges are all worth exploring. A topographical map is most valuable. On it can be noted the suggestions of the local anglers and even if no expert advice is obtainable, a study of the map will show many likely spots which one could not observe without it. Small brooks, for example, are often unnoticeable in wilderness country. A good map discloses them and makes it easy to find them. Land and water contours are readily apparent and much time is saved for fishing because less is used for exploring.

The warming of surface waters signals the beginning of summer stratification. Since brook trout can tolerate water as warm as 75°, and brown trout and rainbows water even warmer, these fish may take flies or bait on the surface until the stratification of the lake is well advanced. If the water be shallow and the bottom habitable, they may come up through the warmer layer to feed. Thus, warm surface water in itself does not make it unadvisable to fish these places, but if the trout are not there, it may explain why.

If surface fishing indicates that the upper layer is too warm for good results, we may as well give it up and decide that the trout have gone to cooler locations. If trolling, we must put on heavier leads to get the lure down to the cold water where the fish are. This may be in the thermocline, fifteen or twenty feet down or even deeper. Admitting that the lure is a proper one, the trolling speed correct, and the location a good one for fishing, the only thing to do is to add lead until we get down to the level where the fish are cruising.

Fly-fishing under such conditions presents a different problem. When surface waters are warm, trout may be found at the mouths of streams and in the spring holes. The very name of the brook trout "*Salvelinus fontinalis*" means "living in springs," and, except in extremely dry periods, spring holes are among the best places to find them during warm weather. One of my first questions, upon visiting a new trout lake in summer, is to inquire, "Where are the spring holes?" If we know these, and the locations of the brooks, we rarely need search further for good warm weather angling.

For many years, I have enjoyed the superb fishing for brook trout or "squaretails" in the Musquacook Lakes of northern Maine. In Fourth Musquacook Lake, there is a spring called the "Barrel Hole." While it is near shore, it is in the lake itself and one must know its exact location to find it. Around noon, when the sun shines down into the water, it is a thrilling sight to drift a canoe over the spot and to watch the great squaretail trout lying in the Barrel Hole. Many of them will exceed five pounds in weight, and several record fish have been taken from there.

Trout like spring holes and stream mouths because the water in these locations is cooler in the summer. Also, it usually contains more oxygen, a factor very important to their welfare. In such places they may not always take flies on the surface. The sunken fly or the deep running lure will often interest them when the surface fly does not.

In the summer, streams which run through wooded country are several degrees cooler than the surface waters of lakes. Trout migrate up these streams to lie in the big pools where it is shady and cool. In the fall, the brook trout and the brown trout go upstream to spawn, as the rainbow does in the spring. When the season advances, we may find trout of these species farther and farther up the streams and little brooks. By October or November, the brook trout and brown trout have reached the gravel bottom of their spawning grounds and are ready to perpetuate their kind. Rainbow trout, normally being spring spawners, make their upstream migrations in April or May and return to the lakes and reservoirs, or to the sea, by summer, to remain in the deep water for the balance of the year.

Many a fishing trip can be turned from failure into success by knowing the habits of trout and the nature of the waters in which they live at various times of year. One fall, I visited friends at a cottage on a New England lake. My host was anxious to go fishing for the large brook trout the lake was supposed to contain. His idea was to troll or fly fish for a while and then, if results were poor, to announce "Guess they are not biting today," upon which he would give up. Although it was late in the season, the surface water was abnormally warm and the fall turnover stage of the lake had not begun. We caught a few trout in the likely spots, one of them being at the mouth of a brook which flowed through a mile or two of woodland and pasture before it reached the lake. At my suggestion we fished the brook for an entire day. "Tried it several times last spring," my host commented. "There are only little ones in there."

We worked up the brook for a short distance, wearing sneakers and enjoying the coolness of the water and the contrasting warmth of the air. Leaves were just beginning to take on their fall colors and drifted down from the trees to bob and swirl around the rocks in the current. The place called for careful fishing. Underbrush and fallen trees made long casts nearly impossible, but by cautiously sneaking up stream and quietly flicking our flies into tiny pools and shadowed pockets we took so many trout that we pinched the barbs from our hooks in order to enjoy the fishing without harming the fish. The males were brilliant in their spotted coats of vivid colors and the less gaudy females were fat with roe. These fish had not yet reached their spawning grounds farther upstream, but they were lazily making their way to the trysting places, evidently postponing their arrival as long as possible to enjoy the wealth of flies and bugs that dropped to them from the multicolored foliage along the banks.

"So that's where the trout are!" exclaimed my host, as we returned home at sunset through the fields and woods of the New England countryside. "The whole stream seemed full of trout, and big ones at that!"

"I know of a reservoir in Massachusetts where fishing is not allowed," I answered. "One may fish the feeder streams. They are not much good in the spring and early summer, but just before the season closes, many migratory trout can be taken from them. When the water is warm in the reservoir, fishing in the streams is apt to be good."

These are instances of a condition which often exists, although the closed season in many states prevents anglers from taking advantage of it often. In my opinion, when trout collect in streams to prepare to spawn, those streams should be closed to fishing. It is not every angler who will enjoy his sport without killing the fish.

Returning to the lakes again, it is interesting to note that, during the summer stagnation period, many lakes can not support fish life below the thermocline. In these lakes, the upper layer may be too warm and the lower layer too lacking in oxygen, thus imprisoning the fish in the area of the thermocline or forcing them to seek shallow spring holes or to leave the lake altogether.

This condition is true in lakes whose bottoms are cluttered with decaying vegetation, or in deep lakes whose waters are so clouded by animal and vegetable organisms that the sun cannot penetrate to the depths. Transparency in lake water is of great biological significance. Without a proper degree of it, the sun cannot penetrate into the waters. Without the sunlight, the photosynthesis of plants cannot take place. This is the function by which they absorb carbon dioxide in their growth, giving off oxygen in the process. Water can absorb both oxygen and carbon dioxide, but if it is saturated with one, it cannot take on much of the other. The rotting of vegetation in a lake bottom gives off gases, the most abundant of which is carbon dioxide, which can be absorbed by vegetable organisms in the presence of sunlight; these organisms giving off oxygen in exchange. In the presence of an overabundance of the minute animal and vegetable organisms called plankton, sunlight cannot reach down into the water and oxygen cannot be formed. Neither can it be taken from the air, due to the stratified condition of the lake. Without proper oxygen content, trout cannot exist. Thus it happens that some lakes in summer cannot support trout very far below the thermocline.

Since fishermen can troll or fish the depths well below the thermocline, this phenomenon is of considerable practical interest. However, with deep trolling rigs such as are used for taking lake trout in the summer stagnation period, even as much as four hundred and fifty or five hundred feet of Monel metal line or copper line, trolled at about three miles per hour, will sink a lure only to a depth of about forty-five feet. This is usually in the vicinity of the thermocline, but it may be in the fishless water below it.

After trolling at such a depth, if fish are not encountered, it may be suspected that the trolling depth is incorrect. The bait may be operating either too far above the thermocline or too far below it. Unless the depth of the thermocline is established by using a thermometer, a trial and error system must be adopted to locate the depth at which the fish are cruising. This may be done by letting out or taking in line, by changing the trolling speed, by adding more lead to the line, or by a combination of these methods.

Once the proper trolling depth has been established by frequently occurring strikes, the same methods should be maintained, of course. It may happen, however, that a boat will get strikes in one section of a lake and not in another. A cause of this may be that the thermocline is tipped, due to wind action piling up surface water on the shore toward which the wind is blowing. Under such conditions, the thermocline will be nearer to the surface on the leeward side of the lake than it will on the windward side. Thus, if we get strikes while trolling on the leeward side and fail to get them on the windward side, we may assume that the lure must be trolled at a constantly increasing depth as we travel to windward.

I have heard fishermen say that speeding of the boat frequently induces strikes. Admitting that there is always a proper trolling speed for each type of lure, this discussion of thermoclines and water temperatures will indicate that there is also a proper depth at which we must troll to obtain best results. If speeding up the boat brings better luck, this may be due to the fact that the added speed makes the lure ride higher in the water. If so, shortening the line or removing a bit of lead may accomplish the same result. It is also true that a steadily trolled bait may not interest fish, but when speed is increased suddenly, the fish think the lure is trying to escape, and they strike at it at that time and for that reason. We have all seen trout follow a lure right up to the boat without taking it. A sudden increase in the speed of the lure may induce them to do so.

Anglers often wonder how deep they are trolling. The general supposition is that their lures are deeper than they actually are. It may be surprising to note that a light line, of nylon for example, will sink a light lure only three or four feet at a three mile an hour trolling speed, even though several hundred feet of line is out. If we wish to test our trolling depth we can mark the line where it leaves the reel [1] so that we later can measure the length

[1] Red nail polish often is used for the purpose.

of line we have had out. Then we can troll near shore until we get hung up. By backing up the boat, we can measure the depth of the lure when we are directly over it by measuring the length of line which was under water when we pulled the lure loose. The results are often surprising.

Some time ago, I invested in a thermometer for use in taking water temperatures. Its scale measures between − 5° and 120° F.,

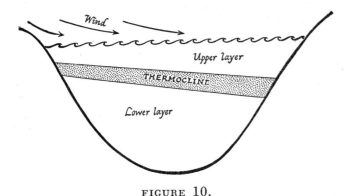

FIGURE 10.

TIPPING OF THERMOCLINE, DUE TO WIND ACTION

A lake's thermocline tips when winds pile surface water toward the windward shore. Food is carried to windward. Trout seek the windward shore to feed.

and it comes in a metal case with a metal screw cap and ring at the top. Rather than spend an hour or more trolling at various speeds and depths, it seems easier to devote a few minutes to a study of water temperatures. To do this, the thermometer is lowered to three feet below the surface and a reading is taken.[2]

[2] While this may be the simplest method, it is not the best one because the reading will change as the thermometer is brought up through the warmer water. Even if done quickly, allowance must be made for this. A better method is to tie a cord around the stopper in a jug and around the handle. Lower the corked jug to the desired depth; jerk the cord to pull the stopper and take the temperature of the water in the jug. The jug may have to be weighted to make it sink.

Then, six feet, nine feet and so on, until a decided drop in temperature is noted. This is the region of the thermocline, and fishing at this depth frequently produces best results in the summer. Depths are easy to measure by attaching to the ring in the thermometer a piece of fish line on which knots have been tied at three foot intervals. By the same means, the lower stratum of the thermocline area may be determined, so that the bait may be trolled at either depth and between the two. Since the depth at which a lure is trolled is mainly based on guesswork, if we can determine the approximate depth of the middle of the thermocline, human error and variations in trolling speed can do little better than to allow us to troll at this general depth. This layer of rapid temperature change is the depth at which good fishing is most likely to be found.

In the summer, surface temperature is of little importance. If the water is warm enough to swim in comfortably, it is usually too warm to provide good trout fishing. Since trout seek out the colder depths at between 50° and 70°, it is logical to fish at the depths where those temperatures exist, in order to catch them.

Summer stratification of lakes imprisons trout in and near the thermocline area where proper living conditions are found. The upper layer is too warm and they rarely pass through it except to feed on the surface at night, when cooler conditions exist. The lower layer, due to decomposition of organic matter and the barring of sunlight from it by suspended organisms in the water, may be too lacking in oxygen to make the area livable. Yet "imprisoned" is hardly the word to use, because avenues of escape or travel are opened up to them by streams flowing into the lake. Even though the water in these streams may be warmer than is desirable, it has been filled with oxygen in its tumbling course over rocks and rapids as it comes down from the hills. It contains food for the trout. It may satisfy three of the principal requirements for their existence: proper temperature, sufficient oxygen and food. This is why trout may be found so often in the mouths of streams, even though the surface water in the lake is too warm to support them.

An aerial view of a stream mouth will show, by the variation
in color of the sand and silt brought down by it as compared
to the color of the lake bottom, that the current of the stream
travels downward far out into the lake. The distance into the
lake traveled by this cool oxygen- and food-bearing current varies

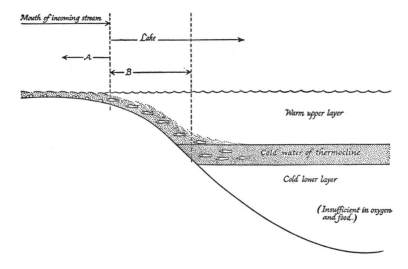

FIGURE 11.

INCOMING STREAMS FURNISH AVENUES OF
ESCAPE FOR TROUT

*Incoming streams bring cold water down into the
thermocline, furnishing avenues of escape for trout.
Fishing should be good in cold stream deltas during
warm weather.*

with the size and force of the stream and the bottom contour. Fish
can leave the thermocline and live above the thermocline level so
long as they stay in the favorable conditions of the incoming
water at the stream mouth. They can travel up the stream without coming into too much contact with the warm upper layer of
the lake. Often, they will pass through the thin upper level at the
stream mouth in order to take the fly.

Many anglers, not realizing that the stream mouth extends beyond the point at which it is visible on the surface, are inclined to run their canoes up into the stream itself, without bothering to fish the very productive waters farther from shore. As is shown in Figure 11, they fish at point "A," when equally good or better fishing may be found at point "B." By passing over point "B" to fish point "A," they frighten the fish farther from shore and unwittingly throw away a golden opportunity.

I enjoy fishing with a guide because the guide can handle the canoe while I handle my tackle. Invariably, a new guide will drift the canoe up into the stream mouth without giving me a chance to fish the surrounding waters. When he does so, we can look down and frequently see large fish which might have been caught if a more cautious approach had been used.

One such stream in Canada comes to my mind. The water is shallow and the mouth extends in a deep channel far out into the lake. My companions fished the place several times and reported that, for some reason or other, there were no trout there. One morning as the mists of dawn still blanketed the lake, I pushed off in my canoe to try it myself. Quietly anchoring the canoe far out from shore, I placed gradually extending casts toward the visible part of the stream mouth and took large fish very near to the canoe. As I worked up toward the point where the stream entered the lake, fewer fish were taken. At the very mouth of the brook, none were found at all. An hour's prebreakfast fishing netted six or eight beautiful squaretails, two of the largest weighing over three pounds each. When I brought these two back to the cabin and showed them to my friends who were assembled at breakfast, no one could believe that Black Brook could yield such fine fish. So, the next morning I took one of the anglers with me, and we did it again! Since then, the outer reaches of the brook mouth have proved to be one of the best fishing spots on the lake.

It has been only during the past year that I have ever heard any discussion of lake stratification by anglers. Recently, two or three articles have appeared in the sporting magazines on the sub-

ject. The anglers who were so surprised to learn of this phenomenon may have encountered the region of the thermocline in
diving. As they plunge into the water, it is warm, but suddenly
they come in contact with a cold layer farther down. "I hit a
spring," they announce. While this may be true, it is more logical
to assume that the cold water they passed into was the region of
the thermocline, and it is not hard to deduce that cold water seeking fish will prefer this area to the warmer water above.

Although too much importance cannot be placed on water
temperatures in fishing, the elements of dissolved oxygen and
food supply are of equal or greater importance. One cannot
arbitrarily assert that trout will live in a certain temperature and
not in waters a few degrees higher, because it is known that the
warmer waters, provided they are not too warm, are excellent for
fish life if an adequate supply of oxygen is dissolved in them.
With both of these requirements met properly, we must remember that trout cruise in water where there is an adequate food
supply, either of surface insects, water-borne feed which comes
down in inflowing streams, or of forage fish. Where optimum conditions exist for temperature, oxygen and food, there one should
find the most trout.

Winds have a way of undulating a thermocline as well as of
tipping it. Under windy conditions, the upper layer of the
thermocline may not be level, but rather, if one could see it, it
would have the appearance of a slowly moving swell.

It has been an often argued question as to whether one should
fish on the leeward or the windward side of a lake for best results.
While it may be most comfortable to fish to leeward, on the side
protected from the wind, more often than not the greater quantity
of fish will be located along the windward shore. This is a logical
assumption when it is realized that surface waters blow water-
borne plankton and larger forms of food life from leeward to
windward. Since the surface currents travel in that direction,
forage fish often are well in on the windward shore. Large trout,
under such conditions, are near shore to feed on them, provided
that the water is cold enough to bring them to the surface.

It may safely be concluded that large deep lakes stratify in the summer. This is even partly true in certain parts of the Great Lakes, and in some areas of the ocean. Large lakes will not stratify if they are relatively shallow in proportion to their surface areas. Lakes exposed to the wind are less likely to stratify than protected waters where the absence of wind-formed water currents prevents the waters from mixing. No definite rules exist for determining which lakes stratify and which do not, except for the general conclusions reached above.

Since this discussion of the seasonal behavior of lakes has been rather detailed, let us briefly summarize the most important parts to see more clearly how this information can be used in fishing. We should fish in cold water, since trout are more apt to be in cold areas than in warm. If water is not cold to the touch, trout usually are not near the surface. When water temperatures of lakes and ponds exceed 75° in summer, we should forsake these waters in preference to colder ones.

After the ice leaves trout lakes in the spring, fishing should be good nearly everywhere with surface lures, but preferably around ledges, in bays, stream mouths and along the windward shore. Trout are inclined to be without appetite and inactive where water is ice cold, so bars, bays and fishing around islands is better because the water is warmer and there should be more food. Later in the season when the surface waters become warm to the touch, better results usually are obtained by fishing at deeper levels, or in the early morning or late evening when surface temperatures are lower than during the warm part of the day.

Warm surface waters indicate stratification in deep lakes. At such times trout are in or near the thermocline at a depth of fifteen feet or more, depending upon the size of the lake. They also seek the cold waters of incoming streams, or springs. If it is convenient to do so, the use of a thermometer is helpful in determining the depth of the optimum range of temperatures satisfactory to trout. Fishing at this depth should bring best results especially near bars, ledges, islands or other sources of food. As surface waters become warmer, trout go deeper or remain in spring holes or cold stream mouths until the surface cools down in the fall.

Cold fall days and nights indicate the end of the summer stagnation period. When surface waters are cold at night but warm by day, early morning or late evening surface fishing should again bring best results if one does not wish to fish deep. Stream mouths and narrows are productive spots. When surface waters remain cold by day, trout again roam the surface and may be taken in the same places as in the spring. For brown and brook trout, fall is the migratory season and fishing should be at its best in the deltas and bays of tributary streams.

We have observed that water temperatures are of major importance in locating trout. If we can locate the places or depths where the optimum temperatures exist; if the spots contain feed for trout and sufficient oxygen, we can safely assume that we are fishing in trout waters and not in barren areas of the lake or stream. To do so is the best guarantee of good fishing.

Catching trout is an art in which knowledge must be combined with skill. Of the two, the former is the more important. An angler may be accomplished in the use of the fly and possessed of expensive, well-matched equipment, but if he lacks the knowledge of where to find his fish and how to catch them once they are found, he will have less luck than the proverbial barefoot boy who fishes with a bit of local knowledge and an alder pole.

CHAPTER FIVE

More about Lakes

Fishable Locations and How to Find Them

ANGLERS who enjoy fishing from boats in the summer frequently locate "hot spots" where fishing in a lake is found to be unusually good. Many of these "hot spots" are far out from shore. Since they often are considered too valuable to mark with a buoy, lest others use the buoy for the same purpose, these places sometimes are located by observing four landmarks on shore, each one approximately ninety degrees from the next so that they are roughly at four equidistant compass points. When these landmarks are known it is easy to relocate the "hot spot" again merely by maneuvering the boat to the spot on the lake where imaginary lines cross between opposite identifying points.

Usually these "hot spots" are encountered by luck. Anglers often do not know why they are good. They merely know that if they fish just off the bottom at certain points they will catch fish. The species they catch may vary, depending upon what types of cold-water fish are in the lake, so the practice pertains by no means to trout only. Since it occasionally pertains to trout and since trout fishermen frequently enjoy trying their luck for other cold-water fish it may be interesting to learn why these are "hot spots" and how to locate such places of our own. It should be noted that while this applies primarily to summer fishing it is of considerable value all year round even though other spots may be better in the spring and fall. I have checked many of these unusually productive fishing locations in several lakes and ponds throughout the United States and have found that most of them conform to a set general rule. Knowing the facts about lake stratification and the existence of the thermocline in summer helps to explain this rule and to understand what might be otherwise a rather mysterious phenomenon.

If the geography of a typical lake is reduced to simplest terms it may be compared in miniature to a wide bowl nearly filled with water. Let us assume that the thermocline in this lake begins at a depth of thirty feet and that the thermocline itself is twenty-five feet in thickness. In summer the great majority of cold-water fish

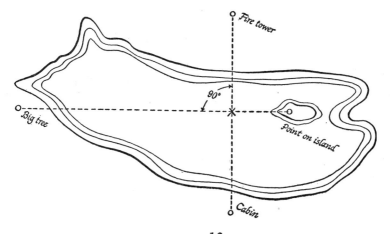

FIGURE 12.

LOCATING A "HOT SPOT" BY LINING UP FOUR LANDMARKS

may be assumed to be in the thermocline or just above it since the waters nearer the surface will be too warm to suit them and the waters below will be too lacking in oxygen. In this instance they should therefore be at a depth of between twenty-five and fifty-five feet, segregated in a slice of the lake thirty feet thick. If we reduce this thirty-foot thermocline area to the simplicity of the simile we have made with a bowl of water the productive area will be a disk proportionately as small. Are the fish everywhere in this disk? Possibly, but when we remember that fish require adequate food as well as ample oxygen and suitable temperatures and when we remember that the greatest abundance of food for the larger fish in a lake is on or near the shore line we can reduce the fishable area to the rim on the outside of the disk. Referring to the lake itself, rather than the bowl, the fishable area then will be a band around the entire shore line from a depth of twenty-five feet to a depth of fifty-five feet. If we fish on or near the bottom of the lake anywhere around this band we can expect to catch more fish than anywhere else in the lake.

Thus we have reduced our good summer fishing grounds from the entire water surface of the lake to a relatively small band extending around it under the surface. We can reduce it still farther.

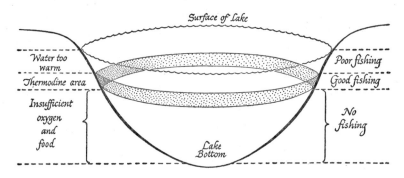

FIGURE 13.

PRODUCTIVE FISHING LOCATION IN A LAKE IN SUMMER

Fishable area of a lake in summer is restricted primarily to the band of lake bottom in the region of the thermocline.

Trout habitually remain in the upper part of the thermocline or just above it rather than in the lower part. This is because the upper area contains more oxygen and a greater food supply. Therefore, it seems not illogical to divide the thirty-foot-deep thermocline area into two disks each half as thick and to discard the lower half, thus reducing the best fishable area to a band only fifteen feet wide, lying at a depth of between twenty-five and forty feet. A weighted sounding line marked somewhere in be-

tween these two distances (such as at thirty or thirty-five feet
from the end) and lowered until it touches bottom will find this
area for us. There is where we should fish. Since the feeding area
is from several feet above the top level of the thermocline to
several feet below it we can set the depth for measuring purposes at the level of the top of the thermocline and let it go at
that. If this level proves inadequately productive we can do our
fishing slightly above or below it. It is at this general depth that
we should find the greatest concentration of fish.

Are the fish equally distributed around the lake along the
band of this disk? No, because some types of lake bottom provide
a greater concentration of food than others. Trout in general (and
some other species of fish as well) prefer a rocky place in which
to live and to feed. If we elect to fish for them in the rocky
places we can eliminate the areas lacking in rocks and thus reduce the fishable portion of the lake to a relatively small part
of this band.

This gives us an answer to where to fish by lowering our bait
to the bottom. How about trolling? Trolling usually is done by
most fishermen in a very haphazard manner. When they find an
area where they catch fish they keep on fishing there, but the
area and depth usually is determined by a process of trial and
error. In this trial and error method of trolling the bait may drag
bottom in some places and be altogether too far from it in
others. If we fish a certain lake a great deal it seems most worth-
while to find out where the thermocline is located and to take
soundings at this depth to determine how far from shore this
band of bottom actually is. We can record these soundings
on a crude map which indicates the distance of each from
shore. By drawing a line connecting these points of equal depth
we can chart our trolling course and thus know with reasonable exactness just how far from shore we should troll to be
over the points where the upper slice of the thermocline touches
the bottom of the lake. Going to the trouble of taking these
soundings and drawing such a map is not always necessary
because topographical maps of many lakes are available on

which the contours of the lake bottom are charted. Regardless of whether this information is provided for us or is obtained by our own efforts it tells us how deep and at what distance from shore we should troll along ledges, around points of land and in spots where the lake bottom levels off. In deep lakes this trolling path may be very near shore. In lakes having a fairly level bottom it may be very far out. Near or far, it is the path of good fishing in the summer.

There are many lakes where nearly all of the bottom will be found to be above the level of the thermocline. When these lakes

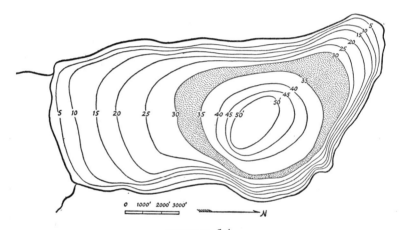

FIGURE 14.

CONTOUR SKETCH OF DIAMOND LAKE, OREGON

Shaded area (where thermocline meets shore line) denotes good bottom fishing in summer. There is little or no summer trout fishing in other areas.

are charted in the above manner, as in the sketch of Diamond Lake above (see pages 251 to 255), the productive trolling area will be confined to a relatively small oval path. Inside or outside of this path the fishing will be relatively poor or nonexistent. Determining just where this path is may require a bit of investigation but the angler who is willing to do this experimenting will be repaid richly in good fishing all summer long, year in and year out, if there are any trout in the lake at all.

In a large lake it may be neither necessary nor advisable to chart the entire shore line. In such lakes we may know, or resident anglers may tell us, that the best fishing is only along a certain part of the shore line. Thus it may be desirable to chart only this part. If one takes the time to do so the results will be far better than those enjoyed by fishermen who do their trolling by trial and error.

This book is on the subject of trout fishing and the suggestions made in this chapter should be considered to be for trout fishing only. They pertain to all species of trout which inhabit lakes, including the lake trout as well as others. I do not yet know how well the method works for other varieties of fish although I know it will do as well for landlocked salmon as for trout. I see no reason why it should not be equally good for smallmouthed bass and many other cold-water game fishes but as this is written there is not sufficient information available to substantiate such an opinion.

Trolling depth is a vital factor in the success of the method. Quite obviously the lure or bait must be trolled near the thermocline to obtain best results. We have noted before that many anglers badly misjudge the depth level at which they believe they are trolling. Since trolling depth is influenced by many factors a bit of experimenting may be advisable, as discussed in the previous chapter, to guarantee that the lure is operating at the proper distance below the surface.

So far we have assumed for the sake of simplicity that the typical lake is in the shape of a bowl. In many lakes islands, bars and ledges disrupt the smooth contours of the bottom. Many of these islands will shelve off into water sufficiently deep to invade the thermocline so that there will be a ringed area where the thermocline level touches the lake bottom around them. These places may provide fishing as good or better than that offered by the shore line.

Here and there in a lake there are humps and ridges which rise almost exactly to the thermocline level. Trout collect around these submerged humps and ridges to feed just as surely as do salt water fish around the Grand Banks off the coast of Newfoundland. These humps and ridges in the lake bottom, if their tops are near the thermocline level, are important in the list of "hot spots" which lake fishermen occasionally find and to which they return time and time again for good fishing. They comprise the majority of the "hot spots" but subsurface springs and channels must be included also. How shall we find these submerged humps and ridges? Contour maps may indicate them but this is the exception rather than the rule. Usually we must find them for ourselves. In trolling this occasionally occurs when the bait becomes caught on the bottom. When this happens it is helpful to back the boat directly over the spot and mark the line at water level so that we can see how deep we actually are trolling by measuring the rest of the line as it is retrieved.

The location of such places also may be found by intelligent guesses based on the topography of the surrounding country. These guesses can be confirmed by taking soundings. When a ridge of land slants down to a point of shore on the lake and lines up with an island farther out it may be presumed that a subsurface ridge connects the two. If two or three islands are in a chain in the lake it is probable that subsurface humps exist in a continuation of this chain. If these humps are at thermocline level a bit of fishing in these places should confirm the fact that there are trout in the vicinity.

In the course of these investigations of a favorite trout lake humps and ridges will be found which are considerably above or below the thermocline level. Those which are below it may be discarded since it will be seldom, if ever, that they will attract trout. Those which are above should be marked carefully on the map, with depths recorded, because they will be valuable for fishing in the spring and the fall, even if they are not productive in the summer. From the preceding chapter we have noted that trout feed more actively on the surface of the lakes in the spring and fall than at any other time of year. As the surface waters warm up in the spring the fish go to lower depths. They go to places in the depths where food is most abundant. Out in the lake these places often are around submerged humps and ridges or ledges in the water. Thus if we have marked on our map spots where there are such protuberances five, ten, fifteen and twenty feet from the surface, for example, we should fish near the five-foot-

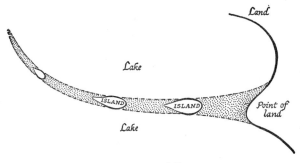

FIGURE 15.

LAND TOPOGRAPHY INDICATES
SUBSURFACE LEDGES

Broken lines indicate estimated location of underwater ledges. Trout may be found in spring and fall where these ledges are near the surface. In summer, trout are where ledges meet the region of the thermocline.

deep ridges when the trout have ceased to feed actively on the surface. Later on, when the surface waters grow warmer, we should try the ten-foot ridges, and then the deeper ones. When these are of no avail it may be considered that the stratification of the lake has been completed for the summer. Then, as far as fishing in the lake is concerned, we should confine our efforts to the thermocline level until the lake turns over again in the fall. If we do not enjoy trolling or still fishing at these depths the warm surface waters in the lake may bar us from fishing there entirely. But the spring holes, brook mouths and streams still may provide good surface or near-surface fishing.

Many anglers, upon reading this chapter, will have a desire to throw up their hands in dismay over the seeming complexity of determining the depth of the thermocline in their favorite lakes in the summer. To find it one may not have the patience to take water samples from gradually increasing depths and record their temperatures until the depth of the level of rapid temperature drop is found. There are other ways of determining this depth which, while less accurate, may prove more acceptable.

From experiences in trolling in the summer it often is observed that some fishermen take trout when others do not, even if similar methods and lures are used. Quite obviously their success, or lack of it, depends upon how deep they troll. In the normal course of events a boat trolling at the proper depth will pass over good water occasionally and will take fish whether or not its trolling path is planned carefully as recommended in this chapter. If the boat takes fish it may be concluded that the lures being trolled from it are being trolled (perhaps accidentally) at thermocline level. We may find this level by adding weight to our line until it sinks to a level where it catches fish. If adding weight causes the lure to be caught on the bottom in the process it means that we are trolling too close to shore. If no fish are hooked in the process we should add more lead and get out farther from shore. In experimenting with adding lead it may be found that lines of braided nylon or monofilament will not sink the lure deep enough, even if considerable lead is added. If so, metal lines should be used. Lead, and perhaps a good deal of it, may have to be put on nevertheless.

When each added bit of lead is put on the line to make the lure troll deeper it may be helpful to run the boat at normal speed for several minutes and then to slow it down gradually if no strikes are encountered. By slowing down the boat the lure will go deeper. When a depth is reached where fish are taken it may be concluded to be the level of the thermocline. If results still do not seem to be good enough perhaps the lure should be trolled a few feet deeper still. In the first instance the lure may be near enough to the thermocline level so that a few fish will come up for it. In the second instance trolling a few feet deeper may get the lure well into the thermocline level and result in hooking the greatest possible number of trout because the greatest number can see it at this depth.

To obtain a general idea of the thermocline level let us take as examples a lake which is very large and deep and a small lake which is so shallow that only a small part of it contains any thermocline at all. Lake Pend Oreille, in the panhandle of northern Idaho, is more than forty miles long and is eight miles wide at its widest point. Even though nearly surrounded by mountains the winds are such that its surface is disturbed by wind action more than might be considered normal. In this lake hydrographic surveys indicate that summer surface temperatures normally are 68°. At a depth of sixty feet the temperature drops to 50°, and down to 40° at one hundred and eighty feet. The lake in its deepest spot is twelve hundred feet deep. At over one hundred and eighty feet the lake remains at 39.2° all year round. Aquatic biologists set the thermocline of Lake Pend Oreille at between sixty and eighty feet where the temperature is about 50°, or as low as normally is enjoyed by trout.[1]

For the smaller one we again may use Diamond Lake in Oregon as an example because considerable accurate biological research has been done on it. Since this lake is at a high altitude (just over five thousand feet) we may assume that the thermocline in the relatively cool summer is as near the surface as in other small lakes anywhere else. Here the thermocline is between thirty and forty feet. From the examples of these two lakes it seems reasonable to conclude that few lakes anywhere have thermoclines shallower than twenty or thirty feet and deeper than sixty or

[1] Note that the surface of Lake Pend Oreille rarely is warmer than 68°, a temperature which is satisfactory for trout. Yet, while cutthroats and small Kamloops occasionally are taken on or near the surface in the summer the big Kamloops, Dolly Vardens and many of the cutthroats descend to cooler waters and rarely are taken with surface lures in summer in the lake itself. Thus, even though surface temperatures are favorable, the majority of trout (and especially the big ones) prefer the colder parts of the optimum temperature range deeper in the lake.

seventy feet. For all practical purposes this limits summer trolling to between these two depths. If we are fishing in a small protected lake it may be wise to attempt to troll at a thirty-foot depth, later varying this depth somewhat if poor results make this advisable. If the lake is larger, forty feet may be a better level at which to operate. In very large lakes fifty or sixty feet of depth may be in order.

In utilizing the procedure recommended in this chapter we may troll in the deepest part of a lake and get our lure frequently snagged on the bottom without taking any trout at all. In this case the absence of a thermocline (due to insufficient depth) may have driven the trout to the streams or to spring holes for the summer. In one lake in Maine where I have fished on several occasions there are very few trout in the main body of the lake in the summer. The smaller ones are in the stream mouths and many of the big ones are in a spring hole in a cove of the lake where the surface of the water is covered almost completely with lily pads. It looks like good bass water and I would have passed it by as trout water if an old gentleman had not showed me the location of the spring hole. The three- and four-pound squaretail trout which lived in this spring hole all summer were almost beyond comprehension. There must have been hundreds of them because we took and released an old tackle-buster at nearly every cast. I think there must have been nearly as many trout there as there were flies and broken leaders wrapped around the lily pads!

Another lake of my acquaintance is formed roughly like an hourglass or like two lakes which are joined together. One half of this lake is shallow but the other half is deep. Trout fishing is good in both parts of the lake in the spring and fall but in the summer the trout which do not run up the streams leave the shallower half of the lake entirely and concentrate in the thermocline area of the deeper half. The shallow half contains no trout at all in the summer and yet when I have been there during that period I have seen many boats hopefully trolling in it. They return to camp in the evening quite discouraged, particularly when they learn that the boats which have trolled in the deeper part and at the correct depth have brought in several big trout. If any of these fishermen happen to read this book I trust that the information offered in these chapters will bring them better luck.

It is occasionally supposed that there is no limit to the number of fish which a pond or lake can support. It seems mysterious to some that certain lakes and ponds possess trout which are large and fat while others are small and thin. The answer to the healthy growth of trout in a body of water, and the number of trout the body of water can support, depends less upon its size than upon the food supply which it contains. After all, even a trout must eat! A farm can support only a certain maximum number of human beings, and a lake can support only a certain maximum number of trout. If there are fewer trout in the lake (ignoring other species of fish for the moment) than is needed to consume its food supply the trout will grow large and fat. If there are too many trout for the food available the trout will grow relatively little from year to year. A remarkable example of this is the giant Kamloops trout of Lake Pend Oreille. In some waters I have taken trout which were five years old and which were less than ten inches in length and yet the Kamloops rainbow trout I landed at Pend Oreille was thirty-nine and a quarter inches long and of the same age! The abundance of food makes a remarkable difference in the growth of trout.

Normally trout obtain only a relatively small proportion of their sustenance from terrestrial insects. Most of their food is derived from the water in which they live. Small trout, minnows and other little fish obtain the greater part of their nourishment from plankton. Plankton, and other similar organisms which may for purposes of simplicity be included under that name, are tiny bits of animal or vegetable life which drift or swim in virtually all waters. These plankton in turn derive their sustenance from algae, bacteria and other microscopic growths. Plankton are more prolific in some waters than in others, their abundance being in a sense directly proportionate to the richness of the soil surrounding the lake and bordering its tributary streams. In some lakes and rivers, and even in the ocean, these minute organisms occasionally are so stupendous in their numbers that they color the water in pronounced shades of the various colors of the spectrum. Mollusks, crustaceans and little fish live largely upon plankton. Since large fish feed to a major degree upon mollusks, crustaceans and little fish it is apparent that the food supply of these large fish also is dependent upon the richness of the soil. Thus it may be said that the more plankton there are in a body of water the more food there will be for fishes and the better will be the fishing. When there are too many fish they eat up nearly all of the available food and are in constant search for more. When this food is eaten up it can not reproduce itself. In consequence the lake becomes poorer and poorer for fishing.

Thus we see that in certain virgin lakes which never contained trout the food may be so abundant that when trout are planted there they grow to very large size. If the lake is such that the trout can reproduce themselves in it they increase in numbers. Ultimately their numbers increase to the extent that the trout have to compete with each other for food, since there is not enough for all. In these lakes the saturation point has been reached. While the trout may be as numerous they will not retain their large size. They will grow smaller as the food supply diminishes.

This may be what will happen to Lake Pend Oreille and its fabulously large Kamloops rainbow trout which have grown to their gigantic size because of the abundance of Kokanee salmon upon which they depend for the greater part of their food. If more little Kamloops are planted in the lake, or if the Kamloops successfully reproduce themselves in large numbers, the trout may grow smaller as their numbers become larger. This may be a good thing for all concerned. Instead of the lake containing but a relatively few gigantic Kamloops it may ultimately contain many times that number of smaller rainbows; rainbows of five and ten pounds rather than twenty and thirty pounds or more. If this comes to pass there may be no more world's records broken at Pend Oreille but the anglers who fish there should enjoy much better sport.

Unfortunately the wilderness lakes which contain too many trout in proportion to their food supply are few and far between. When they are found it is obviously well to reduce the fish population by angling. It usually happens that creel limits are set too high and that these lakes become so popular for a time that they are overfished, thus eventually ruining them from an angling standpoint. It is difficult to keep the natural balance of trout in a lake at the happy medium between too many and too few. This usually is the responsibility of the state Fish and Game Departments. These organizations are not without their troubles and satisfying the greed of the average angler is not the least of them.

During the summer many lakes are afflicted with a scummy growth which floats on the surface, causing it to be said of the lake that it is "working" or that it is "in bloom." Although this growth disappears after a time the fishing in the lake is notoriously poor while it is there. I have noted equally poor fishing during otherwise advantageous conditions when the pollen from trees coats sections of the surface of lakes with a powdery yellow scum. Evidently at these times trout feed far beneath the surface to keep away from these conditions, perhaps because the pollen or floating algae masses get in their respiratory systems if the fish feed near the surface.

More and more good trout lakes are becoming ruined for fishing by the practice of damming them and using the impounded waters for power and irrigation. In the spring they are filled with water, usually to an abnormally high level. If the trout are spring spawners they seek suitable shallow places in which to deposit their eggs. Before the eggs hatch the lake is drawn down to a much lower level. The spawn is left high and dry and rarely is there enough left in a suitable depth of water to allow the fish to hatch and to live. A similar unfortunate condition takes place in the fall. Trout seek what is at the time an ideal depth of water in which to lay their eggs. The lake is drawn down still farther and the eggs of the fall spawning fish die also. Even worse, many of the adult fish die with them. I occasionally visit a lake in Canada which is fished so seldom that it would be impossible for the anglers who visit it to make even the slightest dent in the trout population, even if they killed all the fish they hooked, which they do not. This lake has been deteriorating in its trout population year by year until at present the fishing in it is relatively poor. When I tried to find out why this was so my host took me by canoe to several little bays in the lake which the big brook trout had been using for spawning. This was in late fall and the spawning season had been progressing for a month or more, while water was still being drawn from the lake. As a result hundreds of adult trout had become landlocked in many of these little spawning pockets and were dead and rotting when I saw them! The drawing off of the water in the lake not only was killing the spawn but the adult trout as well. It is no wonder that the fishing was growing poorer and poorer each year! Despite what the proponents of dams tell us, when we tamper with the levels of lakes we tamper with good fishing, even though in many instances it may be necessary to do so.

CHAPTER SIX

Brook Fishing

Secrets Which Add to Angling Skill

MANY ANGLERS never outgrow the absorbing fascination of fishing little brooks. Wriggling excitedly through leafy woodlands, meandering sleepily in verdant pastures or tumbling boisterously down rock gorges, every turn of a brook's tortuous path seems to indicate that it never is quite sure just where it intends to go. Every twist in its course offers a new outlook to the angler, a new problem in presenting the lure to its wild little trout. Men spend small fortunes in fishing famous trout and salmon waters far away yet never grow so sophisticated as to forsake completely the nostalgic pleasures offered by familiar little brooks near home. Rushing rivers with their deep riffles and fighting fish are a challenge which does always compensate for the peaceful angling in musical brooks with their brightly spotted trout, so excited as they dart from cover to pounce upon a fly. Brooks are training grounds for adolescent fishermen as well as nurseries for tiny fish. I doubt that an angler's education ever could approach completeness without the lessons they provide in patience, in caution and in observing the habits of trout. Brooks are rivers in miniature. Their fresh cold waters contain all of the pools, riffles, rocks and glides which merely are exaggerated in size in the larger streams.

It was only after several seasons of youthful blundering that I realized the tremendous value of the cautious approach in fishing little brooks. When my years could be counted on my fingers many a happy day with dog and rod was spent investigating the charm of a tiny meadow stream not far from home. The brook contained many large trout but I did not know it at the time.

When I could race to the brook ahead of the dog I would rush to its bank and hide behind a tree, hopefully peering into the water to see if I could see any trout. If I could not see any trout I would race the dog to another spot and peer again. If the trout were not in plain sight the place seemed too unproductive to deserve my time and attention in fishing it.

Once I was so fast that I began my peering before a nice trout had time to take cover. He darted under a convenient rock and stayed there, completely motionless. Only the tiniest part of his tail was in evidence and I would not have noticed that if I had not known he was there. All of a sudden it occurred to me that there must be lots of other trout hiding in the brook in such places. The fact that I could not see them did not prove they were not there. I fished quite hopefully for the big trout under the rock but of course he stayed quietly where he was until I went away. From that it became everlastingly embedded in my adolescent skull that trout are smart and that it is necessary to fool them in order to catch them. Returning to the place the next day, I sneaked up to the spot and cast a worm to where the trout had been the day before. This time he did not see me and I caught the fish, thus learning for all time the transcending importance of the cautious approach in fishing little brooks. Many times since then I have remembered the incident when my noisy and hasty fishing produced inadequate results.

I often have fished a brown trout stream in New England with an angler who carries caution almost to the point of being ludicrous. He spends four times as long in approaching a spot as he does in fishing it, but he usually ends the day with more fish than anyone else and the trout are invariably of larger size. In watching him from a distance it would be hard to decide whether he was playing Indian or was in an attitude of prayer. If there are no bushes to afford him concealment he will reach the stream on his hands and knees, with little more than his hat appearing above the meadow grass. He rarely sees the place he fishes until after he fishes it, depending upon previous reconnoitering expeditions or upon his intuition to tell him what parts of the brook should be most productive. He does not try to see how near he can get to the water, but rather maneuvers just close enough to make an accurate cast. In doing so his line and perhaps part of his leader will drop on the grass but his fly invariably settles upon the water as lightly as a snowflake. The large trout he catches are tangible proof of the value of his cautious approach.

Meadow brooks are excellent trout waters because of the food, the shade and the concealment which they provide. I know of a brook so tiny that one can step across it in nearly any place and yet its depth and undercut banks afford plenty of water for large trout. Grasses grow along it so luxuriously that parts of it are nearly invisible. Underneath the grasses the hollowed-out banks make the stream three times as wide as the visible part. Being narrow, it is also very deep. Being so well shaded its waters are cool, providing ideal protection for trout. Regardless of the fact that the grasses screen the arrival of the angler, his approach must be quiet and stealthy because the undercut banks act as sounding boards to warn the trout of his arrival; a reverberation evidently is magnified like the echo of a shout in a tunnel. The penalty of haste and clumsiness is to find no trout which are willing to take a lure.

How should one fish such a spot? My friend, the cautious angler, does so by reducing his stealthy approach to slow motion. Until one realizes the importance of this it seems maddeningly and unnecessarily slow. The place for every footprint is selected with care as he crouches forward, sliding each quiet step toward his goal. No Indian stalking game ever did so more carefully. No stone is dislodged; no dead stick broken; no sound whatsoever is made to warn the fish of his coming. When someone chided him for his tactics and commented that his actions seemed rather silly he said, "Would you rather approach one place carefully and take a nice trout or two or rush up to two or more spots in the same length of time and hook no fish at all?" Quite obviously the cautious approach is not necessary on boisterous rocky streams but quiet meadow brooks are quite another matter. Regardless of their small size, there often are remarkably big trout in them, particularly during the migratory season of the species of trout involved. These big trout are notoriously wary in such places; so much so that they are seldom caught except by the angler who takes unusual pains in fishing for them.

On reaching this narrow grass-bordered meadow brook how can we best get a fly or bait into it? After all our time and trouble in reaching the place a poor cast may catch the hook on a little bush and spoil everything. In waters as narrow as this my cautious angler prefers an adaptation of the dapping method. His line is reeled in almost to the leader, which is long and tapered to a fine tippet. Thus he can drop his fly or bait into the brook without casting and with no danger of becoming caught up on the banks. By lowering the rod tip slightly the lure can sink and drift slowly downstream for ten feet or more on a slack line much as if it had dropped from the grasses over the water. If a feeding trout is near by the strike may be sudden and savage. If two or three drifts made in this manner do not bring results the angler slowly works his way along the brook to repeat the maneuver in each new bit of water. He crouches as far back from the brook as is possible. Because of the deep banks and the overhung grasses he rarely sees the water he fishes. He always maintains this maximum distance, realizing that if he ventures closer the undercut banks will warn the trout of his presence, even if they cannot see him.

A long rod is most helpful for this type of fishing because it makes it possible for the angler to stay a foot or two farther back from the brook than a shorter rod would permit. This foot or two may make a great deal of difference in concealing the sound or sight of the angler from the fish. Big brown trout, which often inhabit this type of water, are particularly wary; so much so that even the difference between a long and a short rod may result in catching or not catching the fish. Where there is room to use it, a long rod has decided advantages in brook fishing. It aids the angler in reaching around rocks and over bushes and other obstructions. In fishing brush streams the shorter rod usually is preferable because it is easier to maneuver in congested places.

Whether a brook demands the cautious approach or not, it is very helpful to study its characteristics before fishing it. The angler traveling up or down a stream suddenly may come upon a productive place which he would have fished quite differently if he had known how the spot looked beforehand. It is difficult to retain the geography of a mile or so of brook in one's memory, especially if we visit many streams in the course of the season. Many good fishermen use a pocket-sized notebook as a reminder. They draw a rough map of the brooks they fish, locating each section by a prominent land mark. They cross off the unproductive water so that they will not bother to fish it again. Good pools, glides, rocks, logs and deep holes are indicated by notes or symbols. Wherever a fish is taken the notebook map records the fact. From season to season this information accumulates into map sketches of real value. In brooks, perhaps even more so than in larger streams, where a good fish is taken another will move up to take its place. The "hot spots" may be hard to find and unless we know exactly where they are we may blunder upon them and spoil them for fishing.

One day an angler was introducing me to a brook in Vermont. As he described the water I was to fish he made a point of telling me about a submerged log below a stump on the bank. He called attention to several other places in like manner, rehearsing their characteristics in such detail that I asked him how he possibly could remember so much about this one little bit of brook. In answer he produced a loose-leaf notebook from his jacket. He turned to a rough pencil sketch of the water I was to fish. On it the location of the stump and the log was marked with X's to indicate exactly where each previous fish had been taken. Sizes of fish, weather conditions, flies used and dates were noted. I fished the log below the stump in the manner my host specified and took from the place a brown trout weighing nearly two pounds. If I had not known the characteristics of the spot in advance I am sure I would have fished it improperly and I doubt that a strike would have rewarded my efforts.

That evening the angler showed me his notebook. Favorite

reaches on a dozen streams and brooks were so simply yet so
clearly sketched and accompanied by such pertinent notes that
I am sure any angler, armed with this information, could have
gone to these waters alone for the first time and fished them with
the greatest of efficiency and results. It takes but a few pleasant
minutes to make such records. They save hours of valuable time,
make fishing more profitable and serve as an interesting record
and basis for fireside discussions. In hunting partridge and wood-
cock we map our favorite bird covers in this manner. It is surprising that more anglers do not adopt the practice.

Another meadow stretch of brook which I used to fish never did
produce a trout, yet there were trout in its wooded sections. Recently I fished this brook again but passed over the meadow part
because it was quite obvious that it contained no cover of any
sort to make it appealing to trout. There were no rocks of any
size, no undercut banks, logs, bushes or other means of concealment for fish. The meadow section was wide and shallow, virtually without pools of any depth at all. Even the little trout
seemed to forsake this part. Without depth of water or other
means of concealment certain parts of a trout brook are not
trout waters at all. Yet every season hundreds of anglers hopefully fish this place, even as I did at one time. There is a path
to mark their progress around a dense stretch of alders, leading to
easier waters farther down. On one of my earlier visits I was
following the beaten path around the alder thicket when I thought
I detected the sound of a little waterfall deep in the brush. I
poked my way through this thicket and came upon a fallen log
which had dammed the stream enough to make a little pool.
Cautiously working up to the place I dapped a fly into the water
and let it wash over the log into the pool. Immediately I had a
ten-inch trout. Within a few minutes I caught three more in the
same spot. By appearances no one had been there all season, yet
scores of anglers had passed not twenty feet away.

When I fished the brook for the last time I paid another visit
to the hidden pool. A little boy was in there, quietly fishing with
a worm and the proverbial type of pole which nature affords to

any young man possessed of a knife. I squatted down in the brush and lighted my pipe, watching him while he fished. Three trout lay beside him on the bank and he caught two more while I was there. Finally satisfied with the results he waded up the brook to where I was waiting and proudly showed me his fish. After a few minutes' conversation he poked his way on upstream with a parting admonition to me. "Mister," he said, "next time you come in here, how about wading down the brook? If you go through the brush you'll make a path and then all the lazy fishermen will find this place and catch all the trout." I promised to protect his interests. Before passing from sight he turned once more. "When you wade down the brook, be sure not to break any twigs from the bushes," he said. "Might leave evidence, you know!" He winked at me craftily and was gone. I should like to know how many trout that young man has taken from his little pool. Certainly for every one, another soon moves upstream to take its place in this ideal little sanctuary, thus providing a virtually endless supply. I poked my way up the brook as my young friend had directed and was very careful not to break any branches so as to leave "evidence" which would tempt other anglers to wade down into the place. I haven't had time to go there since but I dare say that the young man has not had to share his secret with anyone else.

The difficult-to-fish places in brooks often are the most productive. They are productive because anglers rarely bother to fish them and also because the dense tangles of brush afford concealment, shade and an abundant food supply of terrestrial insects for the fish. Other conditions being equal, it is axiomatic that the abundance of trout in any given section of stream is in direct proportion to its degree of inaccessibility. Many anglers will not put up with the difficulty of crawling through the tangled mass of branches which shelter many brooks. It is not often that I will do so but occasionally the challenge seems worth the effort. Usually, despite the hardship, an hour or two of this kind of fishing produces double or triple the number of strikes that I would get fishing in open water. I say "strikes" rather than "fish" because a good trout hooked in such a place has an amazing ability to get tangled up in branches and roots and to break away. Even if this does not happen, the branches often are so dense that it is impossible to raise the rod tip high enough to play him properly. It is in this type of brook fishing that the short rod is most advantageous but certainly such a spot, with short rod or long, is no place for a man with a quick temper.

It seems advisable to fish down such a stream rather than up because usually there is little or no room to make a cast. The fly or lure must be drifted downstream and maneuvered expertly and patiently in order to work it into spots which should contain good fish. In doing this, if the current is not swift, the lure may sink to the bottom before it has drifted the proper distance. This can be avoided by placing the lure on a wood chip and allowing the chip to carry the lure downstream on a slack line. When the chip has drifted to the desired position the lure can be twitched from the chip. This method presents the lure naturally since it seems to appear to the fish that it has fallen off the chip much as any insect clinging to a little piece of wood is apt to do. A variation of this method is to cut a branch an inch or two long, with a leaf attached, and to hook the lure to the edge of the leaf. A slight twitch will pull it loose. The method is handy in getting a fly or bait into water infested with branches or roots, where a cast is impossible. Knowing that big trout often lie in such places I try this once in a while but without the assistance of Lady Luck I never did find out how to get a trout out of such a location after he is hooked!

In fishing brooks as well as the larger streams it seems more productive to fish upstream rather than down, wherever the stream is large enough to allow the angler to do so. Upstream fishing is the usual method of handling the dry fly because it permits a more natural float. Many angling writers recommend that, while one should fish the dry fly upstream, he should fish the wet fly or bait downstream. Upstream fishing is more difficult because of the necessity of controlling the length of the line, constantly stripping it in as the lure drifts toward the angler. It is more productive because mud, leaves and twigs dislodged by the angler can not float upstream to scare the trout. It is also more productive because the bait drifts naturally, being relatively unimpeded by the line. The upstream method gets the lure down into the water in a much more effective way than downstream fishing can provide. To me, it is the only proper way to fish a nymph because it is the way a nymph can be presented most naturally.

Anglers who like to fish the artificial fly to the exclusion of bait will have pronounced ideas on what flies to use. Anglers who enjoy bait fishing seem wedded to the worm or shiner in the East and to salmon eggs in the West. Many of them do not observe insects which are obtainable easily and which provide even better bait under many circumstances. In fishing meadow streams when grasshoppers are active there is no more ideal bait. They are not difficult to catch by day and can be taken by the hundreds in the evening when they are lazy due to the cold evening air. Crickets are excellent also and usually may be found under old boards or flat stones. Either can be affixed to a hook with the aid of a tiny rubber band. Their legs should be free to give them a lifelike appearance. At other times of year stone flies, caterpillars and many other insects provide ideal bait. So do hellgrammites and nymphs. For the large brown trout which are found so frequently in little brooks what could be more effective than a little frog hooked through the lips? The banks of streams and brooks are alive with excellent baits if the angler is observant enough to look for them. In using a worm many fishermen consider it necessary to conceal the barb of the hook. Others feel that the worm is less likely to be lost if he is hooked through the collar. It is better by far to use a short-shanked hook and to affix the worm so that half an inch or so of his middle is impaled on the hook with the rest of him wriggling free. In this way he is more lifelike than if he is looped on. Usually a trout will grab him by the middle anyway and there is where it seems best to hook him.

While meadow streams demand stalking skill and brushy

streams require patience, there is to me no more pleasant type of brook than that which splashes over rocks and ledges as it tumbles down a valley to the river below. Whether we elect to fish it upstream or down, to use live bait or the artificial fly; whether we fish in the East or the West, on mountain or in valley, the trout in its waters always are found in the same types of places. To locate them and to know when they are most inclined to be active and thus to take a lure let us refer again to the Temperature-Activity Table in Chapter Three. This tells us that trout generally prefer temperatures of between 50° and 70°. In the early spring or in high altitudes when waters are very cold, at the lower limits of this range or below it, the trout may be expected to seek the deeper pools and to feed most avidly during the warmer part of the day. At the other extreme in summer, if the brook is such that its water temperatures approach the upper tolerant limits, the trout again will seek the deeper pools but will feed more actively during the early morning or late evening hours when water temperatures are cooler and more to their liking. In either case, high or low surface temperatures drive them to the water which is nearest to their optimum requirements. This, under such conditions in a brook, is at the bottom of the deeper pools. To be sure, the temperature difference between the pool surface and bottom may not be very great but it usually is more pronounced than the angler may realize. Like ourselves, when we search for relative coolness in the summer heat, a few degrees makes a lot of difference. Deep in the pools the rocks slow the flow of water and keep it more nearly uniform than that which rushes by on the surface. Trout seek the depths of pools when the temperatures of surface waters are distasteful to them. Thus, under unusual temperature conditions, this simple formula indicates where we are most apt to find trout and when they are most inclined to feed. The use of this formula does not require a thermometer any more than a thermometer is necessary to tell us whether our morning coffee is too hot or too cold. It merely requires enough familiarity with water temperatures so that the angler may judge them with a reasonable degree of accuracy.

From this knowledge of water temperatures we can judge when to fish a lure on or near the surface and when to fish it deep. We can even make an intelligent decision as to whether we should get up early to go fishing or whether it will be wiser to spend an extra hour or two in bed!

Under normal conditions locating trout is less a matter of temperature and more a matter of concealment. In fishing little brooks, as in fishing the larger streams, the pertinent question seems to be "Where are the places where I would hide if I were a trout?" If the angler can answer that question intelligently he can make an accurate guess as to where the trout are. Then, all he has to do is to catch them. It is well to know what species of trout are in the brooks we intend to fish because it has been noted that each has his favorite type of water wherein he is most likely to be found.

Rocky brooks of moderate flow provide waters in which all six major species of trout are happy, with the exception of the Dolly Varden, which likes the big, deep holes, and the lake trout, which does not inhabit brooks at all. In these rocky brooks every boulder in the current may harbor a trout or two, particularly in the protected area of its downstream side. Anglers unused to fishing brooks frequently pass by some of these spots, believing them to be too shallow. If they are shallow they may not contain large fish but it is surprising how big are the trout taken from small runs in the current. Fishing the current is always a good principle. In doing so, every obstruction should be investigated thoroughly. Wherever rocks form a little pool; wherever a log juts into the stream; wherever a ledge or waterfall provides a deep spot, there is where a trout should be found. When bushes or low trees overhang the water trout seek the shade under them, also induced by the fact that an insect or two may drop from their branches. Where the brook turns in its course and forms a deep channel on one side trout seek the deep water and may be resting even behind very small rocks. Concealment is the key to finding trout and caution and knowledge are the keys to catching them.

New England is not unlike other localities possessing good trout waters in that its brooks are crossed at frequent intervals by low bridges on rarely traveled country roads. Regardless of the clatter of traffic on the bridge above, the dark recess underneath usually contains several large trout. Oftentimes these bridges are too small to cast a fly far under them. The water is too filled with rocks to drift a lure in to where the big fish may be lying. Because fishing in such places is difficult is a very good reason why trout are to be found there. In such a place the wood chip trick pays off. On the chip the fly or bait will float far beneath the bridge or into the culvert to be twitched from its little raft when it reaches the spot where the big one is thought to lie.

Little brooks are nurseries for trout. Unfortunately the angler who goes fishing in them for big trout often catches too many little ones. When the angler uses live bait the baby trout often are so deeply hooked that they cannot live if they are released. For this reason many anglers do no fishing in brooks populated largely by undersized fish because they know that every small trout killed means that there will be one less to grow up to respectable size. It seems neither good sport nor good economy to bother the little ones. Yet in these nursery brooks there often are big trout also. How can one fish for the big ones and avoid taking those which are too small? It can of course be done by using artificial flies rather than bait. A small trout which takes an artificial fly usually hooks himself in the lip rather than deep in the gullet. The fish can be lifted from the water by the angler holding only the fly. By turning the fly hook down the frantic little trout will wriggle himself off the hook without being touched by the angler. Since many fishermen will not use flies, what can be done to protect little trout when using bait? The only solution seems to be in using a hook large enough so that a little trout can not take it far into his mouth. In experimenting with large hooks for worm fishing in brooks I have found that I have caught just as many of the large trout but that the small ones are hooked less often. They rarely are hooked deep and the large hook helps the angler to shake them off without injury.

CHAPTER SEVEN

Streams and Rivers

Selecting "Trouty Spots" and How to Fish Them

THE BETTER I KNOW other anglers, and the more I observe their methods of fishing trout waters, the more apparent it becomes that the most successful fishermen do not reach this distinction by chance or luck. Their practices resemble those of the mentally deficient farmhand who found the lost horse when nobody else could do so. He explained that he thought of where he would go if he were a horse; went there and there was the horse. The situations presented in locating trout are more complex but nevertheless similar, because rarely do we bumble upon them by chance. If we remember their basic likes and dislikes of the many varying types of waters in streams and lakes; if we consider their migratory habits and the seasonal variations in water temperatures which cause them to move from place to place, then the processes of elimination and logic seem to make their current abodes fairly obvious. Anglers who have fished many trout waters in all parts of America find it increasingly apparent that trout are to be found in typical sections of any stream while others virtually are barren and a waste of time to fish. Acquiring this knowledge endows the angler with what may be termed "fish sense." Fishermen who have "fish sense" consistently locate and hook large numbers of trout while those who do not have it are successful only in random cases.

Fish sense is relative, since all anglers have it to a greater or lesser degree. It is surprising how little of it is possessed by the average person who invariably fishes the right places at the wrong times or who passes by the good water in order to try his luck in spots where trout are less apt to be. Insofar as stream fishing is concerned, fish sense depends largely upon the ability to pick out the "trouty spots" in a river and then, of course, to present a logical lure to the trout in a proper manner. Whether we wet our lines in Maine or Massachusetts, in Colorado or California, or wherever else there are trout streams, there are in all rivers certain obvious places where trout surely should be, if they are in the river at all.

In selecting such places consideration must be given to the type of trout we expect to catch, since the Eastern brook trout, the rainbow or steelhead and the brown trout all have certain varied preferences in the waters in which they like to live. It will be remembered that the rainbow or steelhead prefers fast water and yet in this fast water he must have a protected spot where the force of the current is broken so that he may rest there with a minimum of effort. The brown trout likes meadow streams where there are deeply undercut banks or boulders and logs near which he may hide. He is to be found in deep pools, which rarely is the case with the rainbow. The Eastern brook trout and his Western cousins, the Dolly Varden and the cutthroat, are found in all of these locations but mainly where there is a moderate current broken by rocks or undercut banks where they can find shade, a suitable hiding place and the opportunity to get the food the stream brings to them.

Such locations are found in countless places on nearly every trout stream. They are standard "holding water" for trout for reasons which soon will be obvious. Our fish sense tells us that trout should be in these places and there is where we should fish for them.

One such place is a large rock which breaks into the current as is shown in Figure 16. The current passing by this rock forms a cone-shaped area of quiet water on both the upstream and the downstream sides. In these two quiet water areas trout can rest with a minimum of exertion. These places are feeding locations as well as resting positions because the currents form back eddies which sweep food into them. If the sun is on the upstream side of the rock, the preferred position is in the shaded downstream area, and vice versa, but both positions should be fished carefully because both are ideal places for trout under all conditions except when the water is too warm to induce them to stay there. Large rocks often harbor big fish. If the rock be large enough and if other holding positions are scarce, it may be that several large trout will inhabit such a position.

From the sketch of the side view of this rock, let us observe that the force of the current hollows out depressions in the stream on both the upstream and downstream sides. It also does so to a lesser degree along the right and left sides of the rock, so that trout may be in these places as well as above and below.

In fishing such places the angler often mistakes the foamy break in the surface at position "A" for the location of the rock itself, if the rock is slightly under water. When he casts at "A" it will be noted that the fly will drift downstream and miss both of the conical holding positions. Just back of the break in the surface there may be noticed a slick, preceded by a slight bulge where the water rises to pass over the rock. It is upstream of this position, at point "B" or slightly above, that the angler should drop his fly in order that it will first float over the upstream holding position, or down into it if a wet fly is used, and then over or into the downstream position. Four casts may be needed to cover the four sides of the rock properly because trout may be on the right and left as well as above and below. Consideration must be given to the force of the current in deciding at what point to drop the lure, especially if spinners or other heavy baits are used. If the cast is made too far upstream, the lure may drop deep down into the pocket on the upstream side of the rock and become fouled unless care is taken to fish it properly. If the lure is dropped at point "B," the upsurge of the water should carry it over the rock and into the downstream feeding position. If no strike is felt as the lure passes the position where the fish is expected to lie, the cast still should be fished out carefully because it often happens that the trout will follow the lure and will take it farther downstream. In using wobbling spoon or spinning blade lures the strike usually occurs when the current has swung the lure down-

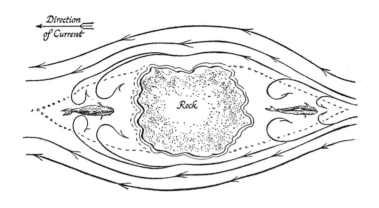

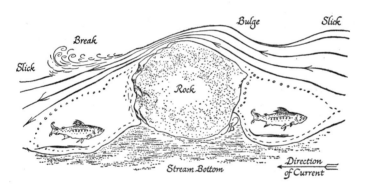

FIGURE 16.

A FAVORITE RESTING AND FEEDING POSITION
FOR TROUT IS IN THE SLACK CURRENT
ABOVE AND BELOW A ROCK

stream at just the time when the angler normally begins to retrieve it. Many anglers get strikes which otherwise would be
missed by fishing the lure a bit in this position, bringing it
forward and dropping it back a few times to tempt a strike if an
undecided trout may have followed the lure. It may be difficult
to place the fly in the proper position just above the rock, because
of the speed of the current snatching it away. One way to overcome this is to cast from below, allowing the leader or line to
drop over the rock so that the fly will land in the desired place.

The situation shown in Figure 17 is complicated by the
presence of two near-by rocks rather than a single one. Both of
these rocks may be fished individually as previously explained.
Between them trout rarely are found since the water is very deep
and fast. Centered behind the two rocks the current branches out
to form a quiet pocket which is indicated on the surface by a
slick above it. Here the currents form an eddy and drop food into
it, thus tempting trout to lie there. This frequently is the best
position of all and should be given special attention by the angler.
A suggested method for fishing it is to drop the fly or lure just
above position "C" so that it will sweep over the rock and down
into the protected area at "A." If the rocks are out of water, it
may be advisable to place the lure in position "D" so that the
eddy currents will carry it into the feeding and resting position
marked by "A." Since several such places should be encountered
on nearly every stream it seems well to memorize the action of
the eddy currents around rocks such as this. Invariably, in any
current, position "A" will be found to be the best. In a moderate
current there may be little choice between the feeding positions
at "A," "B" and "C." When the speed of the stream is very fast,
the size of the holding position at "C" will be so reduced that it
will be of little value, while those at "A" and "B" will improve in
consequence. In this drawing fish should be found where they
are indicated, since these places are both resting and feeding
positions. If a fly is used rather than bait or a weighted lure, it
should be presented by a slack line cast made by casting a bit
farther than where it is desired to land the fly and then jerking

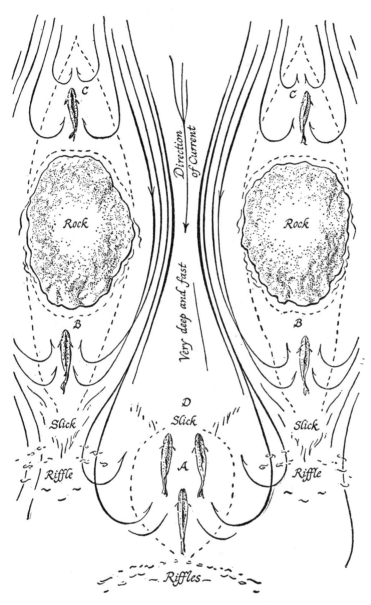

FIGURE 17.

THE CURRENT SYSTEM AROUND TWO ROCKS
PROVIDES NUMEROUS RESTING AND
FEEDING POSITIONS FOR TROUT

back the rod slightly before the fly drops, so that the fly will be pulled back into the proper position with a bit of slack line to keep it from being jerked out of place by the current.

Often the angler encounters rocks or other obstructions in the fast current along the bank which form eddies on the downstream sides. These places should be fished from the opposite side of the stream. Three of them are shown in Figure 18. Behind each rock is a resting place where the downcoming water brings food to the waiting trout. There are at least two ways to fish such spots. Angler number one will fish each one separately, making a slack line cast to spot "X" which should allow the fly to be carried into resting place "A" without drag. If no fish takes it, the current will take the line, forming it into a downstream bow as is shown by the dotted curve, thus dragging the fly out into the stream. Before this happens the dry fly should be picked up, as it reaches point "Y," but the wet fly may be allowed to drift farther downstream in case a trout may be following it. Then similar casts should be made to positions "B" and "C." If a tight line cast is made, rather than a slack line cast, it will be obvious that the current in the main body of the stream will snatch away the fly unnaturally as soon as it is presented.

The highly skilled angler may elect to make a single cast cover all three positions. This is one of the most difficult casts to make properly. In doing so, he will stand in the position of angler number two and make a slack line upstream cast to spot "X" in position "A," at the same time holding two big coils of line in his hand. As the fly on the slack line passes into position "A" and drifts out of it to spot "Y" an upstream loop must be cast utilizing one of the two coils held in the hand to mend the line and allow the fly to repeat the drift in position "B." Mending the line is done by a light upstream roll-cast so made that the line will curve in an upstream direction without disturbing the fly. When the drifting fly reaches spot "Y" in position "B," the second coil of line is released by another upstream roll-cast so that the maneuver may be repeated at position "C."

In the foregoing instances, rocks have been used as examples.

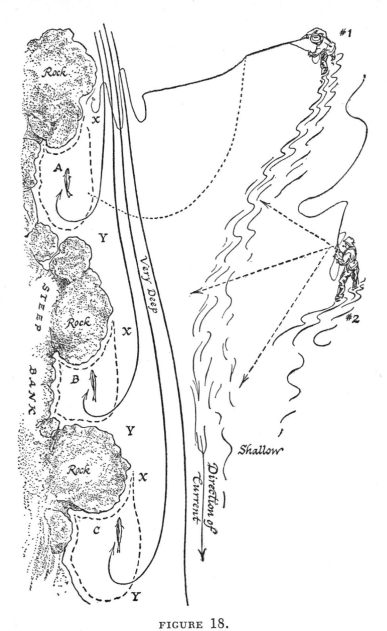

FIGURE 18.

METHOD OF FISHING ROCK EDDIES ON
OPPOSITE BANK

Other obstructions will present similar situations, such as piles of rocks in the first two instances, or even a small island, and a rock ledge or a tree stump in the third.

Logs often fall into the stream and form a barrier to the current as shown in Figure 19. If the log contains many branches it may be a difficult place to fish, costing the angler more in lost tackle than the effort may be worth. If one wishes to chance the investment, there should be fish in the broken current afforded by the log, which offers shade and bits of food to the fish as well. Such places often provide very good fishing. One such log, about a foot in diameter, juts out into a riffle on a thoroughfare in Maine. As we go down the thoroughfare from one lake to another we always stop our canoe a good cast from the log to fish its upstream face. The tiny dry fly dances down the wavelets on a slack line cast toward the moss-covered log, which just breaks the surface of the water. Trout never hit the fly when it is a foot or so away. They wait until it is but two or three inches from the log; then comes a swirl and a good fish has it. It happens at nearly every cast. The fish are only ten or twelve inches long but on light tackle in the swift water they furnish excellent sport with the fly. In this case they seem to be lying just below the log, in the shade, awaiting the food the stream brings down to them. We usually release the trout and there seems to be an unending supply, year after year.

Large logs seem to be more productive than small ones; their size often being in proportion to that of the fish they harbor. I have found many such logs in the smooth running brown trout streams of Pennsylvania and New York. Giant fish hide near them, but if the fly and its presentation is not to their liking, one would never know that are there. In many cases these large brown trout will not bother with a small fly. Their desire for a fly seems to be in proportion to its attractiveness to them and the distance they have to go to get it. Streamer flies may prove more productive than the smaller dry and wet patterns because they imitate a small food fish rather than an insect and thus seem to be more of a meal for the fish.

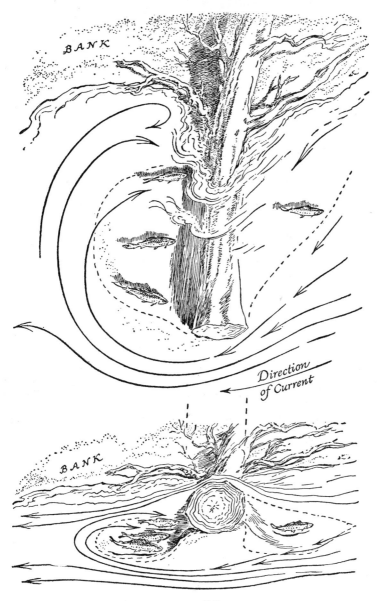

BANK

Direction
of Current

BANK

FIGURE 19.

RESTING POSITIONS IN CURRENT FLOW
AROUND A JUTTING LOG

Logs that jut into the current from a steep bank, providing deep water under them on the bank end as well as out in the stream, may harbor trout all along their length and sometimes more so near the end connected to the bank. Logs anchored in shallow water where there is little or no current should harbor trout only on the end which is out in the stream. If these logs have many branches to snag the fly it seems logical to use a wet pattern, casting it into the current above the log and allowing it to swing and drift with the current in front of the log, fishing it a bit as the line becomes extended and working it down as near to the branches as is possible. When a dry fly is used, a study of the stream currents near the log should suggest how to present the fly to the trout. From the sketch in Figure 19 it will be noted that if the fly is cast near the bank the currents occasioned by the log should drift it down and along the front face of the log, unless the force of the water be so swift that its force will sweep the fly under the log rather than in front of it. When a log is entirely submerged the problem is simpler because the fly then can be drifted over the log and thus presented to the trout which lie both above and below it. Usually, logs which jut out over muddy bottom, particularly when the current is slack, are not as good places for trout as when they are over pebbly bottom in a moderate current. When the current is moderate and the bottom of the stream is cluttered with large rocks, such a place most certainly will contain trout if trout are in the stream at all.

Shelving riffles, as shown in Figure 20, are encountered constantly on all rocky trout streams. Since a riffle indicates a rapid drop in the bed of the stream it must have a pebbly or rocky bottom and must contain a reasonable amount of current. In rocky streams, riffles provide excellent trout water except possibly for very large brown trout or in very cold weather when most of the fish may be in the warmer, quieter stretches of the deep pools. A riffle emerges from a pool where the stream bed is narrow and scooped out or wide and relatively level. Its beginning may be very fast water, foamy and white, indicating a deep and narrow trough through which the water pours, caused by

A Shelving Riffle in Vermont's White River

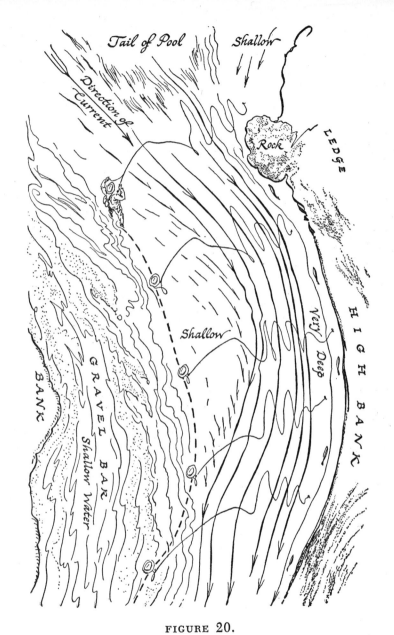

FIGURE 20.

FISHING A SHELVING RIFFLE

the gradually shelving bank on one side of the stream and the steep bank on the other. This throws the main current toward the steep bank and usually causes a bend in the stream toward the shallow part.

The fast, foamy white water usually is too swift to provide resting or feeding positions for trout. At the end of the white water will be a slick where the stream is deep and narrow. This slick is a favorite spot for rainbows and brook trout, but usually the water here is too fast to please the brown trout. If rocks break the current in this slick there most certainly should be trout around them.

Farther downstream in the shelving riffle the deep water will follow the steep bank. On the shallow side, which should be a bed of pebbles and small rocks, the bottom of the riffle will shelve off sharply into the deeper water which starts the main body of the riffle. When trout are feeding they will be ranged along the shallow side just where it has shelved into the deeper part. They take this feeding position because the flow of the stream brings down both floating insects and nymphs or other aquatic food collected in the pool above or dislodged from the bottom by the force of the stream. Riffles are excellent breeding places for insects in the larval or nymphal stages because they cling to and between the small rocks before their emergence as flies. In this feeding position the trout are less influenced by the force of the current, so that they may lie in such places for an hour or more to rise quietly and suck in the floating flies or devour the fat nymphs which drift downstream under the surface.

When the weather is warm, trout most logically take up this feeding position in the early morning or about dusk because at these times the water is cooler and the sun does not reflect into it to make their presence too apparent. These feeding times are more normal in the Eastern states than in the West, where they are inclined to be in the riffles for an hour or two near the middle of the day, as will be discussed more in detail in Chapter Fourteen which relates similar experiences in fishing the Gunnison River in Colorado. It should be remembered that Western mountain streams are uniformly cold, which makes trout less susceptible to water temperatures than they are in the East. For this reason, hatches of insects in Western streams frequently occur at noon, when the water is at its maximum warmth, while in Eastern streams the majority of hatches are in the early evening or at night when water temperatures are comparable to those of noonday in the West.

I remember vividly an occasion when we fished a New England riffle in the early afternoon where I took seven large brook trout on a fly from such a place while my partner took nine. Neither of us changed position since we could cover the entire deep part of the shelving riffle from where we stood. This was in May, when the streams are very cold in northern New England, thus indicating again that trout are influenced more in their feeding by water temperatures than they are by the time of day. It can also be said that trout are influenced in their feeding by the hatching of insects, but again, hatches are influenced largely by water temperatures.

Where the riffle shelves off into deeper water the current will form one side of a long V, the other side being near the steep bank on the far side. From here down, the water steadies into the main part of the riffle. This point is just below the slick mentioned a few paragraphs previously. Where the two sides of the V join at its point there is a concentration of water-borne food from the pool above. Trout are inclined to congregate here or just below this point for this reason and because the speed of the water is to their liking, being midway in force between the turbulent water above and the slower water farther down.

This same condition will be noticed in many cases where the stream enters a pool, the spot providing good fishing for the same reason.

Anglers usually prefer to fish the riffle from the shallow side, casting toward the deeper side where most of the trout are deployed. Their path might most logically take the course of the dotted line in Figure 20. The dry fly angler usually will fish upstream while the wet fly fisherman, or the bait or spinner man will travel downstream, casting across to points just above the likely spots near the far bank so that his lure will drift down with the current, swinging in an arc and covering the water in the middle of the riffle in the process. It may be well to repeat that the trout may be on the far side of the stream but may not take the lure there. He may follow it into the middle of the stream and take it just before the angler begins to retrieve his line. It is important to fish the lure carefully at this point because many strikes are made here. Because this is so, it should not be assumed that the fish are lying in the middle of the stream rather than in the deeper water near the far shore.

Along this far shore many rocks, ledges or other obstructions to the current often will be observed. Nearly all such places are trouty spots deserving of careful attention. They are fished in the manner explained earlier in this chapter. Because of these obstructions the current is slower close to the far side of the stream. Many eddies will be noticed as well as bits of seemingly quiet water. If the trout are not feeding at the head of the riffle, and oftentimes even if they are, the majority of them should be found in the quiet water on the far side of the stream near where the faster current passes.

One can learn a great deal about fishing by watching the methods of good anglers and comparing them with those of others, always asking oneself why some fishermen take trout when others do not. To me, expensive tackle is not the answer and neither, in most cases, is the choice of lure. The important thing seems to be *where* the lure is presented and *how* it is offered to the fish. As an example of this I recently followed two good anglers down a riffle such as is being described. All of us were using wet flies. The leading fisherman made short casts to the proper spots but the fly dropped in the fast water and was whisked away by the current immediately. The second man cast to exactly the same places but his casts were longer and the fly dropped into the quiet water very close to the bank, pausing there momentarily before the force of the current on the line pulled it downstream. In one evening's fishing the second angler took five very large trout while the leading fisherman hooked only one small one. At my suggestion they exchanged flies in process, but the result was the same. There could be no other solution in this case except that the long casts of the second angler placed his fly in the quiet water where the trout were while the first man's casts were too short for the trout to see the fly. The same thing happened very consistently on the Klamath River in California, as will be described more in detail in Chapter Thirteen. In this case the more successful angler was Joe Brooks, Jr. who is well known for his ability in making long and powerful casts. Some of the places along the far banks demanded that the fly be dropped from distances of ninety or one hundred feet or more. Since he could do this with ease while the rest of us came several feet short, he usually led us all in the day's total of steelhead hooked. It often seemed to me that the best spots for these big fish were just beyond the distance I could reach with my fly. After my unsuccessful attempts, Joe would place a beautiful power cast in the spot I had tried to reach and invariably would take a large steelhead from it. It does not seem to matter whether the fishing be for steelhead in California, brown trout in New York State or squaretails in the rivers of Maine. Trout the country over have the same general habits, except for generic differences such as have been discussed, and they are fished for in the same way. A steelhead in Oregon will be lying back of a big rock in the stream just as surely as will a big brook trout be in a similar place in his river in Massachusetts.

Farther downstream the shelving riffle may level off so that all of the water is of uniform depth. Where this is so the current will be even in flow from bank to bank and the trout will be behind or above rocks in the stream in any places where they can find protection. It may be well to state here that resident fish, where water surface temperatures are to their liking, should be near the surface in the deep water of the riffle. The anadromous, or sea-run, trout have a greater dislike for sunlight and are more apt to be nearer the bottom or in very shady spots, regardless of the species of the fish.

In deep riffles where the water may seem to be too swift for trout it may be well to remember that when stones on the bottom are large the current will be slow near the bottom because of the eddy currents formed by them. Thus, water too fast for trout on the surface may be ideal for them near the stream bed. When stones are small, the water will have even velocity from top to bottom. When water is swift and stones are small, trout may not be expected to remain in this area because they would become exhausted from attempting to battle the current.

The split riffle, as shown in Figure 21, holds great fascination for many anglers, perhaps because it demands wading on a bar near the middle of the stream where it sometimes becomes doubtful whether or not a misstep will put the fisherman in water which is over the top of his waders. My adventurous instinct does not influence me to explore the gravel bars of split riffles which are new to me in waters which are deep and fast. There always are local anglers who know how to wade deep riffles and come out dry on the other end. In any event, deep or shallow, east or west, their general characteristics are the same and they are fished almost identically.

Since the shelving riffle has been discussed in some detail, it will not be necessary to do so with the split riffle because, reduced to simplest terms, the split riffle is nothing more than two shelving riffles placed together so that the deep spots are on both sides of the stream instead of only on one. In a split riffle the force of the current puts the flow of a large part of the water along both banks, leaving a relatively shallow sand or gravel bar near the middle of the stream. The proper way to fish it usually is from the stream itself, the angler wading the shallow bar where the fishing is poor in order to reach one or both banks where the trout should lie. It will be noticed that the bar drops off into deep water on both sides. Both sides should be fished in the same way that the same water in the shelving riffle is fished, and for the same reason. Unlike the shelving riffle, the V of the split riffle is at the downstream end, where the two split currents come together, although there may be two minor Vs at the head. Usually, one side or the

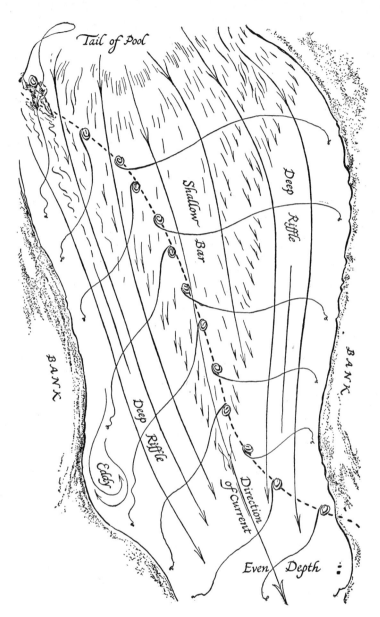

FIGURE 21.

FISHING A SPLIT RIFFLE

other of a split riffle offers the best fishing, since one is deeper than the other. The angler, cautiously wading down the bar, casts to the right or left to rocks and toward the far bank, to the trouty spots which have been described. If he should elect to fish from shore he will be fishing from the good water towards the poor on his side of the stream and he may not be able to reach the best positions on the far side. In large rivers, wading the stream may be neither possible nor advisable and in very small streams it may not be necessary but in many rivers of moderate size it is the only proper way to reach the fish.

The angler's course down the riffle may take the path described by the dotted line in Figure 21. This riffle is in a Western river, although it is typical of similar places the country over. The eddy shown in the drawing is caused by a cave-in of the bank and is not a productive spot because the bottom is muddy, reminiscent of the "sucker holes" in many of our streams, which usually are not tolerated by trout. At the end of the bar, where the water becomes deeper, the river bed will level off so that it usually is possible to wade out of the riffle to one side or the other. At this point there may be a V in the current. If so, it should not be over-looked because it is apt to contain trout.

No general chapter on trout streams would be complete with-out a discussion of that favorite spot of both the expert and the neophyte angler, the trout pool. While I do not mean to dis-parage the productivity of pools, insofar as catching trout is con-cerned, I am firmly of the opinion that many of them are vastly overrated. Typical of this is a pool of my acquaintance in New Jersey. Since it is beside the road it is hopefully fished by nearly every angler who drives by during the trout season. To those who have fished in New Jersey this will indicate that it is fished a great deal. Angler after angler traverses the path to the water and lumbers into the tail of the pool (where the brown trout should be in summer if they are feeding) in order to cast his fly towards the head of the pool where no brown trout should be except when the water is cold very early in the year. Thus, they fish where they should be wading, wade where they should be fish-

ing, and they flounder around in water where they should not
be at all. I have an idea that the very few brown trout in the pool
listen for the car motors to be shut off. When this happens they
swim quietly under a rock and stay there until the moon comes
out and they can enjoy a midnight snack without having some
ambitious angler slap a bunch of feathers in their faces. After
watching scores of fishermen beat this pool without result I
walked upstream half a mile to a good-looking riffle and saw an
angler who was really catching fish. The point of all this is that
pools on accessible streams are such obvious places that most of
them are fished to death. Secondly, it is doubtful that the well
fished pool contains its share of fish, except in the very earliest
days of the spring season. Of course I am referring chiefly to the
pools near heavily populated localities in the East, as differentiated from wilderness pools or Western pools possessing runs of
fish returning from the sea. In the East especially, anglers who
want to catch fish must face the fact that they will have the best
prospects of doing so in the most inaccessible places where the
man who does not want to go far from an automobile will not
bother to fish.

When pools on good trout streams are given a fair chance they
never cease to provide their share of fishing, usually with the
added inducement of a waterfall or an old dam to bring increased
joy to the heart of the angler. The pools of old log dams are so
dear to the man with the fly rod that Chapter Fifteen, and a part
of Chapter Nine, has been devoted to them. Thus, it seems super-
fluous to go into greater detail here. It may be well to bear in
mind that even relatively unfished pools are not as productive to
the fly man all year through as are some other types of trout
waters. Trout which cannot or which do not choose to migrate
downstream to reservoirs and lakes winter in the pools of trout
rivers and many of them are therefore congregated there in the
early spring. At such times the waters are cold and the trout are
deep down where the fly man cannot reach them until the surface
waters warm and hatches of insects emerge. At such times it
seems better to fish the riffles with a nymph or streamer fly be-

cause that is where the fish which have awakened from their winter lethargy will be feeding, nearest to the surface, in the relative warmth of the sunny riffles. In the spring, when the waters are warmer, trout will feed near the heads of pools because there is more subsurface food than surface food coming down to them. Later on, with optimum water temperatures, they may roam the pool more widely. When insects are hatching they drop into the pool in countless numbers, to drift and gather where the pool narrows near its tail. Here is where the big trout may be expected to be feeding in the early morning or late evening, or perhaps near noon in Western waters. Then is when the careful angler will quietly watch them from a concealed position to see how many there are and where and on what they may be feeding. He may count a half-dozen or more in a small pool, gracefully rising to dimple the smooth surface as they suck in the drifting flies. Then, knowing their lie and having attempted to match their food with a carefully selected fly, he can approach the pool from downstream, cast to the nearest trout and attempt to draw him down into the riffles to finish the battle without disturbing the others.

Good trout pools possess many large rocks deep in their waters. These rocks break the force of the current so that, while it may appear swift on the surface, the broken current provides excellent resting and hiding places deeper down. Because of this, when trout are not feeding, the pool may appear to be devoid of fish life, unless the bait fisherman wishes to weight his lure and get it down to where the fish are. When a hatch of insects emerges, if the trout feel that they are unobserved, the pool may come to life and present a radically different appearance; the entire surface dimpling and boiling with feeding fish.

It is unusual for a good trout pool not to contain trout, even if it is small. If there are several moderate-sized ones in it, usually no big trout is present. Conversely, if there seem to be no smaller trout in the pool the angler may well suspect that a very large one is in residence. I know of such a pool not far from my home in Massachusetts. There is a high waterfall at its head so fish cannot get over it. The stream is well stocked with brown trout and rainbows, yet I have never taken a trout in the pool and up to recently I knew of no one else who ever had. Since the spot was ideal trout water it seemed obvious that a big trout was there and had driven all the others away. I fished for him and never even saw him but I was sure he was there. It was not long ago that I read in the newspapers of a seven-pound brown trout which some lucky angler had taken from that very pool. I have not fished the place since but I am sure that by now there are many smaller ones in it, unless some other pugnacious old tackle-buster has moved in to appropriate the domain and drive the smaller fish away.

In Pennsylvania, New York, the Virginias, and other states whose mountains are composed principally of limestone, the trout streams differ in many respects from those in other states. Many of them are smooth, level meadow streams whose deep, cold water is ideal for brown trout. These waters take on a pale green milky color due to the large amount of dissolved lime and are among the most fertile trout streams in the world. Sections of these rivers disappear into the ground entirely to rumble through subterranean limestone caverns deep in the recesses of the bed-rock, later to emerge in full force as complete rivers again, suddenly boiling from the depths of the earth to wind their placid way through mile after mile of fertile meadow land. Luxuriant beds of watercress and verdant grasses line their banks or grow so richly in the stream as to seem to clog its smooth progress through the meadows. If one plucks a handful of these water-borne grasses they are found to be teeming with insect life, crustacea and other foods of the streams. It is no wonder then that in this abundance of aquatic food the trout grow amazingly large and that their numbers do not seem to diminish in spite of the growing hordes of anglers who seek them with rod and reel.

If we did not need to tamper with the natural balance of our streams and rivers there would be little cause for concern as to the future of our fishing. That we must tamper with them is an obvious fact discouraging to the observant angler. We dam them for irrigation, for manufacturing and for power. We cut the protective timber from their banks so that the roots of the trees are no longer there to hold the water. And then we build more dams to retain the floods we have caused. We pollute our streams needlessly and we cause them to become too warm for trout. We prevent the fish from spawning by the dams we have built and then we spend millions for hatcheries to replace in a small measure the baby trout for whose destruction we are responsible. Ignoring in many cases the wealth of income which communities may glean from the peripatetic angler, whose tribe now numbers into the tens of millions and who spends a multiple of that vast sum to pursue his sport, we allow a relatively few men to net our streams of migratory fish to the extent that the formerly fabulous runs of steelhead and salmon are today but an insignificant fraction of their former abundance. In the face of this destruction of our fishing, both necessary and unnecessary, there is fortunately a growing percentage of anglers who have reached the conclusion that the day of the bulging creel is in the past and that the modern fisherman should fish for sport more than for meat. In growing numbers, fishermen feel prouder to exhibit one or two large fish than a basketful of little ones. They are beginning to pride themselves on the trout they battle fairly and release, rather than the ones they kill to bring home. In many communities this sportsmanlike attitude has become imbued even in the families and friends of fishermen to such an extent that the exhibition of too many dead trout is not met with congratulation but rather with contempt.

Some anglers virtually fall in love with trout streams and especially with certain sections of them. After season upon season of fishing their favorite waters they grow to know how best to wade every riffle; how properly to fish each rock, each pool and glide. They come to know the lie of some of the biggest trout and constantly seek to outwit them with the fly rod and the fly. Once taken, the battle fades into reminiscence and the fairly beaten trout usually is returned to his lair to provide still greater challenge for the next angler who tries for him. Tinkering with tackle and the tactics of taking trout becomes a hobby which reaches the point of obsession. Such a man is Harry Byrnes who acquired his love for fishing as the son of a gillie on the river Dargle in Ireland. Harry's affection for West Canada Creek in New York

State is no less than that for the salmon river on which he was born. He came to the hospital to see me the day after I broke my leg on West Canada, bearing the sumptuous present of a dozen delicate dry flies he had tied for me and a bottle of rare Scotch whisky. He seemed greatly disturbed that his favorite stream had treated me so roughly and regaled me for hours with its stocking problems, the dangers of impending dams and with descriptions of battles with the big rainbows and brown trout which inhabit its waters. In his melodious Irish voice he painted the beauty of the sunrise on rocks and riffles and rolling hills making me realize again that fishing means more to the true angler than merely the catching of fish.

One of his descriptions I shall never forget because it is of the mental struggle of every fisherman when he first releases a big trout. "It seemed to me," said Harry, "that I would be happier to let him go than to bring him home dead only to show that I had caught him. He, or I should say 'she,' was a rainbow of better than four pounds, broad of girth and brilliant in the beautiful red stripe down her side. She lay exhausted on the beach gulping the air of which the battle had deprived her. When I placed her into the water she turned on her side, too tired to swim away. I held her upright, gently between my hands, while her gills beat life back into her. When she seemed able to carry on by herself I slapped her lightly on the tail and she swam slowly to the depths of the pool. 'Go on,' I said to her, 'go on upstream and have a lot of babies so that the fishing down here will be better than it is now.' You will believe it," he said to me, "when I tell you that I took more pleasure from watching that trout swim away than I received collectively from all the hundreds I have killed."

Harry's description reminded me of the struggle I had with myself when I released my first big trout. The first one always is the hardest to let go. An occasional trout or two for the frying pan or broiler is the right of every fisherman. But once a man has released his first large fish the intense satisfaction of seeing him return to his stream to add better fishing to our trout waters seems worth far more than the lesser pleasure of carrying him home just to supplement another meal.

CHAPTER EIGHT

Return from the Ocean

Sea-run Characteristics Suggest Ways of Taking "The Big Ones"

BEYOND THE BAR the salmon waited, and with them waited the steelhead, fat and sleek from two years of feasting upon the wealth of shrimp and forage fish supplied by the sea. Two years before, as rainbow trout, they had been brilliant in dark spots and broad scarlet stripes, weighing less than a pound and newly graduated from their adolescence in the river. Returning now to this same river, a complete but temporary transformation had taken place. The bounty of the ocean had added pounds to their size. Its briny waters had encased each of them in a suit of gleaming silver crested by a broad dark back so that they were scarcely distinguishable in coloration from the salmons themselves. Now they rested beyond the bar which separated the river from the ocean, waiting for the feel of rain in the water which would signal to them that their first trip to sea had ended and that it was time to begin the long ascent of the river. Hundreds of miles up the river lay their spawning grounds, the places of their birth whence their instinct compelled them to travel that they might satisfy their reproductive urge before they returned again to the sea.

Others had preceded them in this year's winter run and thousands more would follow. These great schools of fighting steelhead are each a tremendous but separate group. Each had been born in the same tributary and at nearly the same time. Impelled by this instinct of kinship they had made their long journeys together. Now they had returned to their river, their groups eventually to separate each into his own stream. This unfathomable clannishness had bred into each group divergent characteristics scarcely noticeable to the angler but often so apparent to the trained ichthyologist that he can tell a single strain from all others. Some of the schools of fish already had passed over the bar and lay quietly in the estuary and in the pools up to the head of tidewater. In this case, the flow of the river was ample and the bar did not prevent their passage upstream. They lay waiting for the fresh, cool feeling of rain water in the river, the sign to them that conditions were right for the comfort and safety they desired to continue their travels.[1]

Steelhead runs occur in nearly all of our Pacific coastal streams at one time or another during the year. These migrations are separated into two peak periods which are known as the "summer" and the "winter" runs. The two are of such long (even if spasmodic) duration that it may be said that in certain rivers fresh fish always are coming in. These usually are rivers which maintain a swift, even flow all year through, as differentiated from streams which become low and warm during the summer months. Only about one stream in four boasts of a summer run, which starts in some localities as early as May but more usually in June. It reaches a peak in July and tapers off from then until early September, when all of the summer fish should have begun their ascent of the rivers. At the beginning of both the summer and winter runs it is usual for the smaller fish to come in first, followed by the larger ones. Of the two migrations of fish, those in the winter run normally are the larger. While steelhead are known to have reached forty pounds in weight, the largest of record which has been taken by rod and reel is a twenty-nine-pounder which was caught on January 6, 1930 in the Chehalis River in Washington. This fish was forty inches long and twenty-four

---

[1] The impelling motive for the upstream migration of steelhead cannot be ascribed entirely to rising water. In the Klamath River, for example, there is a daily rise and fall due to the Copco Dam, which keeps the river from rising due to rain. Steelhead do not respond to this daily fluctuation but wait for rains before beginning their journey upstream.

inches in girth. Ordinarily, any steelhead weighing over ten pounds is considered to be a large fish.

At the end of the summer run in September the early arrivals of the winter run may begin their entry into the rivers. Usually, the winter run does not start until October, increasing in quantity of fish week by week until the peak is reached in January in some streams and in February in others. Since there are good steelhead runs in many streams as late as March it is apparent that in those rivers where a summer run exists, fishing for steelhead may be enjoyed during nearly any month of the year except for the spawning period of early spring when most streams are legally closed to fishing.

Steelhead fishing can be either a feast or a famine. A stretch of river which abounds in great fighting fish one week may be devoid of them the next and then may offer good fishing again shortly afterwards. Since they ascend the rivers in schools, making an average speed of about eight miles per day, their progress may be predicted. When fishing falls off at one point on the river, it may be expected to be good at an estimated position several miles upstream a few days later. I have camped on famous steelhead streams in Oregon and California at times in between runs of fish and have found the fishing to be very poor, except for a few strays, one or two of which it always seems possible to find. Sometimes these strays are so few and so far between that it seems to some hardly worth the labor of climbing over giant rocks and wading out into turbulent waters to place a lure back of a boulder in midstream where one thinks that the rare fish is apt to lie. At such times it may take a day or two of intensive fishing to hook into a single steelhead, which one may lose among the numerous obstructions in the fast water. Even when fishing is at its worst, just to have a steelhead on one's tackle for a few minutes is to me well worth all the effort expended, but it is very possible to fish Western coastal waters for a considerable time and get no strikes at all.

While eight miles per day is a reasonable estimate of the average progress of steelhead upstream, they may travel much

"Holding Water" for Steelhead Near the Mouth of Oregon's Deschutes River

*The Fighting Fury of the Steelhead Is Conquered by Joe Brooks
on the Deschutes River in Oregon*

faster or much slower, depending primarily upon the intensity of their urge to reach the spawning grounds and the suitability of the water for travel. They will go fast and far when there is a period of high water brought on by rains, but when rivers are low they may remain in the same locations for long periods of time. A summer steelhead entering the river in May or June usually will not reach his spawning grounds until fall. It seems that he plans his progress accordingly. Even with all this time on his hands, he may have a long way to go. He may enter the broad expanse of the estuary of the Columbia River to travel past the nets of the commercial fishermen and over the fish ladders of Bonneville Dam. Surviving this, he must traverse the rapids at The Dalles, where Indians by treaty are allowed to fish for salmon. On flimsy scaffolding over the raging torrent they sweep their long-handled landing nets into the foaming waters below, frequently to be rewarded by catching in them a salmon or steelhead which must enter and attempt to pass through this narrow and rocky gorge in order to get upstream. If his destination is one of the tributaries of the Snake River, he may have more than a thousand miles to go, traveling during high water and resting during low, until his unerring instinct leads him far into Idaho to the very place where he was born and to which he chooses to return.

During his long upstream pilgrimage his appearance changes. His broad sides, bright with silver, begin to show a faint pink stripe. As he remains longer away from salt water, this pink stripe broadens and darkens to become the distinguishing scarlet band of the rainbow. By the time he nears his spawning grounds spots also have appeared and he becomes so identical in coloration to the landlocked rainbow trout that it is virtually impossible to tell one type from the other, except possibly for their difference in size. Thus, in many places, weight is the deciding factor in differentiating between the rainbows which have gone to sea and those which have not. Fish of over ten pounds are termed "steelhead" while those less heavy are considered to be the type of rainbow which has not gone to the sea.

The spawning takes place in the spring of the year on the gravel bottoms of tributary rivers or even in feeder brooks so small that low water may landlock the spring fish in them until the streams raise in level in the fall. The baby fish hatch from their eggs in about six weeks, remaining in the gravel for another month and a half before making their way up from the bottom. As they grow in size they move from their hiding places to work their way downstream, going to the ocean during the second or third year of their lives. Usually they remain at sea for two years, to reach a weight of four pounds or more before they return to the rivers for the first time. Those steelhead which come back to fresh water at the end of their first year at sea are from one to three pounds in weight; termed "half-pounders" by anglers, regardless of their actual size.

Unlike the Pacific salmon, the steelhead does not die after spawning. He remains in the river, returning slowly to the sea, feeding and fattening on the way. Before he reaches tidewater he is again in prime condition, well qualified to give the angler a battle worthy of his name.

Western steelhead streams are fast and turbulent, especially in the winter when steelhead fishing is at its best. For this reason steelhead are less concerned with cover and searching for food than they are with protection from high, fast water. Normally, the fish rest by day and travel during darkness on nights when rain water swells the river, urging them upstream. When the rivers are low, they select typical positions behind large rocks in the current or in water sheltered by ledges or deep pockets in the stream. Rain water or high water is the signal for them to move again; to journey swiftly upstream through pools and riffles, over waterfalls and rapids, until the river again subsides and influences them to rest.

A knowledge of the resting places of the steelhead is of the greatest importance to the angler in selecting spots to fish for them. As I write this on one of the famous steelhead streams of Oregon, this fact is brought out most forcibly. Our host is a veteran steelhead fisherman and in our party is a noted angler with a lifetime of experience in fishing Eastern streams for trout.

It seems quite obvious that Eastern trouting methods bear but faint resemblance to the proper way to locate steelhead in Western streams because, so far at least, the Western angler has beaten the Easterner ten to one. He has beaten me just as badly. Since he has never before fished this stretch of water it seems quite obvious that in his methods there is information of value. Now that our success is increasing under his instruction and since his technique is standard practice on Western streams, a discussion of it may be as interesting to other anglers as it has been to us.

Normally, steelhead do not rest in quiet water such as deep pools. Neither do they rest in the fast turbulent flow of rapids. Their favorite holding positions are in the long, deep riffles where large rocks give them protection from the force of the current; behind ledges which break into the swift flow of the river or in the protected water at the tails of slicks or V's in the stream. Before fishing a stretch of water, it pays to study the stream and to select the places in which it seems most logical for steelhead to lie. A large submerged rock in midstream is identified by a bit of white water on the surface and a narrowing glassy slick extending downstream. Here the current rises over the rock and travels around it, leaving a protected bit of quiet water on the downstream side. It provides an ideal place for a steelhead to rest. The flow of the current around him virtually forces him to remain in his holding position with an absolute minimum of exertion, ready to dart out to one side or the other to pick up any bit of water-borne food which takes his fancy.

A submerged ledge or series of rocks extending across the stream can be noted by the disturbance of the surface water over the obstruction and the wide slick which it causes. Such a place may harbor several fish. There is one on this stream to which the local anglers constantly come, usually taking one or two large steelhead from it. The place is always a "hot spot" during steelhead runs because whenever a fish is taken from it another comes in to take his place. Anglers who have had experience on a stream know these locations and fish them, one after the other, usually passing by all other less likely spots.

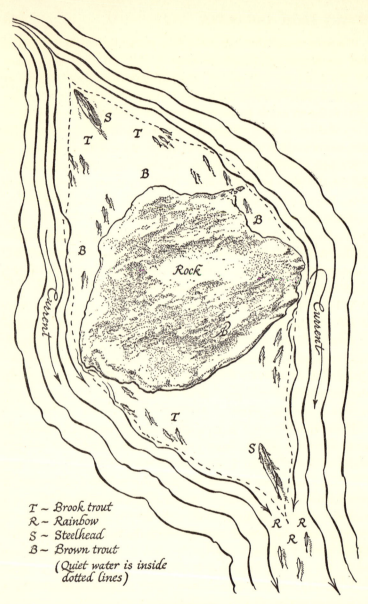

T ~ Brook trout
R ~ Rainbow
S ~ Steelhead
B ~ Brown trout
    (Quiet water is inside
    dotted lines)

FIGURE 22.

ROCKS BREAK THE FORCE OF THE CURRENT
TO PROVIDE RESTING PLACES FOR FISH

*Favorite positions of the more prominent species are
indicated by symbols in this drawing.*

It is safe to say that big rocks in a moderate current, whether they break the surface of the river or not, are ideal sanctuaries for steelhead as well as for other varieties of trout. Wherever there is a glassy slick in the current there must be an underwater obstruction to cause it and to provide a resting place for fish. If one consistently and properly places his lure in such places he certainly should expose it to the maximum number of trout.

Western steelhead streams are fast and turbulent; more so in the winter than in the summer. Wading them is difficult and often impossible, calling for considerable technique and experience and even more caution. Wet and dry flies can be used most advantageously for summer steelhead but the heavy water in the winter places them at a disadvantage, on most rivers, compared to spoons and spinners or bait used with plug casting tackle or spinning gear. The spinning rod and reel is a newcomer to Western streams but it is so amazingly suitable to this type of fishing that its use is rapidly increasing. If a poll were taken of favorite lures, it would be found that the great majority of fishermen who use heavier tackle use salmon or steelhead roe, either with or without a spinner to attract the fish, and nearly always with half an ounce or so of lead to get the lure to the bottom in the fast water.

There are of course local anglers who have special methods some of which are far from orthodox and entirely beyond the realm of logic. When I was fishing the lower reaches of the Deschutes River in Oregon I was surprised to come upon a portly woman crawling on her hands and knees through the grass near the stream and armed with a fly swatter. If she had been a hunting dog, she would most definitely have been on point because, when I arrived so suddenly upon her, the fly swatter was raised for the kill. This stretch of the Deschutes River is somewhat remote, and the volcanic canyons of its banks harbor a large number of rattlesnakes, so coming upon a woman in this territory is a bit of a rarity, especially in such a position. She seemed not the least bit embarrassed that I should find her thus and explained that she was hunting for grasshoppers for her husband who was fishing a hundred feet or so upstream. Being of an inquisitive mind, I sought out the husband to inquire into his rather surprising technique.

He had a plug casting rod with a hook and spinner on the end of his line, with a bit of lead to get it down into the current. He was baiting his hook with the grasshoppers which his co-operative spouse was providing and announced that while he had not yet caught a steelhead on this rig, he firmly expected to do so. He did not explain why he thought that steelhead, just in from two

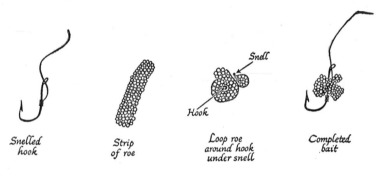

Snelled   Strip   Loop roe   Completed
hook   of roe   around hook   bait
                            under snell

FIGURE 23.

METHOD OF ATTACHING ROE TO SNELLED HOOK

years in the sea, would be interested in grasshoppers and I did not have the heart to ask him. When I returned downstream later in the day, both he and his wife had gone so I shall never find out whether or not his method gave the results he expected of it. Every pool and riffle on a good trout stream should have a distinguishing name. It may therefore be obvious that the place where this gentleman was fishing was known as "Flyswatter Riffle" from that time on.

Anglers who fish steelhead streams have a rather novel and sensible way of baiting a hook with salmon or steelhead roe. As is shown in Figure 23, a size two or four talon-type hook is used with the leader extending through the eye and fastened securely to the shank opposite to the barb by a barrel knot. This forms a noose to hold the bait between the hook shank and the leader. The bait is cut into strips about the size of a little finger, the eggs being held together by the outer skin of the roe.

When the roe is wrapped around the shank of the hook and the leader pulled tight, the bait is held securely in place. Usually some lead is needed to get the lure down into the deep pockets in the fast current. The preferred technique is to use enough lead to keep the lure near the bottom, allowing it to bounce along with the current, keeping the lure just above the rocks. This may be accomplished by the rig sketched in Figure 24.

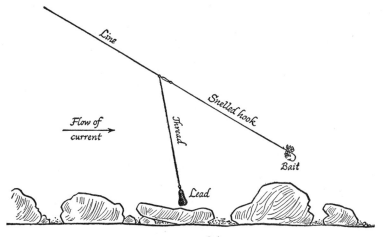

FIGURE 24.

METHOD OF ATTACHING LEAD TO LINE

Since it often occurs that leads get caught in the rocks and must be broken loose, the line which holds the lead is of much lower strength than the main line or the leader. When a break is necessary, only the lead is lost and easily can be replaced.

The more usual method of attaching fish eggs to a hook is to put a bit of roe the size of a marble into a bag made by cutting netting into squares and tying the bag together with thread. The surplus netting is cut off and enough bait bags are made up to carry a day's supply in the tackle box. The type of netting preferred is midway in mesh size between cheesecloth and hair netting. While cheesecloth is used to some extent, most fishermen think that it is too closely woven. The netting is dyed a reddish color to correspond to the color of the eggs. The bait usually is separate from the hook and is fastened to it by embedding the hook in the bag of roe with the barb of the hook pushed through. Fresh roe is preferred but preserved roe in jars often is used.

Many anglers use the usual type of plug casting rod for this kind of fishing. Others prefer the somewhat sportier and more limber action of a "drift rod" which can be either of metal or split bamboo, usually eight or eight and a half feet long, with a grip both above and below the reel seat for two handed casting. With heavy sinkers of between one half and one and one half ounces in weight a stiff rod of this length provides excellent action and makes long casts possible. The orthodox type of multiplying action anti-backlash bait casting reel is used with about two hundred yards of braided line testing in the vicinity of ten pounds. Black line is most popular because it is easier to watch. With such an outfit casts of from fifty feet to one hundred and fifty feet are usual.

In bait fishing, or "drift fishing," the lure is cast across stream. Excess line is taken in and the lure is allowed to swing or drift with the current, the large amount of lead which is used keeping the bait near to the bottom. The arc made by the swinging line is watched closely, the angler striking at the first sign of a pause in the swing. Despite the savage strike which steelhead make at artificial lures they take bait very lightly. Thus, a pause in the path of the line may indicate that the lure is being held up by an obstruction or it may signal the strike of a steelhead. Whichever it is quickly becomes apparent.

With the growing interest in the relatively new sport of spinning with the thread line and the fixed spool reel many converts to this sensible method of fishing for steelhead are being taken from the ranks of both the bait casters and the fly-fishermen. With spinning equipment extremely long casts are possible to reach the promising slicks on the far side of the stream. Such casts often are not possible with any other type of gear and particularly with fly-fishing tackle due to the frequent heavy winds and the canyon walls which prohibit room for a backcast. Bait casters are beginning to find out that spinning tackle is fully as productive as older methods; more sporting and more fun. Fly-fishermen find that with spinning tackle they can get their lures deep down into the water, which is not always possible with a wet fly. Properly used, spinning calls for tackle so light that the fish has as much of a chance to get away as the angler has of landing him. A steelhead caught by such means is fully as much of a trophy as if he were caught on a dry fly.

Large capacity spinning reels holding two hundred yards of line or more are most necessary. Smoothness of drag or brake action is all-important. In extremely heavy water split bamboo spinning rods eight feet long and correspondingly heavy are advisable, but in ordinary circumstances and particularly with summer steelhead the usual average weight rod seven or seven and a half feet long is quite strong enough. There should never be need to use line testing heavier than eight pounds and for all normal use six-pound line makes possible longer casts and is sufficiently strong. Four-pound monofilament offers even more sport and rarely should be broken if reasonable care is used in handling the fish. In company with many steelhead anglers of my acquaintance who prefer spinning tackle for heavy water, I believe that four-pound line is ideal for all but the roughest waters and that it is equal to taking the largest fish, always of course excepting the encountering of obstructions on which even heavier lines might be broken.

Lures for spinning in heavy steelhead waters should be between one fourth and one half of an ounce in weight to provide long casts and to get the lures down deep in the current where the fish usually are found. Those lures such as the Dardevle and the Quilby Minnow, colored red and white, seem to be the most productive. The Harger Lure, with its lead head, revolving Colorado Spinner and hook tied with red and white hair, seems to account for more than its share of the fish. So does the Homa Spinner which has a June Bug type revolving blade at the head behind which is a lead body encased in a bit of rubber or plastic tubing. Other red and white fly and spinner combinations and several varieties of bronze or brass spoons provide excellent results. The old rule of using dull lures on bright days or in very clear water and of favoring bright lures on overcast days or in roilly water seems to hold good for steelhead fishing as often as for trout fishing of other types.

Whenever possible, spinning lures should be cast across stream and allowed to swing with the current down through glassy slicks in which steelhead may be expected to lie. Only enough line should be recovered during the swing to keep the lure off the bottom and to keep the line tight. More often than not, if a strike is to occur, it will happen just as the lure reaches the end of its swing when the angler is about to retrieve it. For this reason the start of the retrieve should be as slow as possible, even allowing the lure to drop back occasionally. It has been noted that steelhead will follow a swinging lure and will strike at it at the end of the swing, perhaps because at that time they feel that the lure is about to get away from them. Since the fast water of most steelhead streams tends to keep the lure off the bottom and acting in a lifelike manner, it is advisable to fish the lure as slowly as the speed of the current allows. The path of the swing should be planned to drop it back of large rocks or into slicks. In such places it should be fished a bit before being retrieved.

For fly-fishing, and especially for the dry fly, the summer runs of steelhead provide better sport than do the winter runs. Usually the fish are larger, the water clearer and less swift, lacking much of the depth and turbulence that make the use of a fly difficult in the winter. Of the summer steelhead streams the Umpqua, the Rogue and the Klamath are among the best known although record fish have been taken from the lower Deschutes and other streams of lesser renown. Fly-fishing for steelhead, when the condition of the water permits, surpasses the taking of them on any other type of tackle. The strike is so savage and perhaps so un-

expected that it could jar the angler off balance on his insecure
footing waist-high in the swiftly flowing stream. With it, the leaping, flashing fury that is a steelhead instantly goes into action
with light tackle and rushing stream decisively in his favor. In
this rapid water a five-pound fish seems as ten; a ten-pounder
virtually impossible to bring to net or gaff. He boils from the
water with a dazzling, defiant leap to display his size and strength.
Into the foam and downstream to the white water he races at
startling speed, stripping off the tapered line and reducing the
backing on the reel. Lest all the line be lost, the angler must get
to shore, fighting the furious fish as he goes. If the steelhead
reaches the rapids and the sanctuary of the pool below, all the
angler may have for his pains is the undying memory of a worthy
foe and a reel stripped bare of line. He must be turned from
the fast water at any cost, even if the leader must break to save
the line. Turned, he sulks in the depths, shaking his head to free
himself from the prick of the hook even as a terrier shakes a rat.
Failing this he leaps again, runs, sulks, shakes, and leaps some
more. Held from the rapids and kept clear of rocks and logs, the
fight slowly turns in the favor of the angler. Little by little the
steelhead's strength ebbs and his runs become weaker. The
angler seeks a stretch of quiet water to lead him to shore and to
draw him to the beach. In the feel of the quiet water the steelhead may make his last bid for freedom, turning and rushing to
his familiar current once more, only to be led again to the beach
and removed from the river for a moment of admiration; then to
be placed carefully upright in the water that he may regain a bit
of his strength and return slowly but proudly to the protection of
his stream.

Taking steelhead on a fly deserves the best in tackle. Since
casts often must be long and driven into the wind, a stiff action
fly rod of six ounces usually is advisable, although a five-ounce
rod or one even lighter may be adequate for the smaller streams.
For the dry fly, a double tapered line to fit may be preferred in
order to land the fly lightly upon the water. For the wet fly, a
torpedo taper will add distance especially if a strong wind be

blowing down the canyon, as is often the case. A large capacity salmon reel is needed to hold the backing which should be from one hundred to one hundred and fifty yards or more in length.

Of dry flies the bivisible or Palmer tied patterns provide an adequate selection in sizes six and eight, with a few size tens for low, clear water. The Wulff patterns also are good, with the Gray Wulff being preferred over the others. All of these flies float well in fast water and are therefore more popular than patterns which sink more readily.

A selection of wet flies will include many predominantly red and white, the most universally favored steelhead colors. Size six is the average, with eights favored for low, clear water and either twos or fours when the streams are turbulent or roily. Choices of patterns vary in the three Western coastal states. Of these, the most popular are the following:

WASHINGTON   Polar Shrimp
Skykomish Sunrise
Red Killer
Kalama Special
OREGON   Umpqua
Golden Demon
Rogue River Special
Silver Doctor
Silver Ant
Royal Coachman
Red Ant
CALIFORNIA   Thor
Cuming's Special
Black Demon
McGinty Bucktail
Gray Hackle (yellow body)
Black Gnat Bucktail
Horner's Shrimp (especially for tidewater areas)
Queen Bess
Bobby Dunn
Van Luven

The last-named three should be dressed on a long shanked hook in size two or four. Many anglers who fish Pacific coastal waters constantly recommend that all flies which can be tied with hair wings instead of feathers be tied so because the hair wings give them a more lifelike action in the water.

The length and fineness of leaders should be guided by the clarity of the water. Normally, seven and a half or nine feet is long enough, with the terminal end 2X in gut or four-pound test strength in nylon. In the winter, when steelhead run heavier, it may be advisable to increase leader tippet strength to .014 inches diameter in gut or six- or eight-pound test in nylon. It never has seemed necessary to increase the length of leaders for steelhead over the lengths given above except when dry flies are used for summer steelhead on small, clear streams. In such cases the angler has the choice of hooking fewer fish with the tippets calipered as above or using twelve-foot leaders tapered to 3X and hooking more fish but taking the chance of losing a few due to the fineness of the terminal end.

The size of leader tippets seems to make a great deal of difference in taking trout of all varieties on dry flies. I have seen expert anglers using the same flies and the same methods and one would take trout consistently while the other would not because the latter used a leader whose tippet was insufficiently fine. Oftentimes 4X will take fish when 2X will not. Small flies have a much more natural action on the water when fine leaders are used. In spite of the probability of losing a few fish, it seems more logical to have the pleasure of hooking them than never to connect with them at all. Color in leaders does not seem to be of major importance, although in Oregon and other states where much logging is done there is a brownish discoloration to the water and when leaders are dyed brown they are virtually invisible.

Earlier in this chapter it was said that steelhead do not rest in quiet water such as deep pools. If there is moderate current in the tails of pools, they may be found there just upwards of where the current breaks into another riffle. In the evening they may move to the head of a pool, just below the fast water, preparatory to running up through the riffle during the night. Ordinarily, steelhead are not found in other positions in pools, excepting always the possible stray fish or those which are moving upstream, which are few in the daylight hours. When rivers are rain-swollen and at flood stage the fish may move out of the riffles into the deep pools for the protection of the quieter bottom water where the current is less swift. As soon as the freshet subsides they will again resume their normal positions in the holding water of the deep riffles. Steelhead are rarely caught in deep pools during normal water conditions.

This may not be true of pools which are formed by a waterfall or dam over which the fish may have difficulty in passing. One such large pool in Oregon was dynamited recently by a person who is now being sought most eagerly by the state authorities. By this wanton act the unscrupulous man killed more than two thousand steelhead, the larger part of the summer run in this river. Evidently he realized the destruction his act had caused because he hastily left the state, leaving all of his belongings behind him. All of these fish had collected in this pool to await high water which would enable them to get over the falls.

Just as the rainbow newly arrived from the ocean universally is called a "steelhead," so is the anadromous cutthroat trout known generally as a "blueback." Its habits have not yet received the careful study enjoyed by its more renowned cousin, yet sea-run cutthroat trout fishing enjoys a great deal of popularity in western coastal waters. These fish, like the steelhead, are silvery of side and bluish-black of back when freshly in from the sea, gradually reverting to their cutthroat coloration as they remain in fresh water. On rod and reel they must be handled with care since too tight holding will pull the hook from their tender mouths.

The sea-run cutthroat appears in Oregon waters early in July, with increasingly large runs into tidewater through August, after which the fish diminish in numbers until a secondary run appears late in October with a peak in December and a falling off in numbers in January. When they can do so, cutthroats spend three months of the year in salt water and the rest in fresh, returning to salt water every year, usually in the spring. They spawn during the midwinter months in very small streams, much like the Eastern brook trout. They average little more than a pound or two in size, and in length they vary between ten and twenty inches.

Fishing for the cutthroat is very similar to that for the Eastern brook trout. They usually are to be found in narrow winding streams not far from tidewater, hiding in the protection of boulders and undercut banks. Many of these streams are very bushy, presenting a delicate problem to the angler, since the cutthroat enjoys the shade of the bushes along the banks and will not travel far for his food. Accordingly, the fly must be so placed that it will drift under the bushes to the waiting trout without being caught in the underbrush. Wet flies are more favored than dry, the principal favorites being the Spruce,[2] Faulk Special, Conrod Shrimp, Royal Coachman Bucktail,[2] Cutthroat [2] and the Captain in sizes six, eight and ten.

The sea-run cutthroat, as does the steelhead, prefers to travel upstream after darkness on high water. Above tidewater he feeds usually in the evening on his upstream run but on his return downstream after spawning he will take flies or bait all day long, with principal feeding periods in the early morning and late evening when the shadows are on the water. He is known to take lures better on dark days than on bright ones. This propensity of his for remaining in the shade of bushes and boulders, of feeding mostly on cloudy days and when the sun is off the water, may be due to his oceanic background when he remained in the depths away from the full glare of the sun. Certainly, he seems to shun sunlight even more than do other species of trout.

In tidewater, where the cutthroat schools frequently come in from the ocean on the rising tide and return on the ebb, he feeds ravenously all day long. To catch him in these places, trolled or cast spinners and spoons bring best results.

---

[2] These flies should be tied on long shanked hooks.

Because of the transcending prominence of the steelhead in Pacific coastal waters the sea-run cutthroat is comparatively ignored. In a way, this is unfortunate because he is a good fighter with bulldog characteristics and an excellent table fish. Like the steelhead, he takes surface feed very little when he is in or near tidewater but as he moves upstream the bountiful hatches of insects become more interesting to him and he gradually becomes used to taking his food upon the surface. Then, a naturally drifting artificial, perhaps retrieved as a nymph in short, sharp jerks, becomes very alluring, providing excellent sport for the angler with his wet or dry fly.

Sea-run Eastern brook and brown trout are so rare in the Pacific coastal streams that a discussion of them would seem to be fruitless. In Eastern coastal streams, except for the far north, anadromous fish of these species are nearly as rare. It may be surprising to some New England anglers to learn that there are small annual runs of brown trout in a few of the smaller streams of Connecticut and that sea-run brook trout come into brooks on Cape Cod. If this book were not confined to trout waters of the United States it would be interesting to discuss the larger runs of anadromous brook trout which enter the salmon rivers of the eastern Canadian provinces. There, big silvery squaretails of several pounds in size share the spring runs with the famous Atlantic salmon, only to be ignored by salmon fishermen who consider that they interfere with their sport.

PART III

Fishing Famous Trout Waters

CHAPTER NINE

Brook Trout in Wilderness Waters

*Finding Big Trout in Remote Places, Such As the
Renowned Musquacook Region of Maine*

MANY A MAN has hopefully traveled to wilderness regions for big trout to find that the locations he fished were seemingly infested only with small ones no larger than those which he could have caught nearer home. Without doubt, during his unproductive vacation this relatively unsuccessful angler was within casting distance of many trophy fish any one of which would have been a source of never-ending joy had it been fairly caught and properly mounted for display on his library wall. Maine is famous for its big trout but one must know when and where to go and how to catch them when the fateful fishing hours arrive. In writing about the big trout of Maine, as about the other famous fishing areas described in this section of *Trout Waters*, my purpose is to narrate specific experiences which, of course, must have definite locations. To the man who has never been to Maine and does not expect to go there I should like to say that the information advanced in this chapter (and in the six more to come) is pertinent to many other similar places even though they be thousands of miles away. Trout behave in the Maine wilderness very much as they do in the wilderness anywhere else. Fishing for them in many places provides experiences which are applicable in countless other places as well. My purpose in writing these chapters about angling in specific lakes and streams is to offer what is hoped will be interesting and instructive reading in proof of the facts established earlier. The facts which apply to Maine, for example, do not apply to Maine alone. They offer practices tried and true which can be adapted to any similar stream or lake wherever the angler chooses to wet a line.

Even if my eyes had been closed to the beauty around me, I would have known when we arrived at Portage Lake by the fragrant odors of wood-smoke, fir and freshly cut timber. This pleasant combination of perfumes always seems to affirm that a year's work in the cities is left behind; giving at the same time a promise of the excellent trout fishing soon to come in the unspoiled wildness of northern Maine.

From Portage Lake there extends west into Canada a primeval domain more than a hundred miles in diameter wherein are no roads or habitations except for a rare fire lookout tower, trapper's cabin or sportsman's camp. This is the land of the moose, the black bear and the white-tailed deer, with hundreds of lakes and ponds shimmering in the forests. In these placid waters, square-tailed brook trout of fabulous size live in peace and plenty, ready to test their strength with the angler and his well-cast fly.

Before the First World War, most of this country fell to the logger's axe, although a few stands of virgin timber still rear their noble bulks among the second growth. The dams the loggers built have fallen to decay, affording sanctuary to the trout who rest and feed in the pools they have made. The old logging roads now are heavy with underbrush, sometimes cleared into faint trails by the axes of trappers and sportsmen. These are the highways of the woods. There are no others, save for the rivers and streams. Many of the smaller ponds and lakes, too tiny for airplanes to land on, are not visited by human beings from one year to the next. Many of the wild trout in these waters have never seen a fly. To clear a trail to one of these unfrequented ponds and to build a raft to fish from may seem to be doing things the hard way, but it often has provided me with angling at its best.

The little logging town of Portage, on Portage Lake, is the end of the highway for this part of the Maine wilderness. From here, in years gone by, it took days for sportsmen traveling by canoe to go distances that now can be covered in minutes by air.

This newer form of transportation has made the deep woods less remote, yet there are still many places which even the airplane can not reach.

On several trips to this region I have been so fortunate as to have for a guide "Old Bill" McNally, last of the old-time beaver trappers and one of the few remaining woodsmen of the old school. Bill's logging days are over, but he and his son, Dana, run one of the finest hunting and fishing camps in Maine. From Portage it is but twenty minutes to the northwest by air, or a day's canoe travel up Fish River, to their base camp on a little island on Big Fish Lake. When the ice goes out in the spring, Big Fish Lake provides some of the best and most consistent fishing for trout, landlocked salmon and togue in Maine. For a month or more, the fish are near the surface and furnish fast action with a fly. Later, when the surface waters grow warm, togue and salmon can be taken only by deep trolling and one must go to the brook mouths and the spring holes for the trout.

The McNally log cabins on the island always have seemed too elaborate for me. I much prefer the lesser luxury and the greater wildness of their remote outlying camps on the Musquacook Lakes, Chase Lakes and Island Pond. From these places, with food, canoe and sleeping bag, so many varied wilderness lakes and streams are accessible that I doubt a man could live long enough to fish them all thoroughly.

At any time during the fishing season, any angler can take all the trout he wants of two pounds or less in these waters. The big ones, if taken on a fly, call for skill and a knowledge of trout habits and water conditions.

One week in June I spent a few days at Island Pond, where Dana was building a comfortable log lean-to and shingling it with "splits" from cedar logs. Island Pond is not more than a mile in length and less than that in width. It is a shallow place with a muddy or sandy bottom, but the dense overhanging evergreens along the rocky shores, the abundance of food and the coolness of several brooks and springs make it a superb pond for large trout.

While we drifted over the water in Dana's canoe, big square-tails were rolling on the surface nearly everywhere we looked. As we cast a fly over one rise, another trout would break the surface behind us with a "plop" as loud as a rock thrown into the water. We used a wide selection of dry flies, wet flies, streamers and spinning lures, yet not a single fish would take anything that was offered to him.

While the coffee was coming to a boil over the luncheon fire, we discussed the matter. "These fish are just playing," someone said. "They won't take a thing when they act like that. I've seen it happen many times before, and never could catch a one."

Dana remarked that he thought the trout were feeding. "When they break water like that," he said, "it could be that they are following a nymph as it rises to the surface to hatch into a fly. I've seen them do the same thing before. They take the nymph as it reaches the surface and their momentum causes them to break water."

"There was no hatch of any importance," I answered him. "No flies on the surface except midges, and once in a while a small may fly drake."

"If they are feeding, and I'm sure they are, they are taking small flies. Either the drakes or the midges or perhaps the nymphs. We have been using large flies, probably much too large. This afternoon let's try the smallest ones we have!"

After lunch, the rise was over, but late in the afternoon it began again. We had tied tippets on our leaders down to as fine as 5X. We had inspected our fly boxes for our tiniest dry flies, and when the rise began, we were ready. The red sun was setting slowly behind the deep green hills and the placid surface of the pond was broken by the faintest of ripples from a delicate breeze. Dana had, after many changes, pulled the wings from a size 18 very sparsely dressed Black Gnat, a fly so small that it would not seem that a large trout would bother with it.

Yet as he cast it out and let it sink just below the surface, retrieving it slowly by almost imperceptible twitches, a boil in the

water came where his fly had been and he was fast to the first
trout of the day.

There is nothing new about removing the wings from a small
fly and fishing it as one would fish a nymph. The point that came
to my mind was that anglers often use too big flies when trout are
being selective. As fishermen will, all of us inspected Dana's fly
and tried to imitate it as closely as possible from the assortments
in our boxes. All of us immediately began to take fish, yet when
we compared notes later, no two of the successful flies were alike,
except in size.

The trout we hooked were all large ones, ranging from two to
four pounds. They were shorter and much more stocky than the
usual squaretails of this weight range, yet they had little or nothing in their stomachs except for a small mass of the tiny insects of
the size of the artificials we had been using.

On another day, Dana and I flew in the Piper Cub for an overnight stay in the moss-encrusted log cabins at First Chase Lake.
The three Chase Lakes are so small and are nestled so deeply in
the hills that Dana is one of the few airmen who dares to land a
plane on them. It can be done only by slipping in on the approach and by riding the updraft of the wind currents in the narrow valley on the way out. Consequently, few anglers ever fish
the Chase Lakes, but those few are well paid for their adven-
turousness by some very excellent trout fishing.

Here again, the big trout frequently are very selective in their
choice of flies. We drifted the canoe over the little lake all morning without hooking into a fish of more than two pounds. Even
so, along the shore line one could catch trout of frying pan size
at nearly every cast. A few for lunch satisfied us with the small
ones. From then on, nothing but a record trout taken on a fly
would do.

When noon came, neither of us had landed a fish of sufficiently
large size to warrant taking it from the water.

"I suppose you think there are no large trout left in this lake,"
said Dana with a grin.

"I'm sure they are here, but either they are not feeding or we are not giving them what they want."

"Let's drift the canoe over the water at the mouth of the brook, and I'll let you pick out one to work on this afternoon," he answered.

The Chase Lakes are very deep and the water in them is so clear that one can see bottom in many places. Where the brook comes in from Second Lake, the current has washed a deep channel of clean pebbles far out into the lake. We put the canoe with the wind and drifted over this spot. The noonday sun shining into the water made the lake bottom, fifteen or twenty feet down, seem much closer than it was. In the slick of the slowly moving canoe, stones and bottom growth stood out as clearly as if viewed through glass. There on the bottom, their noses pointing into the current and their fins gently moving, were fifteen or twenty of the largest brook trout I have ever seen. They were all nearly of a size, and I am sure that the largest one would have weighed six or seven pounds.

After a lunch of the little trout we had taken in the morning, we went back to our fishing again. Twice during the afternoon, a very large trout came up to look at my fly. Each of the two trout followed it in and, fish it fast or slow, nothing I could do would make either of them take it.

Late that afternoon an occasional tiny dimple appeared on the water. There was no hatch except for flying ants, a few of which occasionally would land on the surface. As I idly watched one of them, a dimple appeared and the flying ant was gone. It seemed to me that I saw a dark shape settle down into the water where the insect had been, but at the moment I could not be sure. It is not always small fish which make the nearly imperceptible dimples as they feed on the smooth surface of a quiet pond or pool. Often the tiny fish rise with a splash while the big old tackle-busters suck in an insect so unobtrusively as to make it seem impossible that it could be a big trout feeding with so little disturbance of the surface.

One day while shopping at the famous Angler's Roost in the

Chrysler Building Arcade in New York City, its genial proprietor, Jim Deren, had recommended that I buy a dozen flies tied to imitate black and red ants. I tied a lighter tippet on my leader and put on one of them. No sooner had it settled on the water than a dimple appeared and the lure was gone. In my anxiety to hook my first fish, I struck too hard and the tiny tippet parted at the Turle Knot where the fly was tied to the leader.

Dana and I both tied on imitations of the ants and from then until after sundown, both of us took large trout constantly. We found out that a fine leader aids greatly in hooking fish with a fly as small as this, since when heavier tippets were used, few fish would strike the fly. A 4X or 5X tippet may break if one strikes a fish too hard, but it seems better to lose an occasional fly than not to hook any fish at all.

"This lake is full of forage fish," I remarked. "You can see them everywhere in the shallow water along the edge. In that case, why do large trout prefer flying ants rather than minnows which could be imitated by a streamer fly? Could it be that they enjoy the change in flavor?"

"Maybe," replied Dana, "but you must remember that while it takes hundreds of ants to make a meal for a large trout, there are thousands of them available today from which they can make a meal. Perhaps they think it easier to cruise below the surface and absorb the ants as they come upon them rather than to go into the shallows to chase minnows."

The selective feeding of trout is a constant study of greatest value to the angler. Knowledge of the insect life of trout waters is an integral part of the study of the trout waters themselves. There have been so many good books written on the insect life of trout waters and about the imitations which should be used under various feeding conditions that this book will not attempt to carry these subjects farther.

While trout foods are considered to be concerned only with insects and forage fish, this is not always the case. In the spring when the red buds drop onto the water from the maples, I have seen trout take them. I have seen trout caught under such condi-

tions by using a fly with a red-orange body from which the wings
have been removed. Since it was of the shape and color of the
red buds, the trout took it as freely as they did the buds themselves.

Finding the right fly is not always the solution to taking trout.
First, it is necessary to determine where the trout are; after
which the choice of the right fly may become of paramount importance. When the Chase Lake trout fed on the flying ants, the
surface waters of the lakes were cooler than 70° and the trout
fed on the surface just as avidly as they fed in the waters beneath.

A few years before this, I brought my wife to the same place
in an effort to show her the wonders of wilderness angling. Unfortunately, there had been no rain for weeks. The streams and
spring holes were virtually dry and what should have proved to
be superb September fishing turned out to be almost no fishing at
all. One did not need a thermometer to indicate that the surface
waters were too warm for trout to take flies, even in the morning
or early evening. To prove to her that the trout were there, we re-
sorted to deep trolling with live bait. When the lure was fished at
a depth approximating that of the thermocline, we took one fish
after another. A knowledge of trout waters made it quite obvious that surface fishing was a waste of time. If one desired trout
under such conditions, one had to fish at the depths where the
fish were cruising, waiting for rains and colder weather to cool
the upper layer of the lake so that they could resume surface
feeding again.

The inaccessibility of the five Musquacook Lakes influences
their high rank among the finest trout waters of Maine. They are
big waters, rarely visited except by a few anglers who appreciate
the superb trout, togue and landlocked salmon fishing which they
provide. For many years, the repaired lumber camp on Fourth
Musquacook was operated by Dave Howe, who began running
logs at the tender age of nine and who spent the remainder of his
seventy-odd years attempting to keep out of trouble with the
game wardens. Dave was one of the best white water men I ever
knew; a man born and raised in the woods whose chief philos-

Brook Trout Taken by the Author in the Wilderness of Maine

ophy in life was that the woods owed him a living; the rather diverse opinions of the Fish and Game Department notwithstanding.

A few years before old Dave died on his snowshoes while walking the forty miles of wilderness trail to Ashland to swap some furs for a drink, I wrote to him one spring to inquire regarding the fishing. Dave, knowing that I would not approve of the high water conditions which prevailed at the time, made one of his rare attempts at complete honesty.

"She ain't riz none," he wrote on the back of a picture post card in his shaky hand, "but she's swol some," he added truthfully.

A few weeks later, when the streams were normal, I flew in to his cabins with my old and good friend, Joe Stickney, who did more constructive work in the interests of Maine's fish and game than any man has ever done, before or since.

I shall never forget that first hour when we stood on the rotting beams of Fourth Musquacook Dam and sent a Lady Doctor into the eddy beside the white water in that beautiful hemlock bordered pool. On the first cast, the water churned with silver and gold as several great trout raced for the fly. One of them had it when it had scarcely touched the water. He shook, swirled, bored and raced as only a wild trout of his size can. There was a question of whether the fine leader would hold him, and the equally serious problem of keeping him away from the white water and the tangle of roots and branches which bordered the pool. Just as he was becoming submissive in the slack water eddy below the dam I realized that I had left my net at home.

"Nets are a city feller's contraption only good to catch on bushes," commented old Dave as he placidly lighted the battered bowl of a smelly and ancient pipe. "Pick him out with your fingers like a real fisherman should."

Dave showed me how to slip my thumb and index finger over the trout's gill covers and then hold him in a viselike grip by pressing his throat with my finger tips.

"Now, you can lift him out and kill him or let him go as you choose," Dave advised while Joe looked on approvingly. "He

can't get away even if he wiggles a bit and if you want to release him, you ain't hurt him none."

I have used this simple method of landing a fish countless
times since then and never once has a fish gotten away, when I
had obtained a firm grip on him. Fish that are too small to hold
by this means are usually too small to keep, and rarely does one
hook a trout that is too large to be landed with the fingers. As a
result, I frequently leave my net at home, feeling that when a
trout is played to near exhaustion and then landed by this
method, he is fairly taken and a trophy worth bringing home.

As in most trout lakes, the fish roam the surface waters of the
Musquacook for a month or so after the ice goes out, usually
sometime in May. When the sun warms the surface excessively,
they sink to deeper levels or seek out the spring holes, pools and
brook mouths, where they usually can be found late in June or
in July. In late spring, they often feed on the surface of the
lakes during the early morning hours and late in the evening.
On taking the temperature of these waters, I have noted that they
are often ten degrees or so warmer in the early afternoon, at this
season, than they are at sunrise. While trout may come up through
the warm surface layer in the evening to feed, they are not apt
to do so when the water is in the neighborhood of 70° during the
day.

In the height of the summer, one rarely can expect to take trout
on the lakes' surfaces at any time; even during the early morning.
The mouths of the brooks, unless they be spring-fed or shaded,
are also too warm. Thus, in July and in August, the trout seek
out the spring holes, occasionally coming into the well-aerated
water in the brook mouths in the evening to feed.

Because of this the "Barrel Hole" in Fourth Musquacook and
"Squirrel Pocket," a spring-fed brook mouth on Second Musquacook, are favorite fishing holes at this time. If the angler does
not know a lake, one of the primary reasons for hiring a good
guide is that he may indicate the best fishing locations, since
many of these places are imperceptible, even to the trained eye.
The "Barrel Hole" is a good example of this. It is a large spring

coming from under a ledge fifteen or twenty feet out into the
lake from shore. It can scarcely be seen from the air and is invisible from the land. If one knows its exact location and chooses
to drift a canoe over it, the sight of the gigantic trout which lie
in the "Barrel Hole" in the summer is worth the trouble of travel
alone. I have seen trout lying in the "Barrel Hole" that must tip
the scale at better than seven pounds. At times, so many fish seek
sanctuary there that their numbers and size scarcely can be believed. To catch these wary old trout with a fly is one of the prospects which lure anglers to the Musquacooks all through the summer, when the "big ones" are concentrated in the spring holes
and the black flies or mosquitoes are at their worst. The big ones
feed chiefly at night and rarely can be caught during the day
because they do not choose to rise through the warm surface
layer of the lake for their food until the surface waters cool down
at night. During the cool night hours and before sunrise in the
morning, it is more than presumption to say that they roam in the
vicinity of the spring hole in search of forage fish which provide more of a meal than does a hatch of flies.

During the summer months, early morning is better than late
evening to fish the spring holes. The fact that these trout can be
taken, however, is attested by the fact that their outlines and
other pertinent data are perpetuated in carvings on the hewn log
porch of the McNally base camp on Fish Lake. A fish bigger
than the last recorded is so engraved and it is safe to say that
the biggest ones have not yet been caught. I have seen them in
the water and I know that they are there.

A mile or so of fast water thoroughfares separate Fourth, Third,
and Second Musquacook Lakes from each other. When the trout
will not take the midsummer fly in the spring holes, they can be
caught by deep trolling in the lakes or may be caught with a fly
in the tree shaded, spring fed waters of the thoroughfares. During normal water conditions, a canoe may be carried over the log
dam of either Fourth or Third Lake and brought both downstream and back up again by poling. Under such conditions, the
water is too deep in many places to wade, but in the summer,

wading is possible. It is more convenient to fish from a canoe, if a guide is along to hold the canoe against the current with a pole. At this season, there are fewer migratory trout in the streams than there are during the spawning runs of September and after the season closes in October. Even so, the great rocks, runs and pools are ideal for trout all season through and rarely could the competent angler fish such ideal trout waters without hooking a satisfying number of fish.

It must be that there are many springs which feed the thoroughfares between these lakes, because the water in the streams is always cold enough for trout. As the stream enters Second Lake, it has caused a deep channel to be worn into the pool bed at the mouth. It may also be that there are springs running into the channel. In any event, there are large trout resting there all season through. Oftentimes, they may be caught on the surface of the pool with a fly. If they do not take the fly on the surface, they may do so if the fly is cast upstream so that the current will carry it down deep as the angler fishes it towards him.

There are many days when the sun is too bright and the surface of the pool too calm for trout to take a fly. When there is an overcast or when the surface is rippled by the wind, the fish often take the fly more actively, probably because the visibility is less and the disturbance caused by the angler and his lure less apparent.

When trout will take a fly on the surface, it is a joy to fish upstream in the mouths of brooks in this manner. If the current is so slack that the fly remains nearly stationary, action is encouraged by giving it a scarcely perceptible twitch occasionally. I always prefer to take a trout on a dry fly rather than on a wet because the surface action of the fish striking the fly makes the encounter just that much more interesting. Also, it seems to me that more trout are taken by this means. Accordingly, it seems strange that so few anglers fish the dry fly in Maine wilderness waters. At the time of writing this chapter, with a pad and pencil in the Musquacook country, I remember having seen the dry fly used only in the rarest of instances. From asking several anglers why that is, it would appear that they either think it to be unnecessary or too much trouble. To me, preparing the tackle is part of the fun and the results have seemed always to be well worth the effort.

While I was overseas during the war, both Dave Howe and Joe Stickney passed on to their Happy Hunting Grounds or wherever it is that ex-poachers and good game wardens are allowed to go. Since they were friends in life, they still may be arguing their radically diverse views together on the ethics of the woods. In any event, Dana McNally and his dad, Old Bill, had leased Dave Howe's camp when I returned, and it is the rarest of compliments for me to say that Dana is as good a fishing companion as my good friend, Joe Stickney, used to be.

Although it has nothing to do with *Trout Waters,* I cannot part with a moment of reminiscence without relating a supposedly true story which Dave Howe always enjoyed telling to the sports who visited his camp. There are many black bears in this country and they were always the bane of Dave's existence, since they had the habit of tearing up his canoes and breaking into his cabins, doing damage which old Dave scarcely could afford to repair. After a particularly disastrous raid on his commissary, old Dave used to relate that he left the kitchen window open and tied a string across the window, the string extending to the window of his sleeping cabin near by, where it was tied to a spoon which rested against a dishpan propped up under the sill. With this alarm suitably rigged, Dave retired in peace and contentment. Some nights later, Dave awoke to the rattling of the spoon against the dishpan. Grabbing his ancient and ever-ready shotgun, he pussyfooted to the kitchen window where his worst fears were confirmed by the sight of a large bear joyfully slapping cans of food flat with his paw and lapping up the contents.

Without a moment's hesitation, Dave fired both barrels and the bear expired in a pool of blood amid the shambles he had caused in the kitchen.

"Why didn't you scare him out and shoot him outside," one of his listeners asked him, "so you wouldn't get blood all over your kitchen floor?"

"Dang it," old Dave would reply, "if I had waited until the

poor critter got outside, he never would have known what I shot him for."

Northern Maine, like many other remote wilderness areas, abounds in "dead waters"; ponds, bogs and canals whose surfaces are seemingly without motion. For centuries past the decaying forests have deposited on this land a deep layer of peat. Multitudes of springs feed countless brooks which wind erratically through the nearly level country to wash away the layer of peat and occasionally to disclose the pebbly bottom beneath. Colored by the vegetation, the waters are dark and forbidding; difficult of access to the angler unpossessed of a canoe. This is the land of the moose and the beaver. In these labyrinthine bogs and canals are Eastern brook trout so large that many a sportsman has spent weeks in search of them; perhaps to meet with a selection of trophy fish but often to return home after taking a negligible few of less than skillet size.

It is thrilling sport to push a canoe slowly among the dense islands and hummocks of vegetation and to flick a fly here and there in the deep canals which lie between because one never can tell when a truly "big one" will make a splashing rise to the fly. It is the peculiar sameness of these waters which most discourages the uninitiated fisherman. One can fish all day for time on end and never catch a trout or, by applying "fish sense" and logic one can locate parts of these "dead waters" which bring forth a lusty strike at nearly every cast. What are the secrets of locating trout in such places?

From what has been said earlier it is by now obvious that trout will not live in dead water unless it is cold and possessed of sufficient oxygen. They like a bit of current, too, largely because this characteristic of the trout water also supplies the other two. The brooks, then, are one of the main indications of where to find trout in such places. The brooks flow into the swampy bogs cutting a definite channel which can be identified from the other labyrinthine waters by the presence of current or by areas of washed gravel in the stream bed. Even though there may be trout in near-by places, due to hidden springs or other favorable characteristics of the water, the flowing tortuous channels made by countless brooks are the surest places to find trout in the greatest numbers. Slowly traveling bits of foam or a purposefully moving leaf or twig may indicate where these favorable channels are. The banks of the channels often are undercut to provide the same protection for trout as does a meadow stream. Old logs lie in the channels and under them large trout frequently will be found. The trout may be timid, as are brook trout in more populous places, but they are rarely selective in the choice of a fly. Large, colorful wet patterns such as the Lady Doctor, Parmachene Belle and the Montreal are favorites for this kind of fishing. Where there is a strong current, streamer patterns usually afford good results.

In addition to the difficulty of separating the productive dead waters from the unproductive ones, if one is not fishing from a canoe the dense growth of alders which borders most wilderness brooks and streams provides another discouraging obstacle. A belt axe is handy to clear a path to the stream and to cut a place from which to cast. With a sharp axe one can make such a fishing platform in but a few minutes. The short fly rod is also an advantage here, due to the confined quarters in which one must fish. Waders are hot, bulky and uncomfortable, and, for this type of fishing, are better left at home. A pair of old cotton trousers, wool socks and sneakers are to me the ideal wading equipment because they are light and comfortable and they dry quickly in the sun. I have never yet fished the Musquacook territory with waders and never intend to do so.

To me, fishing in the Musquacook region of Maine always has seemed pleasantest during the last two weeks of September, just before the closed season which starts, according to present laws, on October first. The woods abound in partridge and other game, so that in two weeks or more at this time one can enjoy excellent hunting and fishing. Then, the surface waters again have become cold and the trout, salmon and togue may be taken on the surface waters of the lakes, as they can be also in the spring. If there have been rains, September fishing is ideal. Nights are crisp and cold, insects have gone, and the trees are in their fall colors. The woods are usually dry and the fish are fat and full of fight. In the fall, the spawning runs are beginning, so that fly-fishing in the streams is better than it is in the spring. Since the male trout are in their brilliant spawning colors, they are more beautiful at this time than at any other. It may be debatable whether or not fall fishing is superior to that to be enjoyed during the two or three weeks in May after the ice leaves the lakes. Because the spring fishing generally is more popular, the sporting camps usually are crowded at that time, which to me. is another argument in favor of a trip in the fall.

Near McNally's main camp on Big Fish Lake, several brooks empty into the shores opposite the island. Trout usually start their spawning runs during the last two weeks of September. At this time, therefore, the brook mouths should provide superb fishing. It is not the habit of trout to race up a brook to deposit and fertilize their eggs. The spawning run seems to be influenced predominantly by water temperatures, so that schools of trout in greater or lesser stages of readiness may spend many days in one pool before migrating upstream to another, to the end that they will reach the fine gravel of the spawning beds far upstream at the stage of the cooling of the water when conditions are best for the laying of their eggs.

Thus, many trout in Portage Lake make the long pilgrimage up Fish River into Big Fish Lake and through this lake up the tributary streams where they choose to reproduce their kind. Influenced by the urge to spawn, the trout are on the move when the waters begin to cool off in the fall. In Fish River there are ancient logging dams which provide pools excellent for fly-fishing. Rapids and rock pools interspersed by riffles and glides provide every type of water for which the fly-fisher could ask.

To kill a trout in which roe is developed may not seem like a sporting thing to do. At least, it does not seem so to me. This may be why it is made possible so easily to distinguish the males from the females at this time of year. The colors of the Maine wilderness trout vary markedly between the sexes; the males being brilliantly colored with orange-red lower belly and pure white underneath, while the females are drab in contrast, entirely lacking in the colors which so closely resemble the red of the setting sun when a good day is in prospect for the morrow.

I have mentioned the foregoing instances of fishing in the Musquacook country partially to indicate that the locations of fish during various water and weather conditions follow a definite and predictable pattern. With some slight allowances for latitude and topography, this pattern should be applicable to other lake and stream systems which any angler chooses to fish.

Rains which are sufficiently heavy to increase stream flow markedly have a pronounced influence on fishing. Large trout congregate around the stream and brook mouths during high water conditions because the water in these brooks and streams is then colder and contains a large amount of feed which the rising water washes downstream. It may be that the trout are not congregated around the visible mouth of the stream. More often they are grouped where the tributary current dissipates itself, in the main body of water. This may be a considerable distance from the visible portion of the outlet. In such places, the water temperatures are so marked that the differences in them are readily distinguishable without a thermometer. Where the water in the main body is warm to the touch, that which is influenced by the incoming current will be cold and more suitable for trout.

Light rains, particularly in heavily forested country, may have little effect upon trout feeding conditions. It usually takes heavy thundershowers or two- or three-day rains to so saturate the surrounding country that the levels of the tributary streams are raised to any extent. Under such conditions, however, trout may be expected to remain around the stream mouths for several days, until the incoming waters again become warmer and normal.

Big Fish Lake, like many other lakes, has many small islands and bars or ledges far out from shore. One end of this lake is about twenty or twenty-five feet deep, while the opposite end is double this depth. After the surface waters have grown warm as the lake begins to stratify in the spring, the trout seek the cooler waters beneath. The majority of them congregate in the deeper water around the ledges, gravel bars and islands. The water around these ledges, bars and islands is relatively warm and thus it incubates a large amount of insect life. Small forage fish prefer this warmer water in which to live. Thus, the trout in the deep, cold water around these places have but a short distance to go in search of food. Therefore, fishing may be expected to be good in such places shortly after the lake's surface waters become warm. This is why trolling and fly-fishing in the close vicinity of islands, bars and ledges is so productive under such conditions.

Later in the spring, all of the water in the shallow end of Big Fish Lake is too warm for trout. They have migrated to the spring holes, up the brooks, or to deeper water. At this time, the bars, islands and ledges in the deeper end of the lake furnish nearly as good fishing as the bars and ledges in the shallow end did a few weeks earlier.

It is interesting to sit on the porch of a fishing camp to watch the fishermen come in. When the conditions are not at their best, some canoes will bring in several large trout and others will arrive with no fish at all. "Weren't you lucky!" "Where did you go?" "What did you catch them on?" are usual questions and exclamations offered by the unfortunate to the fortunate. In some rare cases, success in angling may be attributed to luck. Usually, however, a knowledge of trout waters and fishing conditions has influenced the fortunate anglers in their choices of lures and locations, whether they realize it or not.

CHAPTER TEN

Fishing Famous Gravel Streams

*New York's Trout Waters Indicate How to Increase
Angling Results*

WHEREVER there are trout waters there may be gravel
streams whose swift currents scour their beds of settled
dirt to bare the multitudes of pebbles which pave their clear,
cold courses. If the currents are not so powerful as to disturb the
gravel unduly the wealth of aquatic insects which grow on and
in the gravel will provide rich food for trout. The nature of the
typical gravel stream tells the angler much of how, when and
where to fish it and even of what types of lures to use as the
fishing season progresses. In all the world there is no gravel
stream better known than New York State's beautiful Beaverkill
and its tributary, the Willowemoc. If one can fish these waters
properly one can fish thousands of similar streams equally well,
so let us learn of the Beaverkill and the changing conditions which
affect its fishing.

This, in part, is the story of a world-famous trout stream, slowly
dying. Inseparably imprinted on the moss-covered rocks and the
glistening gravel of its dancing rivulets are the footsteps of the
truly great of American angling. Closely interwoven with its
time-honored history is that of the birth and perfection of the
split bamboo fly rod and of several favorite flies still and long
to be cherished by the fly-fishers of this and new generations. So
great has been its renown that those who love to take lusty trout
on delicate tackle have journeyed to it from far corners of the
world to spend a few days floating their tiny flies on its spring-fed
waters and then to return to their distant homelands, satisfied in

the thought that they have at last fished the classic waters of the Beaverkill, the Willowemoc or the near-by and equally famous Neversink.

New York State possesses many remarkable trout streams. Not far from these fabled waters there flows the beautiful Esopus. To the north, West Canada Creek harbors in its wide expanse great trout to test the skill of any angler. Farther towards Canada are the rocky, rushing torrents of the Ausable. There are many others, but none more famous than those of the southern Catskills; more particularly the Beaverkill and the Willowemoc which both flow into the Big Beaverkill to join the East Branch of the Delaware River thus taking their waters to the sea.

It was these historic streams which induced Hiram Leonard, father of the split bamboo fly rod, to settle in New York's Central Valley late in the nineteenth century. To him came his great disciples, Thomas, Payne and Edwards, whose sons still make split bamboo rods in the Leonard tradition, as exquisitely made as any the world produces. More recently there came to near-by Spring Valley the newly famous Nathaniel Uslan whose hand-made rods are no less perfect in workmanship and are often preferred by the scientific angler because of their distinctively powerful tapers and their unusual joining with five strips of bamboo rather than the time-honored six.

The personages who have journeyed to these verdant valleys to purchase the handiwork of these world-renowned rod makers, and to test it on the fighting fish in the pools and riffles of the Beaverkill, are too numerous to identify on these pages. This book would not be complete without mentioning a few who are no less a part of the history of American angling than the rod makers and the streams themselves. It was here that Theodore Gordon tested and developed the American dry fly, inherited by him in 1890 from the great dry fly fisher, Halford of England. On a rainy day in the summer of 1948 I sat on the porch of Game Warden Roy Steenrod of Liberty, New York, and admired the paper of dry flies sent by Halford to Gordon and presented by him to Steenrod as a memento of their years of friendship in fishing these streams together. This historic set of dry flies was the first to come to America and was adapted by Gordon to imitate the insects of American streams. From these came the famous Quill Gordon, the Hendrickson (originated by Steenrod) and many others. Theodore Gordon died in 1915 but not without leaving an indelible imprint on the history of American angling. As with Leonard, the rod maker, the art of Gordon, the entomologist and fly tier, passed on to his disciples, many of whom perpetuate his skill and knowledge near by the waters of the Beaverkill today.

It was here that George M. L. Branche, author of *The Dry Fly in Fast Water*, inherited and developed Gordon's art of fishing the floating fly. It was here that Edward R. Hewitt made his studies of trout streams and angling equipment; gained his background for writing *Better Trout Streams* and *Telling on the Trout*. Here the great Gordon himself made many of his streamside notes, so ably perpetuated by John McDonald in his book *The Complete Fly Fisherman*. Reuben Cross learned the art of fly tying from Gordon and so did many others, notably Harry Darbee and Walt Dette, both of whom still ply their delicate craft near the banks of the Willowemoc and the Beaverkill in Roscoe, New York.

The turn of the present century was the golden day of these famous streams, before the march of increasing population and deforestation had taken its toll of native fish and the ample flow of the rivers. In these early years, downstream wet fly-fishing was the usual practice, although there were those anglers who also fished across and down while others cast their wet flies upstream to sink them deeper in the pools and riffles. These were the days of long, heavy rods of lancewood and greenheart as well as of bamboo. Stout leaders were considered the thing to use, with large number eight and ten flies instead of the more delicate twelves and fourteens in vogue today. The famous wet flies of members of the Beaverkill Trout Club were the Gordon Special, Golden Spinner, and the Cow-dung. When the dry fly was accepted on these waters, records of the club indicate that one most preferred was the Bradley's Special, while the Campbell's Fancy took top honors among the wets. Those were the days when eyeless flies were tied directly to gut snells and two or three flies were used on a cast. Later on, lighter tackle became popularly accepted with leaders of finer gut with which small flies, both wet and dry, were drifted over likely spots to rising trout. Today, as in most other waters where dry fly anglers congregate, the single dry fly is the method most universally used. Anglers from New York City and from places farther away would journey by train and stage to these famous streams soon after the snow waters subsided to try their skill on the Cable Pool of the Willowemoc, the Mountain Pool of the Big Beaverkill or the many other favorite stretches of the river system where they thought the fabulous "big one" would be most apt to be lying in wait for the well-cast fly. In those days, the cold water lethargy of the trout notwithstanding, the fishing began early in the season and was considered to be at an end with the arrival of Decoration Day.

Volumes have been written and stories have become legend about the big trout which were, and still are, taken from these waters. Trout were harvested by the basketful because there was not the need for conservation that there is today. At least it did not seem so to many of the anglers who thought it necessary to prove their veracity by killing every sizable trout they caught. So much has been written about the fabled fish of the Beaverkill and the manner of their taking that nothing seems to be gained by an attempt to add to the yarns bandied about the firesides of the clubs, hotels and farmhouses of the area. The Beaverkill offers us information on trout streams and the catching of trout that is more important than old tales about the taking of fish which have long since passed out of existence.

Not long ago I had the pleasure of spending an evening with Walt Dette, a contemporary and disciple of many of the greatest names in Catskill angling. We sat in his little shop in Roscoe, New York, where he ties his beautiful and exact dry flies in the best traditions of Gordon, Hewitt and La Branche; selling them to the most discriminating of fly-fishers many of whom from experience will use no others. Few men are better anglers than Walter Dette, or possessed of such a lifetime of information gleaned in the study of a single stream. Thus, to me, his pertinent observations seemed worthy of record and I wrote them down almost word for word. Although he did not know the exact nature of the book I was writing or that I was including the Temperature-Activity Table which seems so important in knowing where and when to fish for trout, his comments confirmed this principle so completely that it seems doubly important to stress them here. They are included in the next few paragraphs.

The fishing season on the Beaverkill opens on the second Saturday in April, according to present laws. Because the water is so cold, this is much too early for fly-fishing and even too early for good bait fishing. Opening season water temperatures are between 36° and 40°, causing the trout to be dormant and disinterested in any type of lure. Along about May first the spring sun has melted most of the snow from the source waters high up in the Catskills and has raised stream temperatures to between 46° and 48°. Only then do the trout become active and interested in feeding; increasingly so as the waters continue to warm. About May sixth in a normal season the shad fly (or grannom) hatches on the stream, usually coincident with the appearance of the shad in the Delaware River. This is one of the best hatches of the season; its emergence signaling anglers from miles around to pack their gear and to try for the big trout with a fly.

Many of the trout winter in the deep pools of the Beaverkill. Although these are virtually all brown trout, the migratory run of the rainbows also brings an annually decreasing few of these fish up the stream from the Delaware River. At this time of year all of the fish are scattered, in one place at one time and somewhere else at another, virtually all in the fast water of the deeper pools. Here in the early season they are found most usually at the heads of the pools where the warmer water from the riffles meets the cooler water of the depths.

In late May and early June the sun warms the surface waters to between 60° and 64°, further stimulating the activity of the trout. Influenced by the rising temperatures and the gradual lowering of the water as the spring rains and snow waters decrease, the fish change their locations to the middle of the pools and to the flat water at the tails of the pools; the more suitable temperatures and the increased emergence of insects prompting them to take dry flies on the surface. If the waters stay at an average level this condition continues until the second or third week in June.

When the stream level drops late in June, water temperatures increase to between 70° and 72° and the fish become scarce. Some of them are to be found in the deeper pocket water behind large boulders while others seek out the springs, of which there are many, particularly in the shaded upper reaches of the two main tributaries of the Big Beaverkill; the Beaverkill and the Willowemoc. It is assumed by some that many of these fish drop downstream into the East Branch of the Delaware River.[1] Fish tagging experiments indicate an upstream migration of fish starting as early as June and due evidently to cooler upstream water temperatures. In April and May the tails of fish were marked for identification by clipping. These fish were returned to the water between six and eight miles below the town of Roscoe. In June several of these same fish were caught more than six miles above Roscoe, indicating an upstream migration of more than twelve miles in less than two months.

July and August finds the water in the Big Beaverkill usually very low. There are few fly hatches during these months. The warm surface water conditions make fishing during the day very poor or nonexistent. The fish which still remain in the main stream are lethargic and disinclined to take any fly or lure; evidently eating very little. For these reasons, the best fishing is during the evening or late at night when the absence of the sun causes

---

[1] Although trout may winter in the deep pools of the Delaware and the lower big Beaverkill, it is to be doubted that they migrate downstream in the summer. Recent records indicate the increasing appearance of bass and occasionally of pickerel in the Beaverkill under high temperature and low water conditions. Temperatures which are satisfactory for these warm water fish are almost certainly too high for trout.

evaporation of surface waters and thus provides a temporary cooling effect of several degrees. With the warming of the waters, bass appear and give further indication that the temperatures are too warm for trout.

From late August to the closing of the fishing season in September the fishing improves because cooler weather begins to lower stream water temperatures. During this time, late evening fishing finds the trout in the medium fast water at the heads of the pools where surface waters are cooler and where increased aeration provides more oxygen to compensate for the still too great warmth of the water. It is interesting to note that the trout do not hold these positions during the night. After darkness falls they are to be found usually in the flats and the tails of the pools, presumably because the increasing coolness of the stream during the night has caused the temperatures to become more tolerant, thus influencing the fish to roam more widely than they like to do during the daytime or early evening.

Since these comments of Mr. Dette's are the sum-total of his many years of experience in fishing the Beaverkill, and also those of many famous anglers of his acquaintance, I believe that they may be taken less as personal observations and more as the tangible result of valuable research extending over many seasons of fishing. That they confirm the Temperature-Activity Table (Figure 3) for trout is not surprising to me because this rule is not of my own devising. Rather is it the composite result of the years of scientific research and streamside experience of so many capable experts that all personal opinions and opportunities for error may safely be considered to have been eliminated. The reader may wish to note for future reference the positions of trout in pools under changing temperature conditions because there is no reason why these facts should not apply to any stream under similar conditions.

During the fishing season of 1948 there were more and larger fish caught in the Big Beaverkill between the towns of Roscoe and Horton than at any other time in recent years. These were predominantly brown trout, many of which weighed between four and six pounds. As will be noted by the sketch in Figure 26, a dam is being built on the East Branch of the Delaware River, causing a constant muddy condition in the East Branch at the confluence of it and the Beaverkill. In addition, there were more rains than usual during the early part of this year, causing the streams to remain at a higher level. It would seem logical to believe that the high water and the muddy condition of the East Branch are the causes of the temporary increase of fish in the Beaverkill and therefore that these trout must have come from the Delaware River early in the season. Since under normal conditions this large number of fish do not do so, it is logical to assume that many of them usually remain in the deep pools of the East Branch during the fishing season. There is a pronounced fall upstream migration of brown trout in the Big Beaverkill and from it into the Beaverkill and the Willowemoc. There is a very minor migration of rainbow trout in these streams in the early spring; the increasing smallness in numbers being due to the fact that in recent years very few rainbows have been stocked in this river system. Brook trout which have been stocked, or which are native to the waters, remain in the tributaries due to water temperature conditions, making fall spawning migrations into the feeder brooks in the late fall. The observations of local anglers indicate that the migratory habits of these three species of trouts follow their usual practices as discussed in Chapter Two. In the Big Beaverkill at present brown trout outnumber rainbows more than ten to one and, partly due to temperature conditions, brook trout virtually are nonexistent.

Since Walt Dette provides anglers with his faithfully tied fly patterns year after year and since he so often fishes these streams himself, it seemed logical to ask his comments on favorite flies for these waters rather than to rely on the opinions of other anglers, many of whom are so wedded to one pattern or another that their advice must be considered biased to a large extent.

As would be logical to assume, the extreme coldness of early season waters makes the use of worms, shiners or spinning lures mandatory because trout feed sparsely under these conditions and rarely take artificial flies at all. The first flies that are taken with the beginning of warmer waters in the spring are streamer flies or bucktails, which of course imitate a forage fish rather than an insect. Usually by the third week in April the streams have warmed sufficiently for wet fly fishing to begin. Favorite patterns are the March Brown, Stonefly, Quill Gordon, Gold Ribbed Hare's Ear and the Leadwing Coachman in sizes ten and twelve. Wet flies are preferred exclusively until May sixth in normal seasons, after which both wet and dry flies are used.

We have noted that May sixth should bring hatches of the shad fly or grannom.[2] This hatch consists of both light and dark colored flies. To imitate them, special dry fly artificials are used which are not considered good after the shad fly hatch is over. To imitate the dark shad fly, a local pattern known as Petrie's Green Egg Sack is the favorite. The light natural is reproduced by another pattern called the Light Green Egg Sack. In addition to these, the Quill Gordon and the Dark Hendrickson are popular; all in sizes twelve and fourteen.

Since the advent of the shad fly hatch is a long anticipated red-letter period on these streams, it signals a confluence of anglers from miles around. As a result, while the early days of the hatch offer unusually good fishing, the trout gradually become more and more selective to the extent that the later days reward the angler even more in proportion to his skill and his ability to fish fine and far off. This is a normal condition on many trout waters where the fish have become accustomed to the angler and his flies and grow in wariness in consequence.

In late May and early June changing stream conditions bring

___

[2] Thaddeus Norris in his American Anglers Book (1864) gives a dressing for this fly regarding which he says, "The Grannom has a body of hare's fur; wings of a partridge feather made full; legs of a pale ginger hackle and a short tuft of green floss silk at the tail, to represent the bag of eggs, which this insect carries at the extremity of its body. In this country the Grannom is found on the water towards sundown around the latter part of June; this imitation of it is a killing fly as a stretcher on a No. 8 hook." Since a very similar dressing is described in other old angling books, the grannom must have been a famous fly in those days.

a preference for patterns such as the Light Hendrickson, the
Light Cahill, Dark Cahill and the Red Fox. Early June brings
hatches of naturals such as the Yellow and Green Drakes and
later on the Coffin Fly. To imitate these hatches, dry flies of the
same names are used, plus the Yellow Mayfly, the Spiders, the
Variants and the Fanwing Royal Coachman in sizes ten and
twelve. Coinciding with the dropping of the stream level late in
June and the warming of the water to temperatures scarcely
tolerant to trout, there emerge many hatches of small flies of
numerous species which are imitated by the Light Cahill, the
Conover and various olive-colored dry flies such as the Quills and
Duns in the smaller sizes of sixteen and eighteen. These flies are
the preferred patterns during August and for the balance of the
season in September.

The Big Beaverkill excels in its ability to provide long pools
with riffles in between. It is all good trout water; the favorite
stretches being between Cook's Falls and Horton, with that part
from Roscoe to Cook's Falls playing a close second in popularity.
Below Horton to the point where the river flows into the East
Branch of the Delaware it is wider and is fished less frequently.
The Beaverkill and the Willowemoc converge into the Big Beaverkill at the town of Roscoe. From about one mile above Roscoe, the
Beaverkill is mostly private water. When the Big Beaverkill is
at its high water stage in the very early spring, the lower reaches
of the Willowemoc are popular. As with the Beaverkill, the upper
reaches of the Willowemoc above the town of Livingston Manor
are largely private, although if the angler stays at one of the
numerous hotels along its waters, permission may be obtained to
fish certain parts of the posted stretches.

The Big Beaverkill, perhaps to be followed in due time by the
Beaverkill and the Willowemoc, is a famous trout stream slowly
dying. The signs of its gradual passing are as obvious to the
student of trout waters as the signs of cancer in human beings are
to a doctor of medicine. Before our time, countless trout streams
have died and many are still dying. Unless remedial measures
soon are taken, the Big Beaverkill is destined to follow the rest.

Time was when the East Branch of the Delaware River was a cold water stream teeming with fighting trout as the Big Beaverkill always has been and to some extent is today. With the coming of the settler's axe, virgin forests bordering the stream were transformed into fields. It is said that when a tree which is two feet in diameter at the trunk is cut down, more than sixty gallons of water are liberated to flow downstream instead of being held by its roots in the soil. Trees and underbrush along trout streams hold a vast gallonage of water. When they are present, snows in the winter melt more gradually and release their waters more slowly; that which remains stored in the root systems providing cold springs and a steady flow of cool water all the year through. In addition, trees and underbrush provide shade to keep these waters cool and to serve as an added source of supply of insects and other trout foods.

From this it should be obvious that, as the trees are cut from the borders of a stream, the character of the stream changes in consequence. Piled up snows are released into flood waters by the sun. Floods change the structure of the stream bed and disturb spawning grounds, sanctuaries and aquatic food. Frequent muddying of the water and siltation of the stream bed takes place. When this vast supply of water, too soon released, has passed downstream, there is little more to come. That which is supplied by occasional rains usually is insufficient without the gradual release of root-stored snow waters to support it. The period of spring flood is followed by a summer drought when the flow of the stream subsides to a trickle. The paucity of flow with the absence of shade and cold springs warms the remaining waters above the temperatures which can be tolerated by trout. The trout native to the stream die off or go elsewhere. Spawning runs diminish and the headwaters are a nursery for trout no longer. Eventually bass, pickerel and other warm water fish enter the stream. In their presence, trout can not prosper. What were once superb trout waters are trout waters no more. From the standpoint of the angler, the stream is dead.

This is what happened to the East Branch of the Delaware

River, which in most places is now too warm to support trout. Of this condition the New York State Conservation Department Biological Survey Report of 1935 says "Several factors tend to keep it below maximum production. Among those most harmful, especially to trout, is the lack of adequate shade and bank brush along parts of this river and on several of its tributaries. This not only warms the water but becomes a dangerous flood menace when allowed to proceed to the extent shown in much of the Susquehanna watershed. There is time to prevent such drastic clearing in this watershed and effort should be made to do so."

That this same condition has been growing for many years on the Beaverkill is a fact which should be obvious even to the casual angler and conservationist. Timber and brush have been cut along many parts of the stream and its headwaters for years. Today, this cutting is increasing and with its continuation the conditions noted above are becoming more and more apparent. Anglers are becoming alarmed at the increasing numbers of bass working their way upstream. Pickerel have been killed recently in favorite trout pools. The summer flow of water normally is reduced to a trickle. Under such conditions and regardless of stocking efforts, trout can not long survive.

Anglers and conservationists can now prevent the death of the Beaverkill as a trout stream. It must be done promptly. Action taken a few years hence will be too late. There are other fine trout streams which must, of necessity, be sacrificed to the axe of increasing civilization. The axe is taking too many of them. Let us hope that the classic waters of the Beaverkill and the Willowemoc will not be among them.

CHAPTER ELEVEN

Big Trout of the Deep Lakes

Idaho's Giant Rainbows Prove a Formula for Fishing Success

IN A BIG AZURE BLUE LAKE nestled deeply in the evergreen forested mountains of northern Idaho there live rainbow trout so fabulously large that no angler to this day has thought it necessary to exaggerate when telling of their prodigious size. The lake is Pend Oreille, which was a name the French trappers gave to the Indians who inhabited that locality because of the *pendants d'oreille,* or earbobs which they wore in their ears. From this lake in recent years Kamloops rainbow trout have been caught on rod and reel which have consistently broken the world's record for rainbows, now listed at thirty-seven pounds. In 1947 three hundred and seventy-one of these immense trout, averaging more than twenty-two pounds, were taken on rod and reel.[1] Thirty-two of these fish were heavier than thirty pounds when officially weighed, a record no trout water in America has ever equaled and which perhaps has been equaled nowhere else in the world.

Kamloops trout are not native to Pend Oreille. A few far-

[1] In 1947, which was the best year for Kamloops as this is written, the data on recorded big fish caught is as follows:

	May	June	July	Aug.–Sept.	Oct.	Nov.
No. of fish 30 lbs. or over ..	8	2	2	3	3	14
25 to 30 lbs.	42	14	3	6	5	23
20 to 25 lbs.	17	22	9	19	6	29

The balance of 371 recorded fish were of smaller size. Evidently many more were caught which were not recorded.

sighted sportsmen planted them there as fingerlings in September of 1942 from eggs obtained from the Kamloops District of British Columbia. The results exceeded their wildest dreams. In 1945, two were caught both of which broke the previous world's record of twenty-six pounds, a record which had stood for two decades! These rainbow trout weighed thirty-one and thirty-two and a half pounds, and what is even more astounding, they had attained this remarkable growth in little more than two years after having been planted in the lake! Lake Pend Oreille since then has broken the old world's record for rainbow trout many, many times and indications are that it will maintain its eminence for several years to come.

How these trout came to Pend Oreille and why they grow so large; how and when they are caught and the type of tackle which is used to take them is a story worthy of the telling because nowhere else have such amazing results been achieved in so short a time.

Lured by the prospects of catching one of these renowned tackle-busters, I went to Pend Oreille in the fall of 1948 and was so fortunate as to hook and land one weighing thirty-one pounds and twelve ounces. He was taken on conventional light spinning tackle with an eight-pound test Pequea nylon monofilament line. I am told that he is not only the largest rainbow trout so far taken on spinning gear but that he is also the heaviest rainbow ever landed on tackle so light in strength. He proved to be the largest rainbow taken in 1948 on tackle of any sort.

The saga of the Kamloops begins in his native home of British Columbia. Dr. Charles McC. Mottley, the noted aquatic biologist, who is an expert on this part of his history, has been so kind as to allow the following quotation from his notes.

"The Kamloops trout," he writes, "is really the variety of rainbow trout that is native to central British Columbia. David Starr Jordan of Stanford University was the first to describe it scientifically from specimens sent to him in 1892 from Kamloops Lake, British Columbia. Actually it is not very different from the other varieties of rainbow trout which have been described from

Oregon, Washington, Idaho and Montana. The dominion Department of Fisheries began to stock it in barren lakes about forty years ago. These lakes, as far as can be determined, contained no fish of any kind, but they abounded in natural food for trout. This type of water is very favorable for an initial planting.

"The trout thrived to such an extent in one of these lakes near Kamloops that the department was able to establish a hatchery there, and millions of eggs and fry have been distributed all over the world. A hatchery was also established in 1914 at Gerrard on the Lardeau River, which is a tributary of Kootenay Lake. The native trout in Kootenay Lake are extremely large and produce big eggs which in turn result in large, healthy fry that are easy to propagate in hatcheries. This stock is that from which the Pend Oreille fish have been produced.

"The size of mature Kamloops trout may vary from a few ounces to over forty pounds, depending upon the amount of food available. In 1931, a forty-pound Kamloops was caught [2] at Jewel Lake, not far from Grand Forks, British Columbia, which is just over the border from the Grand Coulee region. The reason that barren lakes produce such large trout at first is undoubtedly the presence of a great abundance of food. Trout seem to have the capacity for taking advantage of such conditions, soon after stocking, by storing up large quantities of fat and attaining an enormous overgrowth in size. If there are poor spawning grounds in connection with the barren lake, only a few large trout may be produced, as was the case at Jewel Lake. If the spawning grounds are good, the trout will increase in numbers but will not attain a very large size because of competition among them for food.

"In the large, deep lakes of southern British Columbia like Shuswap, Okanagan and Kootenay, which resemble Pend Oreille, there is a variety of Pacific salmon which is said to be 'landlocked.' These fish are variously known as kokanee, redfish, silver trout, or landlocked sockeye salmon. In fresh water they feed on microscopic floating animals such as water fleas, just as they do

[2] I believe this fish was not caught by angling since it is not listed in the records of big trout so taken.

in the ocean. In the spring and fall they live over the deeper parts of the lake, but near the surface. In the warm summer months they retire to depths of forty feet or more. In fresh water the kokanee salmon seldom reaches a size greater than half a pound. They provide the main source of food for the large Kamloops trout. When the trout are small they feed on water fleas, fresh-water shrimps, aquatic and terrestrial insects, but after they reach a length of twelve to fourteen inches they begin to turn to a fish diet. In Kootenay Lake it is not uncommon to find half a dozen full-grown kokanee in a single Kamloops trout stomach.

"The Kamloops trout under natural conditions may reach maturity at varying ages. For example, some of the males may mature at two years, whereas others may be four or five years old before they mature for the first time. Likewise, many of the females mature at three years of age but some may be five years old before their first spawning. The attainment of large size in rainbow trout is usually a race between feeding and maturity. Once they mature they do not grow as fast as before. Conse-quently, if a fish matures as a four-year-old, and there is a plenti-ful supply of food, then it is likely to be quite large. Kamloops trout may spawn several times before they die. If the food supply is poor, however, very few survive after the first spawning.

"Kamloops trout spawn in the spring after the ice has left the lakes. When the water temperature of the inflowing streams reaches 40° the mature trout begin to move upstream. The Kootenay Lake Kamloops migrate up the Lardeau River thirty-two miles to the hatchery traps at Gerrard. The large fish usually choose the main rivers, but the small fish seek out the tributaries. The choice of the different streams seems to be guided by the temperature of the water and the volume of the flow. Their nat-ural habit is to sweep out nests in the stones by fanning with their tails. The eggs are deposited in the depressions and buried with gravel. A female Kamloops trout produces about eight hundred to one thousand eggs per pound of fish. A ten-pound trout may lay over eight thousand eggs.

"The young hatch in a few weeks and emerge from the gravel

nests in the summer. Many of them drift downstream at night, apparently losing their way in the dark. On bright moonlight nights the downstream movement is much less. Some of the young remain in the streams for a year or two before dropping down to the lakes. Others may spend their whole lives near the place where they were hatched. These stream residents often feed on the eggs that fail to get buried in the ground at spawning time, and also prey on the young fry.

"In the case of the coastal rainbow the tendency to drop downstream is quite pronounced, and if the body of water happens to be the ocean, the fish returning three or four years after are known as 'steelhead.' Actually there is little difference between the steelhead and the Kamloops. Frequently they can be distinguished only by a trained biologist, and sometimes even he has difficulty.

"Not all of the Kamloops in a population spawn in a given year. While a part of the adult population is spawning, the immatures and the non-spawners remain in the lakes. Two thirds of the population may stay in the lakes. They provide excellent spring fishing. The spawning fish are usually darker and display the rainbow colors in their breeding dress. The fish that remain in the lake, however, have a bright silvery dress with a steel-blue head and back. The marked difference in appearance between the mature and the immature fish has often led people to believe that they are distinct species, but they are really different stages of the same variety.

"The Kamloops trout is perhaps the gamiest of all our trout. It provides excellent sport for fly-fishermen and trollers, provided that they know something about the right time, the right place and the right tackle. The small fish congregate where the inflowing streams meet the still waters of the lake. There they feed on insects in the spring of the year and are excellent for wet fly fishing.

"In the so-called barren lakes, Kamloops of up to sixteen pounds have been taken on a dry fly. In the larger lakes the Kamloops follow the schools of kokanee, and, although they occasionally provide a thrill to a lucky fly-fisherman, they are usually caught by trolling. No doubt the flashing spoons resemble the silvery flashes of the kokanee. In the spring and fall when the kokanee are near the surface the Kamloops may be found closely associated with them. The kokanee is a fall spawner, seeking out streams and wave-washed beaches. The Kamloops trout fishing is good in the late fall because they follow the kokanees into shallow water. In the summer, as the surface of the lake warms up, the kokanees go down to cooler water and the Kamloops follow. By experimenting at different depths it is possible to find these summer haunts. Such secrets, however, are often closely guarded by the successful angler."

These comments of Dr. Mottley describe the manner of fish which were introduced into Lake Pend Oreille in 1942. It was at that time that the group of Sandpoint sportsmen began a new chapter in angling history by planting twenty thousand fingerlings, averaging from four to seven inches long, directly in the lake. Except during the war, consistent plantings have been made ever since. How many of these fish have grown to large size and still remain in the lake is a question which has been debated ever since the first fortunate angler brought in his visible proof of the amazing success of the experiment. When I considered the possibilities of going to Idaho to try to take one myself I was warned that I might fish for a month without a strike. On the other hand there are instances of those fortunate few who have taken their fish on their first day on the lake. Catching one quickly is at best a very long chance, but it is made more possible by a knowledge of their habits, of the correct tackle to use and the proper way to present the lure to them.

There is one instance of an angler taking a twenty-pounder on a Royal Coachman fly. Except for this and my own experience it seems that all other Kamloops so far caught were landed by trolling from a boat with heavy tackle, the lure being fished either near the surface or deep down with the aid of weights or metal lines.

Fishermen describe the Kamloops as "leaping, smashing hunks

of brute strength." They embellish their narratives with every possible superlative, and there is no doubt that much of what they say is true. To catch one on light tackle is a momentous experience which no angler ever will forget.

We arrived at the comfortable cabins at Talache Lodge in mid-October, perhaps too early for the best fishing, since cold weather was just beginning to color the leaves of trees tiered against the mountainsides. From our porch that evening I looked far out into the smooth lake and thought I saw a Kamloops roll on the surface. The widening rings seemed too large to be made by one of the ever-present salmon which are constantly dimpling the surface in their search for food. I had brought with me a large spinning reel equipped with nearly three hundred yards of eight-pound test line and a five and a half ounce stiff action spinning rod which had handled heavy fish successfully before. If I had realized the astounding size and the scarcely believable power of these great fish, I think I might have given up the attempt to use light tackle then and there. Certainly I would have if I had taken seriously the patronizing glances of the boat captains and of other anglers when they saw the equipment which I planned to use. Lines of between one and two thousand feet in length, testing from twenty to forty pounds are the usual thing, with heavy salt-water rods and reels to go with them.

We fished all that day and all of the next and insofar as I could observe there was not a Kamloops in the lake. We fished from a comfortable cabin cruiser whose captain tried to encourage me on the second day by telling me that he had seen a Kamloops roll on the surface. He followed that remark by pessimistically inquiring if I would not prefer to rest a bit and let him put out the deep trolling lines.

That night my arm ached from incessant casting. This, combined with the fruitlessness of the endeavor tempted me to follow his suggestion. It seemed more logical to try to take one of the famous fish by deep trolling than perhaps never to take one at all. Since not a single Kamloops had been caught on the lake for three weeks the prospects of hooking one on our third and last day seemed dim indeed. On the other hand, the nights had been cold. Frost was in the air and the fall turnover of the lake should be near at hand. As we left the dock the third morning my doubts disappeared. Out in the lake I definitely saw a Kamloops roll, his actions closely resembling the surface antics of a small porpoise. His broad back and great tail were unmistakable. I told myself that the cold weather had brought them to the surface in numbers and that the day was lucky, as ultimately it proved to be.

We cast over the spot for an hour but the Kamloops we had seen would not take the lure. I removed my terminal tackle and in its place put an oval-shaped wobbling spoon on the end of my leader-like line, casting it far to one side and then to the other as the boat made the slowest possible headway. Where Clark Fork River enters Pend Oreille the current swings far out into the lake like a whirlpool in slow motion, imperceptible under normal conditions, but there nevertheless. I reasoned that the kokanee (or "bluebacks" as they are locally called) would be there in largest numbers, preparatory to moving up the river on their fall spawning migration. I was confident that the Kamloops would follow the kokanee and thus might most logically be expected to be in this area. I thought that the cold fall nights would bring some of them, at least, to the surface. With this in mind, we planned to fish that location for the balance of the day.

Just before noon, as another cast swung on a tight line made by the slow retrieve and the imperceptibly moving boat, something struck the lure. It was not the smashing strike which so many writers love to describe. The lure simply failed to come in when I instinctively set the hook, much as if I had hooked myself on a log. Then whatever held the lure slowly and inexorably swam away!

As the boat captain stopped his motor I carefully checked the brake on the reel to be sure that the drag was no greater than the delicate line could stand. All the power at my command in the rod, reel and line seemed to provide no more chance of stopping the majestic run of that fish than if my tackle had been hitched to a moving freight train. The fish must surely be a Kam-

Record Rainbow of 1948 Taken by the Author at Pend Oreille

loops, I told myself, because the large Dolly Vardens which are caught in the lake are rarely hooked on the surface and no cut-throat trout could be as big and powerful as this fish seemed to be. I looked forward to the sensational leap so characteristic of rainbows and even of the great Kamloops themselves. There was none. The fish swam deep down into the lake and stayed there, moving slowly and aimlessly about until it seemed that nothing I could do would bring him to the surface.

This was a battle of brute strength against equipment which seemed at the time to be entirely inadequate. To win it I could arrive at but one solution. That was to give the fish all the pressure the tackle would stand. Too little would never tire him and too much would break the tiny line. As the fish swam deep beneath the boat I noted a barrel knot in my line where I had spliced it together some time before. Occasionally I would bring him up a bit but when he went down again that knot always was in sight.

Eventually the continued pressure had its effect. Slowly the fish came nearer and nearer to the surface. When he lagged a bit I would strum the line to annoy him into action. It was so taut that it sounded like a violin string. I used my fingers to partly brake the reel lest a sudden rush should cause the line to snap. Slowly upward came the fish, swimming relentlessly here and there but always nearer to the surface. I looked into the water to see him but he was not in sight and before he came nearer he suddenly changed his mind and rushed swiftly to the depths again. He was more active now and his runs were faster and longer, but always when he was maneuvered under the boat the knot in the line made its appearance. Every time he was urged upward again the result was only to have him swim majestically down and away.

It was nearly three quarters of an hour after he was hooked that I saw him for the first time. Deep in the water his great glistening bulk was startling. He cruised slowly about, finally tired by the relentless pressure of the fine nylon line which held him; a line which he could have broken so easily if the drag had been too tight, or which he could have stripped off on one long run, leaving the reel bare if he had but known. A minute later he came to the surface, seemingly exhausted and lying on his side. It is then in fighting a Kamloops that the angler should beware. The trout that is seemingly beaten may suddenly come to life, snapping the line or throwing the hook and making off to freedom. It happens frequently with lines several times heavier than mine. In this case the great trout was finished. The constant but relatively feeble pressure had been more than he could stand. He was drawn to the boat, gaffed and swung aboard. Unfortunately the big net we carried was obviously too small to hold him. As the boat made full speed for the dock, the great Kamloops lay on its deck, glistening with the silver of the lakes and, like a fresh run steelhead, showing but faintly the pink band of the true rainbow. His immense bulk was of aldermanic proportions, gorged to repletion with the fat little salmon which had made him a record fish, at the same time contributing to his undoing.

Other battles with Kamloops may be more exciting than this, or perhaps they are made so by the stories that grow with the telling. Longer runs and several leaps, even in big fish, are more usual than otherwise, but this is the way it was with the Kamloops I had traveled so far to find and this is the way his taking must be told.

The fact of the frequent appearance of the barrel knot on the line absorbed me afterwards. When measured, it was forty-eight feet from the lure. Scientists have learned that the thermocline of Lake Pend Oreille is normally sixty or seventy feet below the surface (although its depth will vary somewhat, as in all lakes, due to temperature and wind conditions). This great fish, which could have gone far deeper if he had wished, did not choose to do so. He chose to remain just above the thermocline, where countless observations indicate the deep cruising range for trout is located. Anglers will say in all seriousness that this is not so; that they troll at depths of even one hundred or two hundred feet and it is there that they catch fish. This, I am sure, is inaccurate.

Depths of trolled lures usually are overestimated. Earlier in this
book we have learned that fish in summer rarely will go below
the thermocline and we have seen the logic of estimating its
location and of fishing at that depth, or just above it. In spite of
the cold weather in this case I believe that it was too early for the
fall overturn of the lake to take place because the water temperature at the surface was about 60°. It would seem that at this
time the surface waters were cold enough to bring some of the
Kamloops to the surface to feed, but perhaps that the majority of
them were not surface feeding and would not be doing so actively until colder weather had caused the complete overturn of
the lake. It is known that some few Kamloops do come up
through the warmer surface water to feed in the summer, particularly in the evening. It is also known that the best Kamloops
fishing is in November when the overturn of the lake most certainly has taken place.

As another case in point, one angler who has taken many Kamloops by trolling informs me that he has caught most of his fish
during the summer stratification period at forty-five feet in depth.
He determines this depth by marking his line before reeling it
in after a strike. Later on, he lets out the same amount of line
and trolls near shore until his lure catches on the bottom. Then
he reverses the motion of his boat until it is directly over the
lure and measures its actual depth by the length of the line from
surface to lure. To troll at this depth he lets out between four
hundred and fifty and five hundred feet of Monel line or about
nine hundred feet of lead cored line. This being so, one can
imagine the length of line needed to get down to one hundred
feet or more! The trolling speed of the boat has a decided influence on the depth at which the lure will travel. This angler finds
that best results are obtained by trolling at about four miles an
hour.

It will be observed then that Kamloops are not different from
other trout in other lakes in the depths of the water they frequent during the temperature changes in the fishing seasons. In
summer, with rare exceptions, when surface waters are warm they

lie just above the thermocline. In most lakes they are never below it. In the spring and fall, when surface water temperatures are cold (during the spring or fall lake turnover periods) they often are near the surface but may also be deeper because at those times all of the water in the lake is at approximately the same temperature. Lake Pend Oreille is slightly over one thousand feet deep in certain places. It is nearly fifty miles long and is almost seven miles wide at its widest point. Thus the thermocline, which is sixty or seventy feet deep, is deeper in this lake than in smaller lakes.

Being able to estimate the depth inhabited by the trout from month to month is important. Estimating their location in the lake is equally so. Their location depends largely upon the habits of the little kokanee salmon upon which they depend for food. Thus, to find where the Kamloops should be congregated in greatest numbers it is well to learn a bit of the migratory characteristics of the kokanee. This recalls the habits of the landlocked salmon and squaretail trout in Maine, which follow the smelt in the spring. The situation is similar wherever big fish pursue migrating schools of little ones.

Shortly after the ice leaves the lake and the sun warms its surface waters the kokanee salmon come up from the depths and cruise the surface for food. They search for hatches of May flies, flying black ants and other insects, which are found in greatest quantities along the shore lines and particularly near the river mouths and in the bays. With them come the Kamloops, which are caught in greatest numbers in these locations at that season. Then, the Kamloops cruise very close to shore, so that trolling for them is most successful near the river mouths and off the bays or rocky shores. Wherever the prevailing winds blow the insects, there are the kokanees in greatest numbers and there also are the Kamloops which seek them for food. Surface lines are most preferred at this season, with lures of the wobbling spoon or plug type which resemble in size and flashing color the little salmon. Nylon monofilament lines seem to be most popular. Lures all year round are chiefly Martin or Lucky Louie salmon plugs and Roy

Self or F. S. T. wobbling spoons, but many other types of lake lures frequently are successful.

There is another reason for the Kamloops being near the mouths of the incoming streams. Spring is their spawning season, when those of the big trout which are ready to spawn move up into the rivers. Many catches are therefore made near the mouths of the streams and even in the rivers themselves. Because of their preoccupation with spawning, few of these trout are interested in taking lures.

When the lake warms up in summer the salmon go deep to the thermocline region and stay there until the waters cool again in the fall. There they subsist on the microscopic animal and vegetable life, called "plankton" which is suspended in the water and which provides a dominant part of their food all during the year. The Kamloops do the same, so that trolling deep with metal lines is then more productive than surface fishing. The salmon have little reason to feed near shore and both salmon and Kamloops are found deep in the main body of the lake. As will be noted in the table at the beginning of this chapter, very few Kamloops are taken in the warm months of the summer, probably because too few anglers troll at the proper depth. Summer is deep water fishing and best results are found in widely dispersed locations, in fact almost anywhere, where the level of the thermocline is near the bottom of the lake.

The waters of Pend Oreille do not warm up to temperatures intolerable to trout. While both Kamloops and salmon prefer the depths in the summer, occasional big fish are taken on or near the surface. As the lake grows colder with the advent of fall, it fairly boils with the dimpling of millions of salmon feeding on the surface. Therefore it is not surprising that the occasional Kamloops is taken by surface fishing in September and October.

October is the month when the greater part of the spawning of the salmon takes place. Vast schools of them run up the rivers, influencing the Kamloops to follow. The salmon do this in the fourth year of their lives after which they die as do their Pacific cousins which migrate upstream from the ocean. As the waters grow colder, more and more Kamloops are caught on surface lures. While many of them are taken from the main body of the lake itself, the greater majority are caught near the river mouths and where the river waters mix with those of the lake, far out from shore. For all of the foregoing reasons, Kamloops are not as unpredictable as they might seem. The two paramount keys to their predictability are the temperatures of the lake waters and the habits of the salmon. To those who understand these secrets of Pend Oreille go the thrills of taking these great fish on rod and reel. To others who think that the only requisite for catching a big trout is to troll a lure wherever chance takes them goes the neophyte's usual retribution of returning to the dock empty-handed, as even the best of anglers do on occasion.

Pend Oreille is so famous for its gigantic Kamloops that the excellent cutthroat and Dolly Varden fishing seems tame by comparison, yet if there never had been any Kamloops the lake that belonged to the Indians who wore earrings would still be esteemed as a trout water. Like the Kamloops, the Dollies and the cutthroats are rarely taken by haphazard fishing. To catch them other than by chance one must become familiar with some of their habits.

Although the home of the Pend Oreille cutthroats is in the lake, vast numbers of them migrate up the streams in the spring to spawn. They do this before the fishing season opens on May first, so that they provide good fishing in the rivers early in the season. There anglers fish for them in their resting places in moderately swift water, using salmon eggs or artificial flies as lures. These cutthroats usually are adult fish returning from their spawning grounds. Many of them are from eighteen to twenty inches long, furnishing excellent sport on light tackle. In appearance and activity they are not dissimilar to the Eastern brook trout. After the eggs hatch the young fish remain in the river for two years before migrating to the lake. They return to the streams in their fourth year to spawn. The areas around the river mouths, and the rivers themselves, are therefore preferred fishing locations in the spring.

Upon their return to the lake the May fly and the flying black ant hatches bring them into the shallow water over gravel bottoms and near rocks and ledges. As the lake waters grow warm those cutthroats which do not remain in the streams will seek the deeper water and are most difficult to take on artificial flies. They may be caught in lesser numbers by fishing from ledges or other places near shore where the water is deep, using salmon eggs or worms as bait. Trollers also are successful, especially with a number two lure of the spoon or wobbling type in nickel or brass. The choice of these two colors seems to depend upon the clarity of the water and the brilliance of the day; the brass lure being preferred in clear water and under bright conditions.

In the late summer and fall the cooler waters influence the cutthroats into the shallows again and they may be taken near or in the stream mouths or near rocks and over gravel bottoms where they prefer to search for food. Except in the coldest part of the season, early morning or late evening fishing is best because the surface waters are cooler then and the fish are more inclined to enter shallow water.

The Dolly Varden trout has nearly as bad a reputation in Pend Oreille as he has in other trout waters. He is a savage, cannibalistic fish which is rarely taken on the surface with a fly. In habits and as an adversary on rod and reel he is not unlike the lake trout or mackinaw trout of the East, which in the parlance of most anglers could hardly be considered as a compliment. He is a great devourer of the eggs of ripe fish, not only seeking them near spawning grounds but frequently butting into fish heavy with roe in order to make them eject some of their eggs for him to eat. In Alaska his reputation is so bad that for a time a bounty of three cents was offered for each Dolly Varden tail brought in. Fish tails of every description were presented for reward and the practice became so greatly abused that the payment ultimately was stopped.

The Dolly Varden frequently follows the cutthroat migration part way up the rivers in the spring and waits in the deep holes for them to return. His reason for being there is his insatiable

desire for roe, so it is quite obvious that salmon eggs are the
preferred type of bait. Many of these fish grow as large as fifteen or twenty pounds. They must be fished for near the bottom with bait or with the sunken fly and for this reason as well as
their lack of gameness on a fly rod they are in disfavor with anglers who fully appreciate the joys of fishing for trout. Dolly
Vardens often remain in the streams all summer long but also can
be taken in the lakes by deep trolling with plugs or flashing
spoons in the same locations where the cutthroats are found. I
know of no instance when one has been caught on the surface of
deep water regardless of temperatures.

In spite of the virtues which Pend Oreille holds for the angler
in fishing for Dolly Vardens and cutthroats, and also for kokanee
and the introduced or native Lake Superior whitefish, everything
centers around the transcending dominance of the giant Kamloops. Perhaps there is no lake in the world more suitable for
their existence. Even in Kootenay Lake, which is their ancestral
home, they have not grown as large.

It should be remembered that what has happened in other
lakes may also happen to Pend Oreille. If the propagation of
trout is successful they will grow in numbers and as they grow
in numbers they will decrease in size because their size will vary
in proportion to their quantity and to the amount of food available. Thus it may well be that the largest Kamloops in Pend Oreille
has already been caught, although there are citizens who stoutly
maintain that there are Kamloops in the lake which exceed forty
pounds and that world's records at the lake will be broken for
many years to come. This may well be so and if it is it may not
be a good thing. A Kamloops of over thirty pounds is truly a
giant fish; perhaps too ponderous to furnish the best sport on rod
and reel. If their size decreases as their numbers increase the
larger numbers may well provide better fishing. After all, a lively
ten- or fifteen-pound rainbow is a more worthy adversary for any
angler, particularly if he can hook several of them in a day, than
the occasional overfed giant which is now the reward of a day,
a week or a month of fishing.

The stories about these behemoths of the deep are becoming legend. Some of them are true but I am equally sure that many are instigated by the fertile brain of Jim Parsons, Lake Pend Oreille's able publicity director. It is in the minutes of the Army Corps of Engineers Hearing on the Boundary Dam project in 1947 that a farmer at Clarksford, Idaho, testified that he had to build guard fences, when spring flood waters overflowed his meadows, to keep the Kamloops from swimming up into his pastures and making off with his calves. There is also a rumor that the Sandpoint Chamber of Commerce hired lumberjacks with peavies to go along the various creeks to turn the Kamloops around after they finished spawning so that they could swim back downstream. Jim Parsons says that one of them tried to turn around by himself and got wedged sideways, damming up the creek and causing the water to back up and float a farmer's house off its foundations. All this seems to be obviously a case of following fact with fancy but there is no question about the fabulous size of the Pend Oreille Kamloops or that they are terrific adversaries for any angler who seeks them with rod and reel.

CHAPTER TWELVE

Streams with Varied Characteristics

The Deschutes and Crooked Rivers of Oregon Show How to Select Spots Where Big Trout Lie

THE ANGLER need not go West to find a typical example of a stream whose ever-changing nature will disclose where the major species of trout may be found in a single water and how to catch them there. Since many streams the country over are similar to the one described in this chapter he can apply the experiences learned on this river when he fishes many another. Of all the streams I know of, there is none which seems better to illustrate the strangely varied characteristics which a single river can acquire on its course to the sea than the fascinating and diversified Deschutes River system of northwestern Oregon. Its ever-changing waters are abundant in several species of trout large and even fabulous in size. It is rich in nearly every type of stream fishing from the turbulent steelhead waters of its lower reaches to the quieter brown trout and brook trout pools nearer to its source. Into it the Crooked River boils through towering canyon walls. Placid Crescent Creek rewards a stealthy approach and a carefully placed fly with the spine-tingling smash of an immense fish. Wickiup Reservoir provides the sporting hazards of great rainbows amid clusters of tree trunks and snags. In its more than two hundred mile length one can find waters both wild and quiet; ideal either for the dry fly, the wet fly or the streamer. Certain stretches demand spinning tackle to get the weighted lure down to the waiting rainbow. In others, heavy fly rods must be used because light tackle surely will be broken. Again, a baby trout rod and a size twenty Midge will provide delicate and exciting sport with fish that will guarantee the severest test of the angler's skill. It is a river ever changing in fish, in fishing and in scenic beauty.

Twice in the past few years the first prize trout in the Western Rainbow Division of *Field and Stream* magazine's Fishing Contest has been taken from the Deschutes and a winner in the Brown Trout Open Division, weighing over eighteen pounds, was caught in one of its tributaries. Other fish of trophy size have been taken from its waters while many more have broken tackle and still remain to tempt the angler and his fly.

When the fame of the Deschutes finally goaded us into crossing the continent to fish it, we were the guests of Don Harger of Salem, Oregon, whose renown as a fly tier and angling expert had long since reached the East. Since much of the best water on the Deschutes and its tributaries is virtually inaccessible, we used a trailer and tent as our moving base of operations so as not to be dependent upon more dubious accommodations along the way. The virtually insurmountable canyon cliffs bordering many of the best fishing areas along the river will keep it always relatively unavailable to anglers, providing an ideal sanctuary in which trout will remain unmolested to furnish good angling in its more easily reached stretches for many years to come.

The Deschutes has its source in Little Lava Lake, below which the fast, shallow water is open to fly-fishing only as far downstream as the Deschutes Bridge. In this area the trout are small, although numerous, rarely exceeding three pounds in size. This is ideal water for the beginner as well as the expert, since it is not unusual to take a limit of trout averaging ten inches in length from a single riffle and to release many smaller ones in the process. Here is one of the most scenic areas along the entire river. Camping spots are well kept and offer complete facilities to anglers with a tent or trailer.

From the Deschutes Bridge through Crane Prairie Reservoir to the Wickiup Dam there is at present a special bag limit of five fish per day or not more than ten pounds and one fish. In this area the trout run large and it is no rarity to hook into big ones of

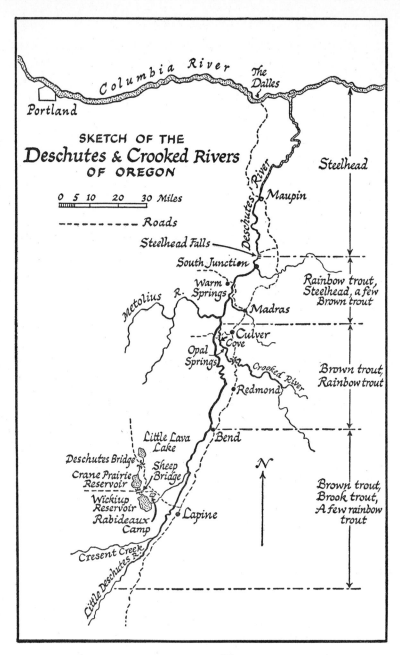

FIGURE 25.

SKETCH MAP OF DESCHUTES AND CROOKED RIVER
REGION IN OREGON

ten pounds and to complete the bag limit with only two fish. Here one finds brown (or Loch Leven) trout, rainbows, Eastern brook trout and an occasional Dolly Varden. In the spring the water is high due to its impoundment by Wickiup Dam, making the angling more accessible if one uses a boat.

In late May and well into July there usually is a tremendous hatch of May flies which can be imitated successfully with a Blue Quill dry fly in sizes ten or twelve. This hatch normally occurs twice daily; the fly appearing in great numbers between ten o'clock in the morning and one in the afternoon and again at dusk in the evening. Trout rise excitedly to these hatches. The slow current of the water is deceptive, there seeming to be no drag to the fly in the evenly moving stream.

A rainbow trout which might have weighed four or five pounds was rising at frequent intervals on the far side of the river close to a few dead trees standing in the water. Several anglers had fished over this trout without success. He rose freely to every fly that passed by him except for the carefully fished artificials. Don, with an expertly placed long cast, would drop a Blue Quill a foot or so above his nose, yet the trout would refuse the offering and rise a minute later to take the next natural fly which passed by. Changing patterns made no difference. After each cast, the result was maddeningly the same. Don changed his leader from nine feet tapered to 3X to twelve feet tapered to 4X and tied a size sixteen gold bodied multicolored Variant to the end. With tackle so light it seemed impossible to handle such a fish in the stream whose deep banks were cluttered with snags and branches. As he made his cast he jerked back slightly with his rod tip before the fly landed to give a bit of slack line in case the drag of the fly might be the cause of the rainbow's refusing to take it. The fly landed about three inches short and a few inches below where the trout had been rising. It remained there for a few seconds and just before the drag of the current straightened the line, he sucked it in. Even as the angler set the hook the trout made for a log and snapped the leader. It proved conclusively, however, that all that had been needed to take him was a fly which drifted naturally without drag, because later on we could see why the preceding casts had been futile. In them, a very slight but conflicting current had taken hold of the fly the moment it touched the water. Even though it seemed to float properly from the caster's position, it had moved across one little ribbon of current just enough to make it appear suspicious to the fish.

Trollers as well as fly-fishermen enjoy good luck in the early part of the season, when a Flatfish or a spinner and worm combination are favorites for taking large trout. Bait fishermen are common sights along the banks, where they do well with preserved salmon eggs, grubs and night crawlers.

As the season progresses into early July on this part of the river, fly-fishing improves. The water has dropped considerably due to releases from Wickiup Dam and the river takes on a new aspect. It is now lower and faster and where boats once trolled there is a jumble of snags and dead trees left by the backing up of the waters impounded by the dam. At this season one can get into the stream and wade the fine, gravelly bottom. By this time, most of the rainbow trout will have moved down into the deep reservoir and the brown trout take their places in prominence as they begin to feed on the surface. Small flies of the Variant and Spider patterns will take large fish if one approaches the stream with caution and fishes it well back from the deep, undercut banks.

From mid-July until early September the weather is hot and the sun warms the water to such an extent that the fishing becomes very poor. The reservoir becomes so filled with algae that it is impossible to see down into the water. By fall, this condition improves so much that during the last few weeks of the fishing season in September anglers again begin to take trout.

Wickiup Reservoir is not a pretty place to fish. The area is so clogged with stumps and driftwood that, while it is not difficult to hook a fish, it is quite another matter to land one. Anglers who have fished this section report that not more than one fish in four can be netted successfully, the others wrapping the leaders around stumps and swimming away with the fly. This would seem to be scant inducement to fish such a place except for the fact that most of the trout are over three pounds in weight. Many large brown trout are hooked, and some are landed, which will tip the scales at more than six pounds. Until recently, when several thousand small trout were released in the Wickiup waters, there were few smaller fish to be caught. The large trout, due to the scarcity of small ones and of forage fish, had not had the opportunity to become cannibals and an eight-pound brown trout would come to the fly as quickly as would one eight inches long. After the hatchery fish were introduced there was a distinct absence of large fish feeding on the surface waters of the reservoir.

Now it appears that Wickiup Reservoir again will be increased in size due to plans to enlarge the dam. In the newly flooded area insect life will flourish for a time and the fly-fishing should improve. Studies of other trout waters indicate that this will be but temporary. Eventually, unless the waters are fertilized and forage fish are added as food for the trout, the reservoir will again be exhausted of food and the fishing will diminish. The artificial rise and fall of the reservoir due to the seasonal draining off and adding to the water desiccates the rich, shallow food-producing areas and thus has a disastrous effect upon bottom food supplies and the propagation of trout. The brown trout and brook trout, being fall spawners, deposit their eggs in the shallow riffles which always have been their chief nesting areas. At the time when the eggs should be hatching the annual rise in the level of the reservoir has caused these low water areas to be so deeply flooded that the flow of water over them stops and the eggs become smothered. The high water deposits silt over the eggs, covering them so completely that few if any survive.

On the other hand, the rainbow trout spawns in the early spring, traveling as far as he can in the high water and depositing eggs where the depth is apparently shallow and suitable for the hatching of young. Again the dams which man has made violate the laws of nature. As the water is drawn off for irrigation purposes the great majority of the eggs die in the dust of dry land when the source waters again return to their normal level. If this condition were true only of Wickiup Reservoir it would be a minor matter. The fact that it is happening in countless trout waters throughout our country where man has built his dams is one of the paramount reasons for the shameful decline in our fishing.

It is but a few miles from Wickiup Reservoir to Crescent Creek, which flows into the Little Deschutes River and from it into the main stream. Crescent Creek is a delightful small meadow stream, slow, winding and deep. Although one often hears that there is no small stream fishing in Oregon, Crescent Creek affords an abundance of sport for the dry fly and nymph angler with numerous brown trout up to four pounds in weight and many more exceeding a foot in length. The stream runs through volcanic lava and pumice formations in which a surprising number of muskrats make their homes. If one lumbers up to its bank heavy of foot it would seem that there is not a single fish in the stream because the muskrat runs which honeycomb the banks are excellent telegraphic channels to warn the trout of the visiting angler. On this, as on many other meadow streams, one must creep up carefully, casting the fly from a distance. This tedious and stealthy approach pays rich rewards. As the fly lights delicately on the stream, with the line and even part of the leader trailing through the grass, one strikes by instinct when he hears the terrific rise of a large brown trout as he takes the fly. Even a cast twenty feet from the bank is not too far away. To approach nearer is to be greeted by a seemingly empty stretch of water. Such fishing may be hard on terminal tackle but it pays big dividends in results.

I remember a stream like it in New England which I fish occasionally with an angler who has taught me much about the merits of the stealthy approach to meadow streams. I remember fishing it several times to be rewarded only by a few tiny trout. Those were the days when I impulsively rushed up to its waters and cast a speculative eye along the runs and riffles before favoring the observant trout with the offering of my fly. By that time

On Meadow Streams Like Crescent Creek a Cautious Approach
Is Necessary

he had of course long since heard or seen me and was unobtrusively hiding under the bank whereon I stood, waiting patiently for me to go away. This obviously foolish method was not confined to me only. Nine out of ten fishermen use it all the time. On the other hand, my angler friend would walk along the stream to make a mental record of its possibilities, if he had not been there before, and then would return half an hour or more later to make use of the information he had stored in his mind. Standing well back from the bank, usually with only his head and shoulders appearing over the grass, he would drop his fly in the places his "fish sense" told him a large trout should be. He might take half an hour to prepare for a single cast but he nearly always would return home with several very large trout when everyone else was taking only little ones.

From a quarter mile below Wickiup Dam there extends downstream approximately thirty miles of the finest dry fly water imaginable.[1] Here, the Deschutes is slow, deep and wide, so boating with a guide is the favorite method of fishing. Here one will find rainbows, brown trout and the Eastern brook trout. The brown trout were introduced into the area by accident rather than by intent, due to the screens being washed from a hatchery during a period of high water. They have gradually taken over the area, driving the rainbows and the brook trout to other localities. Whether or not this is a favorable situation is a matter of opinion because many of the brown trout are seven or eight pounds in size and two- or three-pounders are quite common. Most of the trout will be between twelve and fourteen inches long, which provides an abundance of action to the angler with a light fly rod. During the day, bucktails and streamer flies are the most popular types of lures but in the evening hours the dry fly is more successful. This stretch of water is most productive during late May and early June and again in the late fall, due to the

---

[1] Present indications are that this stretch will soon be ruined by the annual holding back of water for storage behind Wickiup Dam. This reduces the winter flow to fifty second feet. No less than two hundred second feet has been recommended by conservation agencies.

summer fluctuations of water caused by the releases from Wick-iup Dam for the Madras and Bend irrigation projects.

Below the city of Bend, contrary to all the laws of nature, the Deschutes suddenly becomes a small river again, since most of the water has been taken from it near the city for irrigation purposes. The ever-changing river now starts to drop swiftly. The canyon walls become steep and high and the water tumbling and turbulent. Quite obviously this is not brown trout water but several enormous browns have been taken from the pools in this part of the stream. It is ideal for rainbow trout and occasionally a lucky angler will hook into a five- or six-pounder, calling for a maximum of skill to handle him in the fast current. This stretch of the river is not as productive of good fishing as many of the other areas because the dam alters the conditions of the water until the Crooked River joins it to again add to its volume.

The Crooked River from its mouth to Opal Springs is big, deep and fast. One of the most scenic and delightful camping spots in the West is at the Cove area near where it joins the Deschutes. Towering canyon walls reach into the sky on both sides of the camp ground, giving the angler a feeling of being in a far-off corner of the world. Here, the fish are wary but plentiful. The rushing stream is the ideal home of the fighting rainbow. The food supply in the river is excellent and the trout all are fat and in prime condition. The native trout in these waters can be distinguished readily from their hatchery brothers by their dark coloration, their vivid red stripe and their greater weight.

This is chiefly dry fly water although many trout are taken on bait when the big stone flies (locally known as salmon flies) are hatching. Anglers use a size eight or ten bait hook and merely pick the big, juicy bugs from the trees and rocks and bait their hooks with them. During this hatch of big stone flies, which usually occurs in May and early June, the fish feed freely on the surface so that a good imitation of the stone fly, fished dry, will produce amazing results. After the stone flies disappear the trout become more selective and the bait fishermen as well as the majority of the fly anglers seek more productive water. Even so, care and perseverance will always reward the dry fly angler in this area, even in the hot summer months. It may take an evening or two to discover the secret of success, but once the secret is found the fishing becomes amazingly easy, even as it is on other streams.

Don Harger relates an instance of this on an occasion when he was fishing with his uncle, John Atherton, who is as famed as an angler and a wing shot as he is as an artist. Don says that for several days they had difficulty in catching enough fish to eat. In the evenings the big trout were feeding in the pools but nothing in their fly boxes would tempt more than an occasional half-hearted rise. Nearly a dozen rainbows could be seen each evening in nearly every pool feeding greedily on some minute insects which the anglers could not see. Even a fine leader and a size twenty Hendrickson dry fly brought no results. On the fourth evening, with only a half hour of fishing left before the sudden darkness that envelops the deep canyons, Don noticed two small size eighteen Midges in his tackle box, tied to use on a stream near home but which he had never had the opportunity to try. The little fly was made very simply with two turns of black seal fur for the body and only two or three turns of stiff black hackle a little longer than usually would be used on a size eighteen dry fly. There was no tail and neither were there any wings.

In the red afterglow of the setting sun he tied on the fly and dropped it lightly over a big feeding rainbow. There was barely a dimple on the surface as the great fish took it in and made a mad dash for the fast water and the pool below, breaking the fly from the leader in the process. The other fly brought the same prompt acceptance and the same tragic result.

On the next day the anglers used their portable fly tying kit to make up more of the little Midges, eagerly awaiting evening so that they could try them in the pool. When that magic hour arrived they were on the stream again, first trying other flies to be sure that the trout were as selective as before. The fish would take nothing else, but when the little black Midge was offered to them both of the anglers hooked big rainbows on nearly every cast. They caught and released more than thirty fish in an hour and a half, returning happily to camp with the pleasant feeling which all anglers have when they have successfully found the formula for taking trout which are hard to catch.

One who fishes a great deal for trout sometimes runs into similar situations when big fish put on a maddening display of beautiful head and tail rises yet nothing which is offered to them will interest them in the slightest. The big squaretail brook trout of Maine are inclined to do this quite often. Guides and local anglers would say that they were not feeding, but merely playing or, in the fall, that they "were jumping to settle their eggs." I have seen it on Kennebago Stream in Maine, when big trout and landlocked salmon were surfacing all around me while I waded the stream and fruitlessly cast for them. It was only in the evening when we learned that the formula was the tiny nymphs which they were taking just below the surface. I have seen it on a wilderness lake in Maine when they refused everything, even live bait, and would take only a reproduction of the flying ant on which they were feeding at the time. I have even seen it when they would take nothing but an imitation of the little red buds which fall from maple trees in the spring, but I still do not know why a trout will prefer this sort of fare to a live minnow or a wriggling worm.

In Western canyon streams such as the Crooked River one often can see trout feeding in the shade cast by the canyon walls in the early morning hours. They will feed in the shade of the opposite bank in the late afternoon, but when the sun is in such a position that it throws its glare upon the water they usually will cease to feed entirely. When the sun finally sets and evening twilight envelops the water the fish will show increasing activity all over the stream until, when it is nearly dark, the water will seem suddenly to boil with feeding fish.

This trait in Western streams does not always apply. There are times when trout will have a short but furious feeding spree sometime between the hours of ten o'clock in the morning and two in the afternoon. I have seen it happen regularly on the Gunnison River in Colorado and it happens just as surely on many of the streams of Oregon. Suddenly the water is alive with feeding fish. There are a few minutes of activity and then, just as quickly, the rise is over and the stream is quiet once more. It matters not what the weather conditions are or what the phase of the moon may be. At some time during the middle of the day the water suddenly becomes alive with feeding fish.

It is hard to account for such a situation, particularly since it begins and ends with such intensity. In some cases it may be due to hatches of insects which come to the surface in the nymphal state encouraged in their emergence by the warmth of the noonday sun. Even in the Eastern states where there is a rapid daily fluctuation of water surface temperatures this could not always be the answer. In the majority of streams of the West, water temperatures need rarely concern the angler except in cases when they are too cold. These streams are spring-fed nearly all the way from their source to their mouth and the water rarely gets above the lower sixties. The springs in the Deschutes at Sheep Bridge show normal temperatures of 45° in mid-August. The Oregon Game Commission has a hatchery at Oak Springs, on the lower Deschutes, where the temperature is almost constant at 54°. The water temperature at Opal Springs, from whence most of the Crooked River stems, gave a reading of 48° last June during a very warm stretch of weather. Readings taken of the Deschutes River waters at most seasons of the year from the Sheep Bridge area to way below Warm Springs have never found the water to be warmer than 66°, while the Crooked River has never been known to exceed 58°. Western trout are acclimated relatively well to these temperatures and do not show as many of the temperamental feeding tendencies which fluctuating water temperatures instill in the fish in the trout waters of the northeast.

The Crooked River is a series of cascades and long, deep pools with boiling white water surging into the upper end through a narrow chute in the rocks to pile up in waves which gradually diminish in size as they pass from the churning, white frothy water into the deep blue and then into the shallower green of the pool. It is in this intermediate blue water that the big rainbows seem to like to lie. It is difficult to make a fly float in this torrent, let alone to induce it to do so properly, but if it lands with the right delivery and bounces along in the blue and green water at the edge of the race there usually is a good fish anxious to come up and to snatch it away. Such spots are productive throughout the entire day and throughout each season. In the evening the fish may move out into the quieter water to feed and it is at this time that the angler is most apt to catch them in the relatively still water.

It has been standard reading for many years that the rainbow trout loves fast water, yet one rarely sees an angler fish in the one spot mentioned above which is most apt to contain fish. Instead, he will take a precarious position on a slippery rock and dangle a lure in water that is so swiftly boiling and foaming that the fish could not possibly hold himself there long enough to take the lure. There, after a few fruitless casts, the angler will pass by the good fishing and scramble over rocks to absolutely dead water that is perhaps ten or fifteen feet deep and try to coax a fish up from the depths.

In the Crooked River as well as in the lower Deschutes (and in nearly all trout waters for that matter) one always should fish thoroughly the water above underwater boulders which are so prominent as to cause a break or hump upon the surface of the stream. Since this is a general rule for good stream fishing the method for doing so is illustrated and described in Chapter Seven. These waters are so fast and deep that the trout must take advantage of every single spot that might afford a break in the current or a slight back eddy in which they can hold themselves and pick up food. When a fish is hooked in such a place he usually will rush for the fast, big water, often literally cleaning the angler of his fly, leader, line and his backing, if the fish be a big one as he usually is. Many anglers refuse to fish such waters, saying that it costs them too much in lost tackle. For my part, if I am properly equipped to give the trout an even battle, I am perfectly willing that he should race off with everything, including my rod and reel — if he can get it!

All this can be boiled down to say that the Deschutes and Crooked River rainbows in the lower reaches of the rivers are inclined to follow the shade and to hug the banks during the early weeks of the season when the stone fly hatch is on. Then they will move to the deeper water to take up positions around the rocks. If it is possible to do so before fishing a new stream it always seems good strategy to examine it from a high point where one can look down into the water and observe the submerged boulders and other hiding places which are not so obvious at stream level. By so doing, many fishable spots will be noticed which otherwise would be missed. Many anglers seem to think that this reconnaissance work is a waste of time but the few who adopt the practice will affirm that the results are well worth the effort.

From its junction with the Crooked River the Deschutes is a full-fledged stream again, with the waters of the Crooked and the Metolius almost tripling its size. Although the river is still shut in by canyon walls, they are not so high and the country is a bit more open. At the headquarters of the Indian Agent in the Warm Springs Indian Reservation one can obtain a permit to fish on the reservation side of the river, where there is some beautiful water. This area is reached from the city of Madras and is one of the most popular stretches of the lower Deschutes. From there the fishing is said to be good in the North Junction and South Junction areas; especially in the vicinity of Maupin, where it is reported that the rainbows are enormous.

Few brown trout are found in the lower reaches of the Deschutes since the river is not to their liking. The lower river is wild and turbulent and therefore is the home of the resident rainbow and the steelhead. Thus we see that the stream changes its character entirely from the brown trout waters near its source, where it is primarily a meadow-bordered river with deep undercut banks and moss-covered logs under which the brown trout loves to hide and from their shady protection to emerge to feed in its deep, evenly flowing waters.

It seems of interest to know that during July and August the fish in the lower Deschutes and in the Crooked Rivers have a habit of feeding quite regularly on a green moss that is found on the river bottom. When an inspection of the stomach contents of a fourteen-inch trout was made through a high powered glass the large mass of moss he had eaten was found to contain fourteen different specimens of insect life in the larval and nymphal stages. Evidently they find it easier to grab a mouthful of moss than to pick out the individual bits of food. The fare seems to agree with them because they are all fat and full of fight. It should be added, however, that their value as a food fish diminishes considerably during this moss-eating period so that it seems far better to release them than to bring them home for dinner.

Twice yearly there is a migration of steelhead up the Columbia River and into the Deschutes as far upstream as Steelhead Falls, beyond which they cannot go. Recently we visited this area and camped for a week in early September a few miles above where the Deschutes joins the Columbia. Here, the river is so deep and wide that it can be waded only in a few places. One can make his way carefully around the big boulders in the fast flowing stream and suddenly find he is on the brink of a ledge ten or fifteen feet deep. August is the peak month for the run of summer steelhead in this river, their numbers gradually diminishing in September until only the occasional stray fish or resident rainbow remains. The winter run of larger fish occurs in January or February, tapering off in the adjoining two months.

When we arrived in early September the summer run had passed its peak. Without a knowledge of the habits of the rainbow, as discussed in Chapter Eight, we would have taken few, if any, fish. Spinning tackle is at its best on this part of the river because ordinary fly-fishing equipment does not get the lure down into the swift water deep enough to tempt the fish, which are near the bottom behind the large boulders far out in the current. Even weighted flies are of little value in a stream as fast as this and dry flies seemed to be of no value at all.

Our good friend Don Harger, who seemed to enjoy his chosen role as guide to the two Eastern fishermen, Joe Brooks, Jr. and the author, constantly demonstrated his years of angling training by the "fish sense" he exhibited on the stream.

"I think there should be a nice steelhead in that run between the two rocks," he would say, sending a long cast to just above the position so that his lure would drift down into it. Surely enough, there would be. The fish would hit the lure with a reverberating impact that made it unnecessary to set the hook, immediately tearing away to the safety of the fastest white water he could find near by. These sensational runs of the big steelhead, aided by the torrential current of the stream, made it quite obvious why the local anglers recommended that we fish with plenty of line on our reels.

Some of the steelhead were out of the water nearly as much as they were in it. The aerial displays they made, silver sides glistening in the sun against the background of giant rocks and white water, presented a picture which all true anglers dream about and which few are privileged to enjoy. These fresh run fighting steelhead, well in training for their battle after two years in the depths of the sea, proved to be an ample match for the angler and his tackle. It is said that to land one of the big fish for every four hooked is a fair average if the angler uses tackle which gives the fish an even chance. We did somewhat better than that although the wild leaps they made often would throw the hook or the fish would break loose by circling around a boulder. On our last day on the lower Deschutes we saved a beautiful eight-pound, nine-ounce steelhead to take home for the dinner table, having released all of the other fish as soon as they were caught. We photographed him as he lay on the grass at the end of the struggle, dark of back and silvery of sides, with the faint pink stripe of the rainbow trout just beginning to make its appearance as his transformation from steelhead to rainbow began upon his return to the river.

Anglers who visit the West, and many who live there, may be interested in a few additional notes on the tackle and lures which are pertinent to the Deschutes River system and to many other of the streams in the northwestern states. This information, as it applies to steelhead fishing, may be found at the end of Chapter Eight. For resident fish the following notes will apply.

In early season fishing on the Crooked River and the lower Deschutes (excepting the steelhead stretch near the mouth) a goodly supply of stone fly imitations will prove valuable in the large sizes. These flies average nearly two inches over all in length and are tied with a fat orange or yellow wool body, a flat wing of hen pheasant tail or barred squirrel and a blend of black and brown hackle tied on last. Both wet and dry patterns are useful.

Other favorites at this time of year are the Caddis bucktail on a size eight or ten light wire hook and the Coachman bucktail in the same sizes on a long shanked hook. With these it proves useful to have a few small dry fly patterns in grays and browns as there are often hatches of small sedge or alder flies along with the big stone flies. Some of the more popular patterns are the Adams, Light Hendrickson, Gray Sedge, Brown Sedge, Red Quill and Blue Quill. A Blue Dun is excellent if the purchaser can find a fly dressed with a good blue dun hackle.

In the Sheep Bridge and Wickiup area as well as in the Little Lava Lake area the early season will find flies on the water which best can be imitated by a size ten or twelve Blue Quill dressed on a 1X or 2X long shank light wire dry fly hook. Sizes fourteen and sixteen Variants and Spiders do almost as well and often seem to have more appeal than an exact imitation would have. The big Caddis bucktail will do well in this area because the big rainbows seem to like something large and meaty-looking. Many anglers have sensational luck with this fly and use it all the way into British Columbia and at all seasons of the year.

The Variant is a favorite fly with Don Harger and many other leading anglers of the West, several of whom say that if they were to be limited to one fly the Variant would be it. It can be dressed in different combinations as large as size fourteen without defeating its purpose, which is to imitate a light, delicate insect. It seems especially suitable to brown trout which often will accept it while ignoring natural insects.

A good stock of streamer flies and nymphs should be included in the fly box, and some of them should have weighted bodies to get them down into the fast current. At times a condition occurs when the fish seem to be surface feeding and yet they will not take any dry fly pattern which is offered. At such times, in addition to the black Midge previously mentioned a very sparsely dressed and weighted nymph seems to meet with success. The fish take it on a slack line float near enough to the surface to break the water. Examination of the stomach contents of these fish showed that they were feeding entirely on nymphs and fresh-water shrimp. This condition is even more noticeable in the fall than in the spring.

As the season progresses one will have to cut down on the sizes of flies although the patterns can remain the same. Instead of sizes ten and twelve it is well to use fourteens, sixteens and even eighteens during the hot summer months. Here, leader size becomes increasingly important; the finer leader sizes being better because of the more delicate action which they give to the fly. Often trout will refuse a tiny fly tied to a 2X tippet when they will accept the same fly tied to 4X. Under these conditions it would be wise to have leaders in lengths from seven and a half feet to twelve feet tapered in sizes ranging from 2X to 4X. The 5X tippet usually is too light, especially in fast water streams.

It is obvious that lines should be in sizes to fit the rod. It is safer to have one hundred yards of good backing than to have only fifty yards on the reel. Twelve-pound test seems to be the strength most generally preferred. For dry fly use a double tapered line gives a better presentation of the fly but for streamers and wet flies the torpedo or Hedge taper is more popular because it helps to drive the fly out against the heavy winds which occasionally sweep through the canyons.

Two fly rods are virtually imperative if one is to fish the waters of this area properly. An eight-and-a-half foot rod with fast dry fly action is ideal for the streams but will be found to be too light to hold some of the large brown trout which one occasionally hooks. It is also too light for rainbows and steelhead in fast water. The smaller rod is ideal for fishing the brushy streams often encountered; in fact, many anglers prefer an eight-foot rod for this purpose. For the heavier one, a length of nine feet in a stiff action rod weighing between five and a half and six and a half ounces is ideal. Waders can be used on many parts of the stream but a good pair of lightweight shoes with composition soles is also useful. Lastly, a large landing net is important because the nature of the streams in many places prevents the beaching of large trout and the lack of a good net will mean more fish lost than landed.

CHAPTER THIRTEEN

Riffles and Fast Water Fishing

*California's Klamath River Offers Suggestions for
Finding Trout in Similar Streams Everywhere*

WHEN ANGLERS REMINISCE about famous coastal rivers
in which the fighting steelhead abounds, each will extol
his favorite stream, whether it be the Duckabush or Skykomish
of Washington, the Rogue or Umpqua of Oregon or the Eel or
Klamath of California. There are many others equally renowned
and no man can live long enough to know all of them well. Few
men would claim that knowledge of a single one. For an Easterner to visit the West and then attempt to educate Western
anglers on one of their favorite rivers would be the height of
presumption unless the author, as an Easterner, were to preface
his comments with the remark that this is merely the gleanings
of a pleasant fishing trip and is meant to be nothing more.

Our camp on the Klamath was on a bluff overlooking the
shining river as it snaked with disarming smoothness through
the rocky pine and fir covered hills. We were there in late
September and early October, when there was enough frost in
the crisp night air to turn the aspen leaves to the color of
burnished gold, shining brightly against the deep evergreens of
the hills. Thirty miles upstream from our base of operations
Copco Dam furnishes power to the near-by cities and acts as a
barrier to the upriver migrations of the steelhead as well as to the
downstream travels of the large resident rainbow trout and the
few brown trout which occupy the river from there to its source
in the reedy expanses of large and boggy Klamath Lake. Thus,
as a steelhead river the Klamath begins at Copco Dam. From

Copco to Seiad Valley, seventy-five miles downstream, a good road borders the river and makes excellent steelhead fishing easily available. This was the part of the river where we fished for steelhead.

The peacefulness of this section of the Klamath is disarming. In a matter of twenty minutes it can turn from a low water stream into a raging torrent, swift and deadly for all but the rambunctious steelhead resting behind the boulders which breast its rocky riffles. As the turbines at Copco produce power the dam releases water, causing the river to rise once a day more than twenty inches in as few minutes. Many an unsuspecting angler, gingerly wading a deep riffle in the middle of the stream, has been swept from his feet by the flood and there are those who have not lived to tell of it. To guard against such mishaps, the sportsmen's clubs of northern California have erected warning signs near the most popular riffles. Anglers who fish there soon learn the wisdom of heeding the warnings and cast constant apprehensive glances at the ripple marks along the shore, the disappearance of which will indicate the rising of the water in case it should be ahead of schedule, as it often is. The flood waters travel about three and a half miles an hour so that, upon meeting them at one point, fishermen can drive downstream for five or ten miles and have an hour or two more of low water before the rise again overtakes them.

Steelhead fishing is much better when the water is not high. The fish migrate upstream during high water and are difficult to locate and to interest in a fly when they are traveling. High water makes many of the riffles unwadable. It discolors the water and makes it all the less likely for the steelhead to notice a lure. Even during low water, long casts of about eighty feet often are needed to enable anglers wading the riffles to reach some of the favorite resting places of the fish near the deeper bank.

Anglers who know the Klamath love it as a steelhead stream because nearly its entire course is a constant and delightful succession of riffles. Riffles are the favorite resting places of steelhead, which, unlike the salmon, prefer them to the pools. Each riffle is given a name, which may vary between different groups of anglers but which oftentimes becomes so well known as to be a permanent and universally recognized appellation. Manzanita Riffle acknowledges the manzanita bushes which grow along its banks. A fisherman told me that when high water caught him one day in Blackberry Riffle it took him more than two hours to cut his way through the thorny vines. Horserace Riffle is more than one hundred and fifty yards long and often accommodates ten or a dozen rods at one time. After wading through it, anglers frequently walk back to the upper end and begin all over again, thus earning for it the name of "Horserace." By the same token identifying names have been given to "Sevenmile," "Peachtree," "Barkhouse," "Butterfly" and many others.

After fishing each riffle a few times one would grow to know where to expect a fish and thus could hurry over certain sections to place a cast into a bit of "holding water" where a steelhead had been taken before. During a run, even of moderate intensity, there are spots which always seem to hold a good fish. When he moves on upstream, a later arrival usually likes the position well enough to take his place.

When there is a good deal of fishing on the river each favorite riffle may be visited by an almost constant succession of anglers. The leading one sets the pace for the rest and may be so entranced by a bit of water that his over-careful fishing of it impedes the progress of the others. On one such occasion the culprit was waist-deep in the middle of the stream, industriously refishing an eddy back of a rock and totally oblivious of the stalled line of several patient or impatient anglers behind him. As luck would have it, the next angler hooked a nice fish, unobserved by the obstructionist in front. The big steelhead chose to make a run to a spot two or three feet behind the man who was holding up the procession, there erupting from the water in a beautiful leap and covering the angler with a geyser of spray. The surprise of this sudden onslaught so overcame the man that he lost his balance on the round stones in the swift current and disappeared neck-deep into the river. While he was ashore emptying the cold water from his waders the stalled line of fishermen moved on.

The angler who had hooked the fish made his way to shore to play the leaping steelhead from the bank. After several long runs the exhausted fish was led to shallow water and drawn to the beach. The angler weighed his prize, admired him momentarily and carefully removed the fly. He carried the steelhead into the water and held him upright below the surface, facing upstream. In a few moments the fish had recovered sufficiently to swim away. By this time the waterlogged fisherman had repaired the damage enough to be ready to resume fishing and stood by watching the sportsman release his fish. "Funny thing!" the wet one remarked to the lucky angler, "I never used to let my fish go until this year. It's really more fun than killing them, isn't it!"

The Klamath is a river famous both for salmon and for steelhead. Although both occasionally are taken from the same pools, this usually is not the case. The fact has been stressed that steelhead prefer moderately fast water where they have the protection of large rocks. They also prefer to lie in the eddies in the current formed by the indentations or obstructions along the bank of the stream. These resting positions, in which they remain when they are not migrating upstream during the periods of high water, are more commonly found in riffles than in pools. On the other hand, the salmon concentrate in the larger pools, moving from one to another, always influenced by high water as are the steelhead. In doing this, a few large steelhead may accompany the salmon but the angler who desires to fish for steelhead is better advised to try for them in the areas they usually prefer, rather than in the pools. From the statements of other anglers and from my own experience it seems that the best steelhead water ordinarily is on the deep side of the riffles where the water is neither too fast nor too deep. Oftentimes this is on the outside curve of a bend in the stream. Thus it is necessary often to wade the riffles in order to reach close to the deep bank with a cast the length of which is within the ability of the angler. The ability to make long casts, in a stream like the Klamath, often makes a great difference in the number of fish which the angler is able to hook. A secondary position is in a defined channel where the fish can rest in the quiet water afforded by depressions and large rocks. When runs of steelhead are well established, the tail of a pool is an excellent temporary position because they are inclined to rest there for a few moments just after passing through the fast, white water below the pool. This is also true of salmon, so that the angler who fishes this position may hook a salmon rather than a steelhead, although it is rare to do so with a fly.

In Chapter Seven there was a considerable discussion of riffles. Their characteristics are important in fishing the Klamath because it has been noted that the river is nearly a constant succession of riffles, dropping on an average of ten feet to the mile. Those which are known usually to contain fish are termed "holding riffles" because they have the depth and speed of current desirable to the fish, together with the necessary rocks and back eddies which break the force of the current and thus induce the steelhead to rest in them. Their location may be a factor also, in that when they lie above a long run of fast water the fish may be more tired and thus more apt to tarry there.

"Holding riffles" are known as either "early" or "late" riffles, the names pertaining both to the season and to the time of day. Anglers know from experience that this is so but usually do not search for the reasons. While the reasons advanced here may be more opinion than fact, so many fishermen agree with them that they may be worthy of note. Some riffles which are good early in the season are barren of fish later on, and vice versa. Water level and the speed of the current seem to have a lot to do with this. It has been noted that steelhead prefer water that is neither too fast nor too slow. Some consider that the proper speed is between three and six miles an hour, or as fast as a man can walk, which can be estimated by the speed of objects floating on the surface of the stream. Thus, when the river is low in the early fall the steelhead may prefer the narrow riffles which are deep, while in the late fall or winter when the river is running full, these places may be too fast and too deep and the favored riffles, or "late riffles," may be the wide ones where the current was too slow and the depth too shallow earlier in the season.

Many anglers will not fish certain "hot" riffles except at definite times of day, maintaining, for instance, that Slippery Riffle is no good in the morning, while Pinetree Riffle is fishable only before noon. One explanation for this is the position of the sun on the water. When the fly is between the sun and the fish they feel that the glare on the surface is such that it can not be seen clearly. Advocates of this theory prefer to fish riffles at the time of day when the sun is behind the fish (which will be facing upstream) rather than in front of them. A somewhat similar belief is that too much glare on the water is not conducive to good fishing, so that riffles are fished at a time of day when they are in the shadow of the bordering hills.

King salmon (often called Chinooks) and a few silver (or Cohoe) salmon journey up the river as far as Copco Dam near which there is a hatchery where the eggs are stripped from the fish and hatched to stock the river. It is said that today there are ten times as many steelhead as salmon because the salmon (and the steelhead to a large extent) have been radically reduced in numbers by the greedy netting of commercial fishermen.

When we arrived at our camping place we were met by the heartening news that the salmon were running up the river and had been seen in a pool not far from where we were staying. These were glad tidings because it is usual for a fresh run of steelhead to follow the salmon, perhaps because they both have the same urge to travel during high water or perhaps because the steelhead like to pick up the eggs which the ripe salmon lose along the way. This is the first and last return to the river for the salmon, which die after spawning. If the steelhead are successful in running the gantlet of the anglers and of the nets of commercial fishermen they will go back to sea and may return to the stream annually to lay or to fertilize their eggs, perhaps repeating the migration as many as five times before death overtakes them. On these nuptial journeys the salmon eat nothing, whether because their reproductive urge overshadows all else or

This Angler Releases a Steelhead Properly by Holding It Upright until It Can Swim Away

New Type Rotary Fish Screens Like These Prevent Small Trout from Dying in Irrigation Ditches

because they realize the futility of nourishment no one seems to know. They strike a lure usually on account of anger or habit rather than because of the desire for food, evidently feeling that it is something dangerous to the success of their journey which they want to kill in order to get it out of the way. On the other hand, the steelhead feeds regularly on his course upstream and down, seeming to know that an abundance of food is necessary to sustain him on his arduous travels.

The initial migratory runs of both the steelhead and the salmon usually reach this part of the Klamath by late September, possibly having come into the mouth of the river as early as July. The early steelhead are small ones, averaging only three or four pounds, although an occasional one is hooked which is much larger. For each ten fish which we hooked and landed at this time of year there was one which would weigh seven or eight pounds. Mixed in with these fish which had spent two years or more in the sea were occasional "half-pounders," as the one-year fish weighing less than three pounds are called. Each succeeding run brings in larger steelhead, so that it may be said that the average weight increases by a pound or a pound and a half a month. By December, January and February the river abounds in huge, fighting fish but they are less readily taken on flies because the river is high and discolored due to the abundance of rain at this season. Even the large, weighted bucktail flies are of little value but spinning lures, wobbling spoons or bait often are successful. The months of March and April are closed to all fishing because this period is during the height of the spawning, when the fish should be unmolested. In the first two weeks of the open season early in May steelhead are caught in incredible numbers in the smaller streams, where they usually have finished spawning and are concentrated in small areas before they begin their journey back to the ocean. During June, July and August the weather is warm and the water in the river is low because there is little or no rain in the summer and the greater part of the water is drawn off for irrigation.

One day I accompanied a biologist from the State Bureau of

Fish Conservation on a short trip to see a new type of rotary fish screen which had been installed on Beaver Creek to keep the little steelhead (perhaps more aptly termed "rainbows" at this stage of their lives) out of the irrigation ditches. He pulled up from the by-pass a cage trap used for estimating the success of the project and counted more than five hundred baby steelhead which had been saved from destruction during the previous twenty-four hours. During the height of the seaward migration of young steelhead, more than five thousand have been recovered from a single trap overnight and have been returned to the stream. These cage traps are used for census taking only. Ordinarily the fish are stopped by the screen and are guided by the flow of water in the by-pass away from the irrigation ditch and back into the stream again. Since water is used extensively for irrigation in California, thus making thousands of ditches necessary, the importance of fish screens in the conservation of young steelhead (and salmon) can not be overestimated. Without them many of the baby fish running downstream would enter these ditches and would die when the water is shut off at the beginning of the rainy season. Their instinct is to move ever downstream and the irrigation ditches thus become death traps.

These new fish screens are being installed rapidly at the entrances to many irrigation ditches but unfortunately today many of the screens are old in type and inefficient. The number of good ones is altogether too few. On the new type a paddle wheel operated by the current in the ditch moves an endless chain connected to the rotary screen. The screen blocks passage of the fish but carries leaves and other clogging matter over it so that it can not act as a dam.

Klamath feeder streams and brooks are loaded with small rainbows up to six or seven inches long. Many of the larger of these young fish are underdeveloped, with unproportionately big heads and emaciated bodies. The spring runoff of water in these small tributaries is often of freshet proportions, rushing down the mountain gorges, rolling rocks and sweeping food before it. This so effectively scours the stream bottoms of nymphal and larval insect life that the stream becomes too depleted in food to nourish any but the smallest fish. As the trout work down into the main body of the river, its abundance of food compensates for this infantile semistarvation period and the fish rapidly gain a normal, healthy appearance.

Little fish have other hazards to overcome on their way to the sea. This is particularly so in the Klamath, due to its rise and fall of water. Thousands of them become stranded in the pockets made by gravel bars and ledges when the water subsides and leaves them high and dry. There they become the favorite food of racoons, mink, merganser ducks, kingfishers, pelicans and other predators who devour them so voraciously that their presence rarely is noted by the angler.

Klamath Lake, the source of the Klamath River, is an immense body of water, shallow and rimmed with acres of tules, or cattail rushes, which rot in the water, discoloring and polluting the river for many miles downstream. As the steelhead move into the upper reaches of the Klamath this pollution affects their flesh sufficiently to give them a decided "mossy" taste often found in fish of other streams and lakes where a similar situation exists. For this reason, many anglers who catch the fish for food save only the obviously fresh run steelhead and return the others to the water. The fresh run fish are brightly silvered, showing little if any of the pink band of the resident rainbow. This natural pollution of the Klamath, more noticeable in the summer than at other times of year, is much like the decay absorbed into the water of stagnant beaver ponds. Obviously it is more pronounced near the source and becomes dissipated as the clear water of the tributaries enters the river farther downstream. Somewhat like the Ganges and the Nile, the Klamath does not seem to purify itself as other rivers do.

Lest this fact discourage anglers from visiting the Klamath, it should be added that this type of pollution, in the Klamath at least, does much more good than harm. Aided by the oxygen which the rushing river absorbs from the air, these bits of vegetation provide food for snails, nymphs, crawfish and other aquatic life which in turn make food for the fish. The Klamath so abounds in natural food that it is one of the richest rivers in the world. No angler can tread its riffles without observing the profusion of aquatic life clinging to the rocks of its bottom or scurrying between them. Nearly every day during warm weather its riffles give birth to clouds of flies which rise to the surface as nymphs and spread their wings to add to the abundance of these favorite foods which all trout so greatly love. Thus the steelhead grow fat and active in the river and, despite their mossy taste, are as preferred by anglers as any others of their kind anywhere in the world.

Many anglers who have fished the best steelhead waters of the West have told me that for sheer dash, wild power, high jumping and long fighting qualities they would rather tie into a five- or six-pound Klamath River October or November buck steelhead than any larger steelhead in any other water. There are those who will not agree with this statement but the thirty or forty minute battles I have had with them leads me to believe that it contains a large degree of truth. The biggest steelhead of the Klamath are more usually taken on spinners or with bait than on artificial flies. It also is a well-known fact among advocates of light fly-fishing tackle that the largest fish invariably break away. One of the standard bets on the Klamath is that the newcomer will lose three out of every five fish he hooks when the larger steelhead are running up the river late in the fall. If he accepts the wager he normally has to pay. One of the best-known fly-fishermen told me that he lost every big fish he hooked last season, and added that there were many of them! Another said that he lost seventeen in succession and still a third affirmed that out of eighteen fish he hooked in a day on the river he successfully landed only a single one. My own observations are not as pessimistic as this, but the statements indicate that Klamath steelhead fishing for the man with the fly rod cannot be listed among the simplest forms of angling. The fish have the advantage of a swift current with many rocks and rapids in their favor. In addition, men who prefer fishing on the Klamath to the other famous steelhead streams of the West maintain that the Klamath steelhead is of a gamier race than his brothers in other streams. Anglers from Washington and Oregon may dismiss this statement with the remark that those who make it quite obviously must be Californians, who are inclined to be optimistic about everything in their beautiful state, even including the weather!

In Chapter Eight there was a considerable discussion of flies and other elements of tackle preferred in fishing for steelhead. The popularity of weighted flies was not mentioned because they

FIGURE 26.

PETER J. SCHWAB'S "QUEEN BESS" IS A TYPICAL STEELHEAD FLY OF THE WEIGHTED TYPE

Drawings 1 and 2 show method of weighting body. Drawing 3 is completed fly. (Method of dressing is as follows: Tail — gray squirrel showing the black bar and white tip. Body — silver over weighted wire [or plated wire]. Wings — yellow bucktail topped with gray squirrel.)

are not as often employed on other streams as they are on the Klamath, due to the swiftness of its waters. Weighted bucktails are used in fast water to furnish quick sinking qualities, enabling the fly to get down into the deep riffles in spite of the heavy current. Their original sponsor was Peter J. Schwab, famous as a steelhead angler and author, who described them in two articles in the June and July 1946 issues of *Sports Afield* magazine.

Some weighted flies are tied so that the wire which weights them acts as the body of the fly as well. In others, the body dressing conceals the wire which is wound on underneath. In either case, gold, silver, brass or copper finished wire may be used, preferably in size .018 inches diameter for size six hooks, .023 inches diameter for size four hooks and .028 inches diameter for larger sizes. The wire must be soft and, if dressing is to be placed over it, the next size smaller should be selected.

Briefly, the hook is wound with thread over the second and third quarters of that part of the shank of the hook on which the wire body is to be applied and the thread is then varnished to provide a secure base for the wire. The end of the wire is grasped with small pliers or by the fingers of the left hand. It is bent over the hook and wound forward in close, tight coils, starting on the bare hook three sixteenths of an inch above the bend and going forward over the varnished or lacquered foundation and over the bare hook again to within a quarter inch of the eye. The surplus wire is cut off with small cutting pliers, the loose ends are pressed in close contact with the body coils and the burrs and rough ends are smoothed to a taper with a file. The wire body may then be burnished and should be lacquered to keep it from tarnishing. The thread base adds width to the middle of the body. Properly applied, this body is so secure that hooks have been broken beneath it and the fish have been landed because the wire held the two parts of the hook together. The rest of the fly is tied as the desired pattern dictates. The method of application of the wire body is mentioned here because of its importance in fishing fast steelhead waters and because flies with correctly tied weighted bodies are difficult to obtain.

As in all trout waters, the temperature of the Klamath has a decided effect upon the activity of the steelhead and upon their interest in taking a lure. In the summer, when the stream is low and relatively warm, with much of its water being drawn off for irrigation, the fish are in the deepest, coldest water they can find and do not respond well to flies and to other surface lures. Conversely, in the winter when the stream is coldest the temperature of the water approaches the lower tolerant limits and causes the trout to be lazy and disinclined to feed. For this reason, cold winter weather in December, January and February does not provide the best steelhead fishing on the upper Klamath, even though the largest fish are in the river at that time. Anglers who have caught them then report that, instead of taking the lure with the crashing strike for which they are famous, the steelhead take it so unobtrusively that the fisherman may think at first that it is caught on a rock on the bottom. As well as being less gamey under these conditions, the coldness of the water so reduces the trouts' metabolism that they may take as little as twenty-five per cent of the food they consume normally during the optimum water temperatures, thus reducing the probability of the angler hooking them to approximately that percentage.

Men who walk the riffles of the upper Klamath tread on gold. Spotted below the towering cliffs of the river are many old, abandoned mining claims, with here and there a few which still are being worked. The dredgers came up the river many years ago, scooping up the river gravel and washing it to get the gold which had been washed downstream and had settled deep in the river bed during ages past. They took the gold from the land of all who would let them, leaving in its place great ditches and high piles of gravel which even the spring freshets cannot smooth down. Today the old dredgers rust in the river but the bed is no longer being sifted for gold because the price it brings is not worth the labor of digging it out. When such work again is resumed, new laws state that the gravel must be re-spread as it was before and that topsoil must be replaced so that the beauty and the fishing qualities of the stream will not be impaired. In the river many fabulous strikes have been made such as the famous one at Humbug Creek, where thirteen million dollars in gold was taken from only nine miles of this small stream.

Below Seiad Valley the river enters a series of gorges wherein good trout riffles are less frequent. The rise in level due to releases from the dam forces the angler who fishes there to endure high water all day long. Here, the river is too fast and too deep for the fly, but fishing with spinners or bait usually is successful.

It is sixty miles from Seiad Valley to Somesbar. Although this part of the stream is bordered by a road, its present state of repair is so bad that traveling over it is difficult. At this point the Salmon River enters the main stream, so stabilizing its volume that the previous fluctuations in water level are no longer apparent. Twenty-four miles farther downstream the mighty Trinity River joins the Klamath at the town of Weitchpec. The Trinity is a fine steelhead river in its own right and well deserving of greater attention than the writer shall give to it. This stream, even more than the Klamath, has been and still is being exploited by gold mining interests who wash mud and gravel into it, keeping it badly discolored most of the time. The mouth of the Trinity is a part of the Hoopa Indian Reservation. It is a custom of the Hoopa Indians to obtain winter food by catching salmon and steelhead in weirs made of willow poles and sticks which they set into, and often across, the bed of the river. As a mark of progress, the Hoopas have adopted from the white man another of his bad habits; this time the use of gill nets to catch the fish. As a result of the mining mud and the gill nets, fishing in the Trinity has deteriorated to an alarming extent.

Between Weitchpec and tidewater the Klamath is broad and fly-fishing is good, but many parts of this stretch of the river at present are inaccessible except by boat. In tidewater, the fishing is mostly for salmon and trolling with spinners is the accepted method.

The Klamath is a river which long has been exploited by gold miners, by commercial fishermen and by some of the anglers themselves. Only in recent years has it been defended. In the meantime, like most of the famous salmon and steelhead streams of the West, its fabulous runs of fighting fish have been reduced to the danger point. Today, the West is growing to realize that the most valuable gold in the Klamath is the income which can accrue to its communities from the visits of anglers who travel from afar to fish its famous waters. Modern conservation practices are being enlisted to increase the migrations of fish and to safeguard them in their travels. If these conservation practices are continued the glorious game fish of the Klamath will prosper, bringing to angler and non-angler alike rewards far greater than those the destructive exploitation of the river ever has been able to supply.

CHAPTER FOURTEEN

Typical Mountain Lakes and Streams

Why High Altitudes Require Different Tactics in Catching Trout

FROM the peak-bordered city of Colorado Springs it is an awe-inspiring 140-mile drive over the 11,200-feet high Monarch Pass down into the valley of the Gunnison River. The Gunnison is one of the finest high altitude trout streams in the West. It is predominantly a dry fly river, rarely equaled anywhere in the world for the majestic grandeur of its colorful, towering canyons and its constant succession of rushing riffles and swirling pools filled with brilliantly colored fighting rainbows and fat, crafty brown trout. In and near the town of Gunnison anglers congregate in the many excellent tourist cabins from the present opening of the season on May twenty-fifth until its closing on October thirty-first to compare notes on tackle and tactics and to find out where some lucky fisherman caught the biggest one of the day.

While the Gunnison is noted for its beauty and the never-failing abundance of its fishing, it is of special interest because the behavior of its waters and its trout are typical of the difference between high altitude streams and the waters of lower elevation found so commonly elsewhere in the United States. Here, as in low altitude streams, several valuable deductions may be drawn to make fishing more enjoyable and more productive in all streams whose characteristics are similar. The truth of these deductions becomes obvious when the reasons for them are understood.

The headwaters of the Gunnison accumulate in the melting snows of the gigantic peaks on the western slope of the Continental Divide. From heights approaching fourteen thousand feet they run their icy courses through rocky clefts in the mountains, cascading rapidly downward to merge into the two main tributaries of the Gunnison, the East River and the Taylor River. These join and become the Gunnison at Almont, Colorado. From Almont, the Gunnison provides forty miles or more of superb fishing as it winds down the valley through canyon and meadow to disappear into the awesome gorge of the Black Canyon and to join the Colorado River at Grand Junction, nearly two hundred miles downstream. The best fishing is from ten miles above to thirty miles below the town of Gunnison, where the air is crisp and dry at an altitude of between seven and eight thousand feet.

When we fished the Gunnison River in late August it was half again higher than normal and the water was between 46° and 48°, which is colder than usual. Both of these conditions were due to bottom water being drawn from Taylor Dam on the Taylor River slightly above its confluence with the East River. At this same time the water in the East River was 54°, which is normal for the temperature of the stream around noon at that season. This was of interest because the trout were taking dry flies voraciously on the East River while their feeding on the colder Gunnison was almost entirely on nymphs and other subsurface food except for a sporadic rise when the water temperatures came up slightly during the warmest part of the day around noon. This condition, borne out by the experiences of anglers who have fished the stream for a great many years, indicated that the Temperature-Activity Table (Figure 3) holds as true for mountain trout as it does for fish acclimated to lower altitudes and warmer temperatures. Fishing experiences in the high altitude streams of California, Oregon, Washington and Idaho also confirm it. For example, temperatures were taken on July 21, 1948, one of the hottest days of the year, on Bear Valley Creek which is one of the headwaters of the Salmon River in Idaho at an elevation of sixty three hundred feet. Since this is a shallow, unshaded and moderately large stream, these temperature variations are greater than in deeper streams with more shade, having reached a maximum difference of fourteen degrees during the day. They were as follows:

5:00 A.M.	50° F.	
5:55 "	50°	(sunrise)
8:00 "	51°	
10:00 "	54°	
11:30 "	56°	
1:30 P.M.	61°	
2:30 "	62°	
5:00 "	64°	
7:40 "	62°	(sunset)

On this day early morning fishing with flies was poor during the cold water period of the early morning, few trout even responding to bait or artificial lures. During the early afternoon sub-surface fishing increased in success. The ten-degree rise in temperatures in the afternoon stimulated hatches of insects and brought on a feeding period in which surface fly-fishing was most successful, reaching its peak just before sunset. Here again it was indicated that trout are more active and fishing is better as water temperatures move higher into the optimum range than it is when the waters are in the tolerant temperatures of approximately 50° or below.

In high altitude streams the trout do not seem to move around as much as they do in the greater temperature range of streams of lower altitudes. Since the waters do not get abnormally warm there is no need for them to seek brook mouths or spring holes. It appears that they often remain in the same areas all season through, feeding near the bottom when the water is in the tolerant or lower optimum ranges and increasing in their hunger as the rising temperatures bring on hatches of flies influencing them to feed on or near the surface.

Since I had broken my leg fishing a stream in New York State six weeks previously, it was somewhat difficult to cover a great deal of water with this rather necessary appendage encased in a plaster cast. This may have been a blessing in disguise because it forced me to confine my fishing to a small stretch of water where I could observe the success of other anglers and the habits of the trout as conditions changed during the day. It will be remembered that the water was cold and high. In mid-morning it was 45°, gradually rising about ten degrees during the day as the sun appeared over the canyon walls. I sought an advantageous spot where I could fish the runs and riffles with a dry fly and the deeper water with spinning lures. Early in the day the flies had netted me nothing. Tiny spinning lures fished deep resulted in the taking of three beautiful rainbows of a pound or a pound and a half in size. Few fish are more beautiful than the Gunnison rainbow with its brilliant red stripe and its gill covers of purple red. It is particularly pleasant to fish for them in the clear cold water of the Gunnison with its background of weirdly shaped towering rocks ever changed by the sun as it colors the bluffs with brilliant hues of sage-green, gray-blue and red-brown. Magpies flit over the rushing water to light in the cottonwoods on the far shore or to sweep far off into the sagebrush of the hills. In the distance farmers are loading hayricks in the green meadows and cattle are peacefully grazing.

Certainly on this lovely morning the famous Gunnison trout were feeding very little. I had released the first two of my prizes because we had agreed not to kill more than one fish apiece for dinner. The third one seemed to be an ideal size for a meal, so I opened him to see what he had been eating. His stomach contained but half a teaspoonful of nymphs and other subaquatic organisms, indicating that he had been taking very little of the bountiful food supply the Gunnison affords and that that little had been taken entirely from under the surface. Other anglers who passed by had had very poor results that morning, even including those who had been fishing with bait. My companions returned occasionally to report equally mediocre success with their dry flies.

Gradually, as the sun warmed the water, conditions changed. Degree by degree the water temperature rose and with the rise the response of the fish was in proportion. In the water which had appeared devoid of life there came the resounding splash of a lusty rainbow as he jumped for one of the flies which suddenly began to hatch and flit over the water. A rise came by the willows on the far shore and another trout arched his broad back in the riffles. More flies were born to skitter gracefully over the surface. They appeared by scores, by hundreds, and then in countless swarms. The river suddenly came to life. Big trout dimpled unobtrusively in the dark water of the slick, deep glides. Smaller trout splashed and shook themselves joyfully in the white water. Fish were everywhere and all were active. To have seen the quiet river an hour before one would not have believed that it would hold so many. From upstream came the shout of an angler as a big rainbow made off with his Ginger Quill. In the pool below there echoed the tolerant curse of another as a big brown trout broke his leader. My spinning rod was long since put away in favor of floating a Multicolored Variant down the glassy riffles. After leading in and releasing one exhausted fish one would hook another on the next cast. On this day the feeding period lasted for half an hour. It was over as suddenly as it had begun. The dancing hordes of flies diminished to a few stragglers. The rising fish ceased to rise and the river was quiet once more. The noonday hatch on the Gunnison was over.

From noon to sundown the rises were few but the warmer water made dry fly-fishing at least as successful as fishing with bait or spinners. Our hosts apologized because the water was too cold to make the fishing really good. To an Easterner, used to overfished streams underpopulated with trout, such an apology seemed unnecessary. To me, the fishing was superb even though my broken leg prevented me from traveling to the more inviting spots which always are farther on. I sat on the bank to watch the others and to see where the trout were. The far bank, overhung with willows, seemed undercut and an occasional rise in that direction indicated that a few fish still were feeding from insects which dropped from the branches. The water was warmer in the riffles and many of the trout which were still feeding were there. When we took stock later in the day, one angler who had fished the riffles consistently had taken fifteen fish while two others who had worked the deeper water had netted but two trout apiece. The angler who had been most successful had fished the Gunnison for more than twenty years. He waded the riffles and floated his fly from them to where the water dropped off deeply. Under these conditions of temperature and season the great majority of the trout lay in the deeper water just below the riffles before they shelved off into the pools. Here was the favorite feeding position where the hungry fish were strategically located to await the bits of food which the current bore down to them. If the water had been warmer they might have been in the tails of the pools because they then would have preferred the relatively cool feeding position of such a location.

Anglers who fish the Gunnison consistently find that in the spring when the days are long there are feeding periods of an hour or so both in the early morning and in the evening. In the summer and fall, when the days are shorter, the morning and evening periods merge into a single time of pronounced activity when the fish feed for an hour or two while the sun is high at noon.

From opening day on May twenty-fifth to the time of the first fly hatch, the fishing on the Gunnison is confined entirely to the use of live bait, nymphs or streamer flies. The streamer which seems to be the local favorite is tied with a silver body, red throat and with wings of gray-barred hackle feathers tied over gray squirrel tail. The first fly hatch is known as the willow fly, which appears on the lower Gunnison about June tenth, moving upstream at the rate of one or two miles a day and lasting for about a week in each vicinity. This hatch signals the beginning of the fly-fishing season and may be expected at the town of Gunnison between June fifteenth and eighteenth. It is imitated by the artificial of the same name. Oftentimes the natural fly is used as well as the artificial, anglers picking them off the willow trees, impaling them on a size ten or twelve salmon egg hook, and allowing them to float downstream. After the trout have gorged themselves on willow flies and the hatch has ended, the most

Colorado's Beautiful Gunnison River Is a Fly-fisherman's Paradise

Pack Train Camp Tread to Remote Mountain Lake

popular dry fly is the Adams, closely followed by the Ginger Quill, Blue Quill and the Multicolored or Red Variant in sizes twelve or fourteen. With the cessation of the willow fly hatch, these artificials are used all season through.

In the early weeks the trout usually are to be found in greatest numbers in the heavy, deep water at the heads of pools below the riffles. They feed actively on hellgrammites, which often are used for bait with a split shot or two to get them down into the deep water of the pools. Since these deep pools often harbor the largest fish, many three-, four- and five-pound trout are caught by fishing them near to the bottom at this season particularly. When the flies emerge, the feeding trout move up into the shoal water of the riffles and are found there most usually during the remainder of the season. Since it has been noted that there is little variation in the seasonal temperatures of high altitude streams, there is small necessity for the trout to move about except to leave their resting positions temporarily to feed.

In addition to being one of the most beautiful of America's famous trout streams, the Gunnison River is one of the most productive of trout. It is productive because it abounds in rich natural food, making the trout fat, healthy and full of fight in the clear, cold water in which they live. There are rainbow or brown trout in virtually every foot of its many miles of riffles and pools. Some sections of it, such as the part which flows through the Black Canyon National Park, are almost inaccessible, furnishing sanctuaries in which the trout living there grow amazingly large. For this reason, although the usual Gunnison trout is less than two pounds in weight, fabulous fish of five and six pounds or more are not a rarity. A multitude of feeder brooks afford natural spawning areas and safe nurseries in which the little trout grow to maturity before venturing into the larger river. The greater part of the stream is followed by a motor road, making it so easily accessible to anglers that it is fished to a greater extent than this rather Utopian description might indicate. If all the anglers who fish it were true sportsmen, this fortunate condition might continue and furnish equally fine sport for anglers of generations yet unborn. In common with other trout waters, this desirable situation is more of a wish than a reality.

In the cabin next to ours there were two elderly gentlemen of obvious means. Both were so fond of fishing that they were spending the entire summer on the river. In conversation with us one evening one of them boasted to us that he and his partner had each taken their limit of trout nearly every day during the entire summer and that they were planning to stay for nearly two months more. A bit of questioning brought out the fact that both men killed every fish they netted, only stopping their fishing when the count of the fish in their bulging creels indicated that they had reached the legal daily limit of twenty trout for each rod. Moreover, they had brought their wives along. The wives did little or no fishing but they owned fishing licenses so that our two anglers could help them out a bit if the taking of their daily limit left their lust to kill still unsatiated.

"What do you do with all the fish?" we asked, trying for the moment to conceal our feelings.

"Oh, we give away the little ones to anyone who wants them. We freeze the big ones in dry ice and take them to our frozen food locker. Have to catch enough to give some dinner parties this winter, you know," they answered, evidently without embarrassment.

A quick bit of mental figuring indicated that, if these statements were true, these two despoilers of the Gunnison would deplete the river of more than two thousand trout before they returned to their homes. When we mentioned this to them and intimated that it was a bit more than their rightful share they seemed rather incensed.

"We buy licenses and we do not exceed the bag limit," they told us. "If it is wrong to kill so many fish, why doesn't the state reduce the number of fish a person is allowed to take? If the state says we can have twenty fish each day, it must be all right to take them."

There is something to be said for this point of view. The conversation is quoted because the attitude of these gentlemen is not unusual. What they do not realize is that the competent Commissioner of Fisheries, or whatever he may be called, often is powerless to reduce bag limits even if such restrictions be sorely needed to provide good fishing in future years. In many states the Commissioner is subject to the vote of a commission made up of men who often have little or no knowledge of conservation and an equal lack of interest in sport fishing. They want to please the sportsmen and they think the sportsmen want a lot of fish. They act for today and give no thought to tomorrow. That is, they do until organized sportsmen's groups educate them to the errors of this type of penny-wise and pound-foolish reasoning.

Before bringing out additional conclusions which may be drawn regarding high altitude trout waters some observations on Diamond Lake may be valuable. Diamond Lake, one of the sources of the Umpqua River, covers an area of three thousand acres near famous Crater Lake in southern Oregon. Since it is little more than five thousand feet above sea level it may not be considered a high altitude lake in the full sense of the word. However, it presents two facts of more than passing interest and thus will well serve the purpose particularly since lakes of higher altitude are but rarely visited by the average angler.

Diamond Lake was stocked with rainbow trout about 1910. As in many other suitable lakes in which trout are newly planted, the relatively few fish grew large with the abundance of food they at first found there. Fish of six or eight pounds were not uncommon and records indicate that a few weighing more than twenty pounds were caught with rod and reel. Live bait fishermen brought chubs to the lake and those which were not used evidently were liberated in its waters. The chubs (a member of the minnow family) multiplied beyond all reasonable proportion. As they multiplied, the rainbows decreased in weight and in numbers until, less than ten years after the illegal introduction of the chubs, few trout of larger than two pounds were caught. Today the lake abounds with chubs and the rainbows average less than a pound in size. Few chubs are ever found in the stomachs of the trout, leading to the assumption that the chubs are too dif-

ficult for the rainbows to catch. Evidently they would eat them
if they could because when parts of the lake have been spot
poisoned from time to time it was noticed that the trout devoured
the dazed chubs avidly. The conclusion must be drawn that the
chubs multiplied so fast that they decreased the food in the lake
until it became insufficient for the rainbows' normal growth,
which is now much slower than it was before the chubs were
introduced.

Many anglers believe that chubs are good food for trout.
Others who catch big chubs occasionally wonder if they should
kill them or let them go. It may be that small chubs furnish food
for trout in some lakes but it should be obvious that large chubs
compete with the trout for food and thus retard the growth of the
glorious old tackle-busters that all of us love so much to hook.
I have caught chubs weighing as much as two or three pounds
and some are known to be larger. The support of conservation
officers is given to the statement that trash fish such as chubs
should be killed whenever possible and especially when they
reach a size too large for trout to eat. Many members of the
minnow family never reach large size and are ideal trout food,
but this is not so with chubs, roach, carp, suckers, and similar
trash fish. It seems obvious that minnows obtained for bait should
not be released in a lake and that they should not be transplanted
from one lake to another, lest this same thing happen elsewhere.

On Diamond Lake a float line was installed from shore to shore
to reserve the smaller part of the lake as a sanctuary for the
propagation and growth of trout and fishing accordingly was forbidden in this part. Since the trout moved from place to place,
this did little good and the barrier was removed. While it was
installed, fishermen found that if they tied their boats to either
of two of the floats and bait fished on the bottom of the lake
they always would catch trout in summer. They knew this but
they did not know why these two spots always produced good
results. It was also observed that those who fished near the bottom
of the deepest part of the lake (which is fifty feet in depth) never
caught any fish at all.

The reasons for these locations being either productive or nonproductive are provided by the aquatic biologists who are making a study of the lake. They confirm the previous suggestions in this book on the successful fishing of trout lakes. The two floats the fishermen found it so worth while to use as markers for good fishing locations were both directly over a depth of between thirty and forty feet. The lake, which stratifies in summer, has its thermocline located at a maximum depth of forty feet (see Fig. 13, page 92). In other words, these fishermen unwittingly were fishing at the approximate depth of the thermocline or just above it, where is located the coldest level in the lake containing the highest concentration of oxygen. The surface waters, which reach a temperature of approximately 70° in summer, are less desirable to the trout than the cooler waters near the thermocline level. Deeper in the lake below the thermocline there is insufficient oxygen in the summer and winter stagnation periods to support trout because the algae in the water prevents the sun from penetrating to this depth, thus eliminating the growth of plant life which would provide oxygen. Quite obviously there are many other places in the lake where these fishermen could have caught trout near the bottom. All of them lie in the rim of bottom approximately between the thirty- and forty-foot contours, or at the general depth of the thermocline. In the spring and fall, when the lake waters mix, this situation is not so, but in the summer it provides an example of where trout may be found and where there are no trout at all. Another point of interest is that bait fishing near the bottom can best be done where there is little or no vegetation. In Diamond Lake there is virtually no plant life beyond a depth of twenty-five feet. The most successful summer trolling in the lake is done at a depth of between thirty and forty feet for the same reason.

Hatches of flies in high altitude waters grow less as the altitude increases because as the altitude increases the time between frosts is less and there is correspondingly less time for the insects to appear. In Diamond Lake there is a caddis fly hatch in July and a May fly hatch somewhat later. The caddis fly is imitated by a Caddis bucktail. Anglers report that no attempt is made to imitate the May flies and that virtually any dry fly pattern in sizes eight or ten produces results if it floats well.

As in other lakes in summer, the trout seek out the creek mouths when the surface waters become warm because the incoming water from the tributaries is colder. Thus, for fly-fishermen, the only surface fishing is found at the inlets of the two creeks which provide a constant flow of water. Fly-fishing is at its best in the evening, rather than more evenly distributed during the day as it is in lakes at higher altitudes, where surface waters are colder. As in lower altitude lakes, the trout in summer are inclined to move into the shoal areas in the evening to feed. Fishermen notice them breaking the surface far out in the lake early in the evening and gradually working toward shore.

As lakes and streams increase in altitude the growing season for trout grows correspondingly less because the waters are correspondingly colder and the metabolism of the fish decreases in proportion. For this reason the average size of trout in mountain trout waters grows less as the altitude of the waters increases. The growing season for trout is considered to be the time between killing frosts. In a lake at five thousand feet of altitude such as Diamond Lake the time between frosts will be approximately from one hundred and twenty to one hundred and forty days, allowing only this amount of time to the trout for intensive feeding. At seventy-five hundred feet the growing season will decrease to about ninety days and in lakes higher than eight thousand feet this period may be of not more than sixty days' duration.

In high altitude waters another reason for the smaller sizes of trout is that their food supply is greatly restricted in type and abundance. While the high winds may blow terrestrial insects into the water, the water itself furnishes little but fresh-water shrimp, scuds, midge larvae and pupae which are eaten as they swim to the top of the water to emerge, and the ever-present plankton, which is a general name for tiny or microscopic aquatic animal or vegetable life. Stomachs of countless mountain trout have been found to contain nothing but plankton. In these high altitudes very few flies are available for food due to the long cold weather seasons. There may be small hatches of May flies and alder flies and even a few stone and caddis flies.

Lakes in areas which have been subjected to volcanic action invariably are richer than lakes in sedimentary or glaciated basins. Foods are more abundant because volcanic lakes contain more dissolved mineral matter and thus have greater alkalinity, which promotes fish growth.

It is even more important to anglers to note that the feeding periods of trout in high altitude waters are more predictable than in streams and lakes nearer to sea level. Because of the coldness of the water in high altitudes, fish are less active and are less inclined to feed in the morning and at night. It was noted on the Gunnison River that there was a definite feeding period every day during the summer at midday. This is typical of high altitude waters and is more pronounced as the altitude increases. Under these conditions trout feed when the water is warmest, which is at midday. At high altitudes the clouds are fewer, the air is purer and the full force of the sun is felt on the water more than it is upon streams and lakes at lower altitudes. Thus it may be concluded that those who fish for trout in high altitude waters may enjoy sleeping late before having a late breakfast and may look forward to returning from their fishing before sunset because they will find the trout most co-operative during the middle of the day.

CHAPTER FIFTEEN

Trout Pools, Large and Small

Experiences with Big Trout in Pools

OLD LOG DAMS on good trout streams always have held a special fascination for me ever since my first large trout broke away many years ago by wrapping my leader around the submerged logs of Schuster's Dam. Old dams present a beautiful and ever-changing picture dear to the heart of the angler. The shimmering spectra of tiny rainbows glisten in the updraft of cool spray where the cataract thunders into white foam in the rocky, tree bordered pool. May flies dance over the churning waters to tempt rising trout. An old angler cautiously works his way over the rotting timbers of an ancient millrace the better to be in position for the long lash of his line to land his Quill Gordon delicately where the great trout should be waiting in the quiet water near by the foam. The tiny straw-hatted lad with his alder pole dips his bare feet in the coolness of the current and carefully selects a wiggling worm from the tobacco can beside him on his rocky perch. All is quiet save for the rushing of the water, yet there is a tenseness in the placid scene because at any moment the great trout may take the drifting worm or the floating fly.

Each old log dam seems to have a personality all its own. Many of them are famous for their picturesque beauty and for the great trout which live in the sanctuary of their rotting timbers. Such a place is the famed Upper Dam Pool in the Rangeley region of western Maine. For more than fifty years the fabulous trout and landlocked salmon to be caught there have lured anglers from far and wide to its remote location where the waters of Mooselookmeguntic pour down into those of Richardson Lake. One

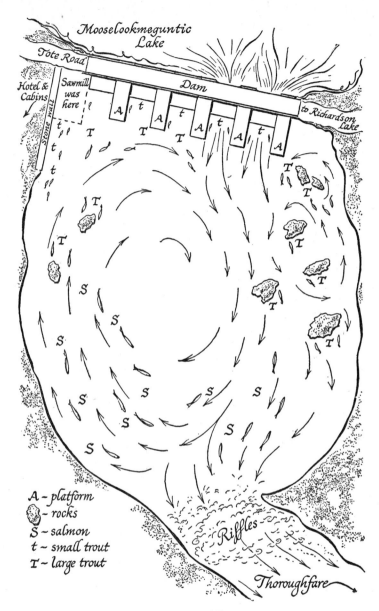

Labels within the figure:

Mooselookmeguntic Lake

Tote Road

Hotel & Cabins

Sawmill was here

Dam

Stone wall

to Richardson Lake

Riffles

Thoroughfare

A ~ platform
~ rocks
S ~ salmon
t ~ small trout
T ~ large trout

FIGURE 27.

UPPER DAM POOL, MAINE

*Sketch of water currents and locations of fish. Two
sluices at right are open.*

must go there by boat because there is no road. At the journey's end log fires light the cabins and a delicious meal in the little hotel on the water's edge fortifies the angler for the superb fishing to come.

It was many years ago when Joe Stickney, Bill Edson and I made our first visit there. The great trout which had seemed to be a myth were soon to become a fact. I walked down the stairs to one of the ramps built between the sluices and cast a streamer fly into the swirling current. In the many years which have passed between then and now I never have quite recovered from the shock of seeing the scarcely believable size of the squaretail trout that came out from under the dam to refuse my fly. Suddenly his great length appeared in the water so near the surface that every motion of his majestic approach toward the fly was colorful and clear. He eased slowly forward with a casualness born of years of experience. As he reached the fly his progress slowed while he critically watched my intense efforts to fish it in a lifelike manner. Since I stood in plain sight of him, nothing more could be done except to remain motionless, hoping that he would take the fly before my presence became too obvious.

If a trout ever made contemptuous remarks in pantomime, that one certainly did! He seemed to want to assure me that he knew I was there; that this sort of thing had happened to him many, many times before. "How could a fish as old and as wise as I live so long," he seemed to say, "if he snapped at every bit of fur and feathers that flitted about in the pool?" His only interest seemed to be in criticizing the styles and sizes of flies that currently were in fashion. His reaction, as he slowly turned and passed from sight below the dam, was uncomplimentary in the extreme. Since the fly was a Gray Ghost which I had tied myself, my disillusionment was all the more acute. There was the record trout I had been seeking; so near, and yet so far away!

As I was regaining my composure, Joe Stickney walked down the stairs. I moved back away from the water and told him about the big trout. "Try for him with a Lady Doctor," I urged. "Maybe he will come out again."

"He may come out," Joe replied, "but he won't take the fly. Even if he did, he would break you in an instant by wrapping your leader around the logs under the dam."

Nevertheless, Joe tried a cast and the trout drifted out again; disdainfully inspected the fly and haughtily returned to his lair. Nothing we could do that day would interest him after that.

"We are fishing for him from the wrong spot," Joe commented. "Maybe we can hook him by casting toward the dam from a boat anchored in the pool. We'll have to use heavy tackle to hold him away from the piling and to get him out into the current. He has been hooked many times before, but hooking him is one thing and landing him is another. Let's try it at dawn and we'll see what we can do."

That night was a sleepless one. The big trout, and the strategy of catching him, was on my mind so much that I had my tackle rigged and was at the pool long before daylight. As pale dawn showed in the east, Joe arrived. We chose a spot a fair cast from the dam and anchored the boat in the swift current. We fished until long after breakfast that day and the next, but nothing came of it except for a few fish that would have seemed of respectable size if the big one had not been foremost in our minds. We tried everything logical within the ruling of "unweighted flies only," but nothing we offered would interest the big trout. In desperation we reduced the strength of our leaders to strands so fine that they could neither have held him nor prevented him from going under the dam. Fine leaders did not prove to be the answer.

In searching through my fly box that night I selected several untried possibilities for use the next morning. One of them was an imitation of a large bee whose fat black and orange body was tied from closely cropped dyed deer hair. It was virtually unsinkable and therefore should float well in the whirlpool of the flume near where the great trout lived. The angler who gave it to me had said that he had taken many large trout with lures identical to this, so I hopefully put it aside for use.

The dawn's early glow found us in our Rangeley boat anchored again within casting distance of the dam. "Try the bee first," Joe advised, so I cast it into the air and dropped it where the current would drift it in front of the apron of the dam.

Eagerly I watched the little bee dance on the wavelets. One minute I saw it and the next it was gone. No splashing strike occasioned his taking it. He sucked it in so unobtrusively that at first only my intuition told me he was there. As he went for the protection of the dam I held him so tightly I thought the delicate leader surely would part, but it did not. The current was in my favor and suddenly he was in it, dashing down the white water toward the tail of the pool.

Joe raised the anchor enough to let the boat follow the fish in the current downstream and dropped it again in the quiet water where I had room to handle him. The great trout would race for the dam again and again, only to be held by the tackle and coerced into the fast water which brought him downstream to my boat again. When he had the strength to seek the dam no longer he rolled on the surface, brilliant and heavy, his great back and fins assuring that here indeed was the trophy brook trout I had been seeking, tired of fighting and almost mine.

As he was drawn nearer and nearer to the boat, I took the net which Joe handed me. This trout I would land myself. With the net wet and ready I led him in and it was then that I saw that in his struggles he had pulled against the hook until it was held to his jaw by the merest thread of flesh. As a great trout should, he made a last lunge for freedom. The last I saw of him was the defiant flip of his tail as he sank into the depths and swam slowly to the safety of the dam.

Joe looked at me with a sympathetic smile. "Big for a brookie," was his casual understatement. "He's better off there than mounted on a log slab anyway. How big do you think he was?"

"He was so big," I replied sadly, "that no one would believe how big he was. He would have weighed about eight pounds, I think."

"Eight pounds and then some. They look smaller in the water. Let's get breakfast and then I'll show you some of his brothers."

After breakfast we walked to the sawmill (since torn down) at the near end of the dam and downstairs to the lower level above where the backwaters meet the seepage through the logs. We raised a trap door in the floor and lay on our stomachs to watch the life in the slow current below. Schools of minnows drifted about the log piling in the dim light. Then we saw the trout. By ones, twos and half dozens their great shapes drifted into sight as they rested quietly in the water, occasionally to lash forward to snap up a minnow which imprudently had ventured into their path. Here was the sanctuary of some of the biggest brook trout in Maine, yes, in all of America. Trophies, all of them, there was not one which would have weighed less than four pounds. Here and there some were much larger; even as large as the big one I had hooked that morning.

"Now you see what goes on under a dam," said Joe. "You can fish a pool when it would seem that no trout are in it. During the day, many of the big ones rest in the cool shade under the dam where there is safety and feed for them. The big trout diet almost entirely on minnows. Backwaters of old dams abound in them. When they come out into the pool it is usually in the late evening, at night, or early in the morning. During the day most of them are where you see them now."

Many times have I hooked a large trout at the base of a little dam where the downcoming water meets the eddies beside it. There, where the fast water blends into the slow, trout like to lie in wait for feed. In the heat of summer it is cooler there. The tumbling waters are saturated with oxygen. All conditions are to their liking. In the early morning or late evening they may venture to the tail of the pool. During cold weather they should be in the deepest part of the pool itself. Trout for protection travel in sizes; the biggest ones in one place, the medium-sized ones in another and the tiny trout somewhere else. Rarely will tiny trout be found where there are big ones, and conversely. The small ones, for their own safety, keep to themselves among the rocks, riffles or brook mouths. They may be in safe places under the dam itself, but if one catches little trout it should signal the fact that the big ones are not near by.

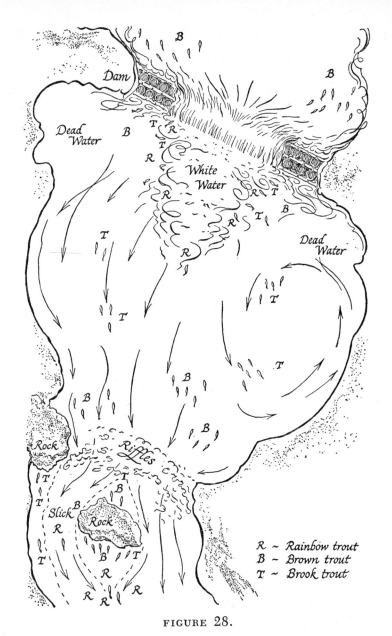

FIGURE 28.

TYPICAL FEEDING POSITIONS OF TROUT
AROUND LOG DAMS

If one ever has climbed beneath the downcoming sheet of water under an old dam, he should be surprised by the great area of safe water there, hidden behind the waterfall, where trout can live in

FIGURE 29.

BROOK TROUT AND LANDLOCKED SALMON RECORD OF UPPER DAM POOL

(1897 to 1921 inclusive)

Year	No. of Trout Recorded	Weight in Lbs. and Ozs.	Average Weight	No. of Salmon Recorded	Weight in Lbs. and Ozs.	Average Weight
1897	121	534.12	4.421	7	32.14	4.7
1898	77	334.3	4.207	5	25.14	5.2
1899	34	136.10	4.029	10	47.1	4.272
1900	39	154.14	3.974	34	145.14	4.294
1901	42	173.5	4.119	31	135.5	4.354
1902	30	124.10	4.166	63	295.5	4.682
1903	23	95.10	4.173	58	301.2	5.189
1904	21	88.4	4.19	96	456.6	4.75
1905	20	74.7	3.7	68	287.4	4.191
1906	25	104.13	4.2	62	247.8	3.983
1907	28	118.10	4.25	126	519.5	4.119
1908	22	109.9	5.	82	346.8	2.411
1909	13	52.8	3.23	63	254.10	4.047
1910	26	87.7	3.346	60	235.7	3.916
1911	36	134.3	3.444	81	323.6	3.987
1912	31	115.5	3.709	104	385.3	3.701
1913	6	25.15	4.333	58	212.	3.655
1914	22	85.9	3.909	69	249.13	3.623
1915	18	66.12	3.722	117	432.15	3.7
1916	9	33.14	3.777	58	206.7	3.555
1917	10	32.11	3.3	43	161.13	3.534
1918	12	46.4	3.833	27	96.6	3.555
1919	10	36.10	3.7	43	159.8	3.697
1920	17	58.12	3.47	66	253.3	3.833
1921	23	83.7	3.608	60	222.3	3.07

peace and security. Rarely can the angler put his lure into such places. If so, there are so many obstructions there that broken tackle surely must be the result of a strike. The only alternative is to fish the fly as near to the downcoming flood as is possible, where the fast white water meets the slow. From under the dam the trout are watching for food. A well cast fly in such places should reward the angler with the flashing strike of a trout waiting there to rush out to take whatever the current brings down to him.

Since 1895, Upper Dam Pool has been famous for landlocked salmon (*Salmo salar sebago*) as well as for trout. Since the salmon were introduced into Mooselookmeguntic and Richardson Lakes they evidently have thrived at the expense of the trout since each succeeding year has produced fewer large trout and more salmon. From the standpoint of the angler as well as the ichthyologist the increase of the salmon and the decline in numbers of the trout, together with the diminishing average weight of big fish caught, seems worthy of note. The figures, as taken from the records of Upper Dam Pool are preserved in Figure 29. They indicate only fish of over three pounds in weight, taken from this pool alone. Doubtless many more large ones were landed than are shown in these old records, but the actual numbers are less important than the yearly change which has taken place in those which are recorded.

There are still many large brook trout in the pool at Upper Dam, although not as many as in the earlier years. There will be record trout there for many years to come, but the famous old tackle-busters are growing harder to find and still more difficult to catch. The table on page 265 is a record of trophy trout of seven pounds and over which have been caught and recorded there between 1897 and 1911. It shows that the record fish weighed nine pounds and eleven ounces, taken by Mr. R. N. Parish on September 23, 1897.

One of the interesting facts about this record is that the great majority of these trophy trout were taken during the last two weeks in September, just before the season closes on October first. At this period the lakes should be at their fall turnover stage, causing the trout to come to the surface from deep water and to roam more widely; this being intensified by the fact that the fall

1897	Sept.	1	7 pounds	1	ounces
"	"	1	9 "	4	"
"	"	10	8 "	4	"
"	"	13	7 "	15	"
"	"	16	7 "	7	"
"	"	18	7 "	6	"
"	"	23	8 "	12	"
"	"	23	9 "	11	"
"	"	28	7 "	6	"
1898	"	14	7 "	10	"
"	"	14	8 "	7	"
1900	Sept.	19	8 "	0	"
1901	"	13	7 "	3	"
1903	Aug.	10	8 "	6	"
"	"	26	7 "	1	"
1904	Sept.	19	7 "	4	"
"	"	26	8 "	2	"
1906	June	21	8 "	10	"
"	"	22	7 "	3	"
1908	Aug.	26	7 "	5	"
"	Sept.	1	9 "	7	"
1909	"	8	7 "	2	"
1911	"	22	7 "	1	"

migratory period is beginning. No trophy trout are recorded in certain years, perhaps due to unusually dry or late seasons. That an occasional big fish was taken in August may have been prompted by premature cold weather. It should be noted that all of these trout were taken with unweighted flies on the surface rather than being hooked in deep water. The spring season for good trout fishing in Maine is short, reaching its optimum water temperatures usually in June. It will be noted that only one large trout was caught in the pool in June and that none were taken in July. Due partly to logging operations in the early spring, the pool harbors very few large fish as permanent residents. Most of them are transients journeying from one lake to the other and resting in the pool for a few days or weeks when water conditions are to their liking and when logs are not being run from Mooselookmeguntic Lake through the flumes in the dam and through the pool into Richardson Lake. In the summer it may be concluded that stratification of the lakes causes the large trout to seek deeper water and that very few of them spend their summers in the pool. With the exception of small trout, which are residents of the pool throughout the year, few fish are to be caught there during warm weather, due to warm surface water conditions. During the spring and fall turnover periods, fishing at Upper Dam usually is excellent; the best anglers preferring the months of June and September for that reason.

The great majority of trout (and salmon) taken at Upper Dam are caught on streamer flies. The question of who originated the streamer fly has been argued ever since it became generally popular twenty-five or thirty years ago. There is no doubt that it reached its present state of perfection at about that time in the little cottage of Mrs. Carrie G. Stevens near the famous pool at Upper Dam in Maine. To my mind, Mrs. Stevens ties the loveliest streamer flies ever made. It was she who originated the popular Gray Ghost which bears such a faithful resemblance to a smelt that it is generally acknowledged to be the most successful streamer of all time. Certainly, the streamer fly began its present popularity at Upper Dam Pool, where many large trout and salmon were caught on Mrs. Stevens's creations in the early nineteen-twenties. From there the success of the fly which imitates a food fish rather than a winged insect spread over the nation, to bring back to Mrs. Stevens the gratitude of all anglers and to add to the fame of the pool at Upper Dam.[1]

To understand where trout lie in the pools made by dams one must fish the same pool many times under all seasonal conditions. Every time I have fished around the old broken-down log dam on Third Musquacook Lake I have been increasingly fascinated by the behavior of the large trout that nearly always are to be

---

[1] Among the most popular streamer flies for Maine are the Gray Ghost, Black Ghost, Supervisor, Colonel Bates, Lady Doctor, Edson Tiger (both Dark and Light), Mickey Finn, Dana, Jane Craig, Sanborn, and Nine-Three, dressed on number 2, 4, or 6 extra long shanked hooks. Marabou patterns are also popular.

found there. This dam was built originally by loggers about the time of the First World War. It is so remotely located in the north woods of Maine that few people ever go there. Rotted by the snows of thirty seasons and burned by several fires, it is today more a pile of misshapen driftwood than a dam, but it still retains some of the lake's waters and serves admirably as a haven for many of the biggest brook trout in the eastern United States.

I have fished it in the early spring when the big trout were still deep in the lakes. Even streamer flies were of little avail. Those trout which did respond were thin and lifeless, rarely taking anything except live bait fished deep. One would find them only in the deepest part of the pool, where the waters running through the broken dam had cut a channel in which they seemed to lie. On a warm day in the early season a streamer fly fished near the riffles at the tail of the pool would bring response from several small fish of a pound or less, but the big ones were nowhere to be found.

I have fished it in the late spring and the late fall when a fly dropped upon its waters would bring up the flashing shapes of several large trout from the depths, each one determined to be the first to reach the fly. This is the time of optimum surface water temperatures when the trout prefer the coolness of the tree shaded pool and are avid for any bit of food which may drift down to them. Under such conditions it seems that the big trout are everywhere, fat, hungry and full of fight. I have fished it in the early summer when the black flies settled around one in a billowing black cloud, investigating the openings in one's garments and biting the first bit of flesh they could reach. I don't like fishing in Maine during the black fly season because every single bite itches for weeks, making me wonder if it would not be better logic to forget the whole thing and to stay at home. In the heat of the summer, there are very few big trout in the pool. Those that are there are close against the logs, seeking the cool water and the shade. There are always small ones which will respond to the fly, with an occasional large one showing interest in the early morning or late in the evening.

In this pool, as at Upper Dam, the best months for fishing are during the optimum water temperatures of June and September. Last June, Dana McNally and I flew in there, landing the little Piper Cub on the lake and mooring it to the dry-ki that had accumulated for many years in a tangled mass above the dam. During the afternoon we took several trout on flies but none of over two pounds, which is considered less than average for those waters. Another airplane appeared overhead, its colors identifying Warden "Sleepy" Atkins of the Maine Warden Service. Noticing our yellow plane on the ground, he wobbled his wings at us in recognition and went about his business, an hour later returning to pay us a visit.

"Sleepy, where are all the big trout?" I asked him. "They should be here, but we haven't taken a 'keeper' all afternoon!"

The warden considered the matter thoughtfully. "Would you invest a few leaders and flies to find out?" he smilingly replied.

Since the obvious answer was in the affirmative he led me over the dry-ki to the upper part of the dam, where the current from the lake disappeared in black swirls beneath the maze of logs and into the pool below.

"Drop a fly between the logs and see what happens," the warden suggested.

The spot was scarcely a yard in diameter; merely a hole in the mass of driftwood. I flipped my fly into the spot and before it had floated a foot's distance a big trout had it with a smashing strike, at the same instant snarling me around the submerged branches and breaking away.

"You can't catch them with that light tackle," the warden said rather needlessly. "You asked where they were and said you were willing to pay to find out. It will cost you a fly and a tippet at every cast!"

After three or four such investments, I gave up. The trout were big ones of two, three and four pounds, but it would take heavy tackle, a strong arm and a complete lack of sportsmanship to remove them from their lair. The day was hot and the trout were in the shade in the safest and most comfortable place they knew. Since we had to leave before dark, we could not wait for them to return to the pool. When I have camped there overnight under such conditions I have noted that they have dropped down into the pool soon after sunset to prove again that in the late evening or early morning the fishing of pools in warm weather is better than at any other time during the day.

When the trouts of all species make their migratory runs the fishing in pools below dams is at its best. Pools are the resting places for trout in their travels. In them they pause for days or weeks to enjoy the diversity of swift water and still; to feed in the luxury of their bountiful expanses; to share the safety and coolness of their deep waters, their rocks and their shade. To stand in the eddy of a tree-bordered pool, casting a long line to rising trout with the music of the waterfall in one's ears, always has seemed to me one of the pleasantest occupations imaginable. To hook a big fish under such circumstances, holding him from the dam, coaxing him out of the fast water and easing him into the eddy and the net is an episode of angling which helps to make fly-fishing the glorious sport which it is.

In the Eastern United States, fishing in pools below dams usually is allowed, although many states rightfully restrict many of these pools to angling only with the unweighted fly. Perhaps this should be done in more cases, certainly at times of the year when migratory trout fill the pools in such numbers that too many can be removed by the use of bait. In many Western waters it is illegal to fish around dams because hordes of anadromous fish ascend these coastal rivers during their summer and winter runs, waiting in stupendous numbers in the pools for the high water which will enable them to negotiate the dam. At such times in Western streams these pools could be veritable "slaughter pens" if angling of all types was not prohibited.

In fishing pools below dams during normal water conditions it will be noted that brook trout, brown trout and rainbows select typical feeding positions in the pool. If we know what type of trout the stream affords, these typical positions, as shown in Figure 34, make it easier for us to locate them. Rainbow trout (including steelhead) have a propensity for fast, foamy water, providing it is not too swift for them to maintain their usual resting or holding positions in the protected spots behind boulders or even in the fast water itself. Unlike the brook trout and the brown trout, which are inclined to travel widely in search of food, the rainbow habitually adopts a resting place which also is a feeding position. He is inclined to stay there and not to leave it except to migrate farther upstream or down. For this reason we usually will find him in the fast water where it comes into the pool or in the eddies behind rocks farther down in the pool where the current is swift.

The brown trout normally seeks the opposite type of water. He will be in the quieter portions of the tail of the pool, if hiding places are offered to him there, or in deep spots just before or beside large rocks in the current. If there is a fissure in the ledge of the pool bottom; if a large log or rock offers a shady hideaway beneath an undercut bank; if trees and bushes protect deep places along the shore, these are the logical spots in which to fish for him. He will leave these places in the early morning and more especially at dusk to roam the pool and riffles in search of food. From either his resting position or his feeding area he constantly is on the lookout for the drifting fly or nymph and the unsuspecting minnow if water conditions are such as to whet his appetite.

The brook trout chooses the middle ground and may be located in the same places as the brown trout and the rainbow but more usually in moderate water which is neither too fast nor too slow. He hugs the fringe of the current near the fast water and will dart into it when food tempts him there. He enjoys the sanctuaries of protective rocks, undercut banks and bushes but will travel to the riffles or roam the pool when necessity demands, more particularly in the early morning or late evening hours.

All trout, and especially the sea-run varieties, have a decided distaste for bright sunlight. When the full force of the sun is on the water it is the exception to find them where its glare penetrates. When the day is bright, it has always seemed to me to be most important to specialize on the likely spots which are in the shadow and usually to pass by even the promising feeding or holding positions which are in the direct light of the sun.

Among anglers there seems to be a decided difference of opinion as to the merits of beaver dams for the protection of trout. In discussing this matter with game wardens and conservation officials it seems agreed that such dams are never of any lasting value and that if they are maintained in trout streams it eventually causes the decline or elimination of the trout. When beavers throw a dam across a brook or stream, considerable water above the dam is impounded, often to such an extent that large ponds result. In the first year after the dam has been built this pond may offer a sanctuary for the trout imprisoned above it, providing a great deal of food in the flooded area. Fish in the brooks which enter the pond may descend into the pond itself and thus provide good fishing for a time. Since the dam is a seepage dam it is a barrier for the migration of these trout; those above it being unable to go downstream to the lake or river below and those below being unable to ascend the stream beyond the dam to spawn.

If the area in the beaver pond possesses an abundance of cold water springs, the trout may thrive for a time and perhaps permanently. Usually, this is not the case. The impounded waters have spread into a shallow but wide area the surface of which usually becomes so warmed by the sun that all of the water is above the tolerant limit of trout. If they cannot go elsewhere they must die. Even if the waters of the beaver pond do not warm to such an extent as to become lethal for trout, there is another condition which usually takes place to cause their death. In the impounded waters is an abundance of partially submerged vegetation composed of trees, bushes and grasses. The majority of these die and rot, using up oxygen and giving off carbon dioxide. As they do so the acid water becomes saturated with carbon dioxide and other deadly gases. Replacement of oxygen is virtually eliminated because there is a minimum of water flow and a minimum of oxygen-producing plants. With the preponderance of destructive gases over the life-giving oxygen, trout cannot survive. This was brought most forcibly to my attention when I watched a beaver trapper cut a hole in the ice of a beaver pond. The stench of the gases which were emitted from the hole was indescribable. In some cases this goes so far that the beavers themselves sign their own death warrant because often they cannot live in the gas-saturated waters of the ponds they have built. The water in the pond may be so warm that the seepage through the dam makes even a large part of the brook below the dam unsuitable for trout. The obstruction dams up food in the pond and causes it to settle and to strain out, preventing it from going downstream. I have visited beaver dams where there was no fishing whatsoever for several hundred yards downstream and not a fish of any sort visible in the beaver pond itself. The presence of the dam entirely eliminated the source waters of the stream as a breeding place for trout.

It is unfortunate that there must be so many dams on our trout streams. While negotiable dams occasionally may be an asset to the production of trout it is certain that in general dams do much more harm than good;[2] their presence often entirely ruining the stream as a trout water. In the newspapers from time to time we read statements by public utility interests to the effect that the water impounded by dams increases fishing. While this may be true in the cases of certain warm water fishes, it rarely is so with trout. If the building of a dam is necessary to the common good, most farsighted anglers will join in supporting the enterprise but they do not like to be confronted with the obvious untruth that the dam will be an asset to trout fishing. Even large dams, wherever their construction is necessary, can be so built as to provide proper means for migratory fishes to pass over them.[3]

[2] There are occasional exceptions to this, such as the mountain meadows of the Sierra Nevada and Cascade Mountains which were formed by beaver dams filling the area with silt. In some cases beaver dams provide late summer water flow on streams that otherwise would dry up.

[3] This applies to large dams not over 100 feet in height. While fish ladders on lower dams have done much for Western waters, their value for residential non-migratory species of fish is questionable. In the West, striped bass and shad seldom, if ever, use fish ladders and smallmouthed bass have

If this were properly done and if dams unnecessary to the common welfare were forbidden, we could in a large measure enjoy the fruits of progress and have good fishing too.

---

never been known to do so, according to Dr. Paul R. Needham, former Commissioner of Fisheries of Oregon and presently Professor of Zoology at the University of California. On this subject he writes, "Fishways have long been used in Western waters to get anadromous fish past dams to their upstream spawning beds. Steelhead and salmon are the principal fishes in Western waters that have been aided by the construction of fish ladders. One of the best sets of fish ladders ever built was installed in Bonneville Dam on the Columbia River at a cost of over $5,000,000.00. This is a low dam operated with a head of only sixty feet. No fish ladders were installed at Grand Coulee or Shasta Dams because of their height. It is well known that fish ladders will work only in dams of less than 100 feet in height. It would have been a futile waste of money to have installed fish ladders in the two dams just named." In both the East and the West, if dams which are not excessively high must be built on trout rivers, there should be installed in them fish ladders for the passage of trout.

PART IV

Development of Trout Waters

CHAPTER SIXTEEN

Brook Improvement and Stream Conservation

How Bits of Work Build Better Fishing

A FEW YEARS AGO several anglers were fly-fishing a small, rocky woodland stream in western Massachusetts. This was a stream they had fished many times before, so they knew every trout-bearing hole and riffle by heart. Many brook trout lived here all year round but they were small, for the most part; so small that the anglers used flies with the barbs pinched off so the little fellows could be released unharmed. The larger trout were few and far between. It was only the occasional taking of a sizable fish that tempted the anglers to fish there. They wondered why the big trout seemed to forsake the little stream for the heavier waters farther down in the river. If it had not been for the fact that the place was so near to their homes it is probable that the anglers never would have fished there at all.

On this day they met for lunch and discussed the reasons for the poor fishing. "Recently I obtained some government booklets on trout stream management," one of them said. "The booklets indicated that a stream such as this could be improved with a very small amount of work and that this bit of work would increase the fishing remarkably in only a season or two." The angler went on to relate what he had read about how it could be done.

As a result of this streamside chat the fishermen put away their rods and went to work to improve the water. They picked out a site for a little pool where the rocky banks narrowed from a bowl to a V caused by a ledge of rock. They filled the V with boulders as large as they could lift, interlocking them in place as best they could so that high water would not wash them away. When the big boulders were in place they filled in the crevices of the rock dam with smaller stones and then with bits of sod, leaves and shovelfuls of gravel. They spent two hours at their task. Even as they finished the water level rose and where there had been a gully there was now a beautiful little pool whose overflow splashed happily over and through the seepage dam they had built. They had raised the level of the water in the pool by nearly two feet, thus providing a deep, cold pool that seemed to be an ideal sanctuary for trout.

Encouraged by the visible results of their labors they went upstream to a similar place and built another rock dam. When darkness came they returned home happy in the realization that, even though they had sacrificed the catching of a trout or two, they had accomplished something else that was ultimately to be more worth while.

During the following week they read all the information available on the improvement of trout streams. On the following Saturday they returned to the place with shovels, brush hooks, crowbars and axes. The two rock dams they had built held back the stream so well that most of the water cascaded over the tops of the structures, adding to the aeration of the stream and making it easy for trout to leap over them in their travels. For the sake of safety they added a few more large boulders and then started similar projects elsewhere.

Here and there in the banks they found little springs which they cleaned out, digging channels from them to the main stream so that small trout and forage fish could find protection there; so that the spring water would add its coolness and volume to the stream in the summer. Where a bank had been eroded they cut a dead tree and anchored it to the shore with its branches in the water to protect little fish which might wish to live there. Upstream from this place they made a deflector of rocks to deepen the channel and to decrease the erosion of the bank.

Where the wideness of the stream caused silt to be deposited in the stream bed they built a single log dam, anchoring both ends

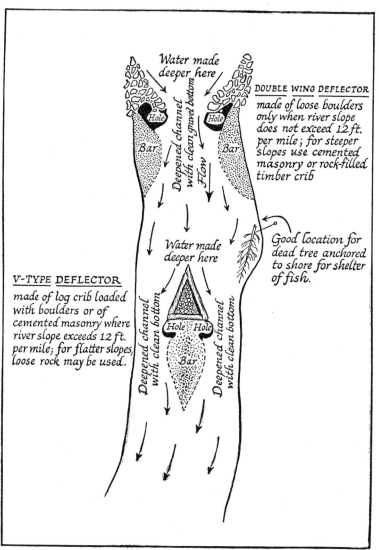

Water made
deeper here

Deepened channel
with clear gravel bottom

Flow

Hole

Hole

Bar

Bar

DOUBLE WING DEFLECTOR
made of loose boulders
only when river slope
does not exceed 12 ft.
per mile; for steeper
slopes use cemented
masonry or rock-filled
timber crib

Water made
deeper here

Good location for
dead tree anchored
to shore for shelter
of fish.

V-TYPE DEFLECTOR
made of log crib loaded
with boulders or of
cemented masonry where
river slope exceeds 12 ft.
per mile; for flatter slopes,
loose rock may be used.

Deepened channel
with clean bottom

Deepened channel
with clean bottom

Hole

Hole

Bar

Courtesy U. S. Forest Service, Division of Wildlife Management

FIGURE 30.

DEFLECTORS FOR TROUT STREAM
IMPROVEMENT

of the log into ditches cut into the banks. Farther downstream they anchored a similar log across the current so that the water flowed under as well as over it. In another spot they planted big boulders in the stream bed. All this increased the speed of the water flow, causing the silt which had accumulated to be washed away and preventing the deposit of more. Silt is a type of stream bottom distasteful to trout but when the gravel which lies under the silt is uncovered the trout will collect there to rest, to feed and possibly to lay their eggs.

In many places they installed deflectors of logs or piles of boulders to narrow and deepen the channel and to furnish hiding places for trout. They carried rocks from places where they were valueless and put them in spots where they would add to the productivity of the stream. They dug up little trees deep in the woods and planted them along the banks where shade was needed. All this they did during several pleasant week ends in the spring. Then they waited to see what good would come of their labors.

One sunny day in the following spring the anglers took me to their stream to demonstrate the results of the enterprise. They had improved nearly a mile of its course at a cost of virtually nothing except their own efforts. The difference between the improved section and the unimproved stretches was remarkable. The beauty of their water had been increased manyfold by the addition of deep pools and natural-looking rock dams. No dead stretches of stream existed. Everywhere was cascading water with its deep runs and glides. Everywhere were gravel bottoms filled with ideal hiding places for trout.

We joined up our rods and fished the stretch. Of course there were many little trout; even more than during the year before. The happy discovery was that there were big trout there too. They seemed to have come from all the rest of the stream to live in this improved stretch which proved to be so much to their liking. It seemed that they no longer chose to go downward to the river because in this part of the little stream on which the anglers had labored they found water as they wanted it to be.

That day we caught and released more trout than we could have taken from any other part of the stream. The average size of the trout was much larger than I ever knew the water to produce. The success of the project attracted other anglers, of course, but many of them saw there the benefits to be gained from trout stream improvement and they offered their help in doing the same with other stretches of the river.

This example is but a single instance which is typical of what a few enterprising men can do to improve trout fishing near home. If a stream contains inadequate facilities for trout it will support very few of them. In this case, stocking the stream with trout is relatively ineffectual. If the stream is improved by the addition of low check dams, deflectors and shelters, trout pools will be gouged out and deep runs and stretches of fast water will exist where none were before. Stocked trout will remain in this improved water and fish from other parts of the stream will seek it. Stocking will yield more results because the stream then contains better living accommodations for Mr. and Mrs. *Salvelinus fontinalis* and more food for them to grow on.

In planning stream improvement let us again give thought to water temperatures. If the stream becomes too warm in the summer trout will not stay there. Opening up the springs and deepening and shading the water will cool it down by several degrees, which may make all the difference in the world between attracting trout and driving them away. Between 60° and 65° is an ideal summer water temperature. If the brook is five degrees warmer or colder than this its temperature can be adjusted by proper stream management. A stream which is too cold can be warmed by widening it just as a stream which is too warm may be cooled by narrowing and deepening the flow of water. Appropriate to this is the following quotation from the Bureau of Fisheries (Department of Commerce) Memorandum I–133.

It frequently happens that where streams are warmer than 70° F. for a considerable time the environmental conditions are more favorable for other fish than for trout and consequently they become so abundant that the trout are re-

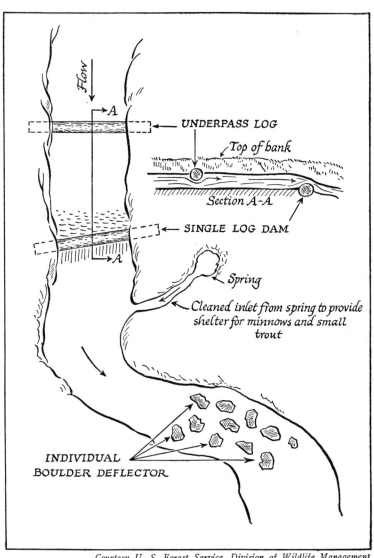

FIGURE 31.

STRUCTURES FOR TROUT STREAM
IMPROVEMENT

duced in numbers or driven out entirely. This is a common occurrence in streams in deforested regions, where as a result of the removal of shade and other factors, once famous trout streams are now inhabited chiefly by minnows and suckers. In such cases it will require more than the construction of dams or deflectors to restore conditions favorable for trout. The remedy is evidently reforestation and the planting of shade trees along the banks. The elimination of wide, shallow areas will also help materially and, in general, the channel should be narrowed as much as possible.

While streams are often too warm for trout they may also be too cold for good trout production. Water which is too cold retards the growth of both food organisms and trout and is therefore less productive than warmer water. Streams and lakes too cold for satisfactory growth are common at high altitudes in the west. This condition is aggravated by the short growing season with the result that several years are required for trout to reach legal size. When the temperature is constantly below 55° F. on hot days it is too low for satisfactory growth and an effort should be made to warm up the water. This can be done by removing shade or by building low dams or holding ponds to spread the water over a large area where it will be exposed to the full effects of the sun. The creation of back water, sloughs and quiet pools will produce warm areas favorable to the growth of young trout. Such areas will also be more productive of food since they are not only warmer but they are not exposed to the scouring action of floods which are so destructive to food organisms in swift mountain streams.

An excellent "before and after" impression of what trout stream improvement can do may be gained from the photographs of Prew Savoy's brook in the Catoktin Mountains of Maryland, as shown in the illustrations facing pages 284 and 285. This was a rather ambitious undertaking and there is no doubt but that it cost a great deal of money. As such it will be less pertinent to the requirements of most readers than the first instance of stream improvement already noted, which cost virtually nothing. Prew Savoy's brook is called Otter Valley Run. He owns a mile and a half of this stream which winds down through the wooded hill-sides into a fertile valley below. Before he redirected the forces of nature this brook was no more prepossessing than many others, as the first of these two pictures will show.

In this mile and a half of brook he built one hundred and twenty rock dams to form a continuous succession of large pools which constantly cascade cool, musical water into those which lie below. Although masonry often is used to hold the boulders in place in low dams of this type I believe that very little, if any, was used in the construction of these. The added strength of masonry was considered unnecessary because the stream does not reach freshet proportions due to the almost complete absence of snow in this part of the country. The abundance of forestation holds back the release of heavy rains and causes a fairly even supply of water all year through.

While building this succession of dams more than sixty springs were found and opened up so that they could contribute their maximum flow to that of the brook itself. As a result of the building of the dams and the cleaning out and channeling of the springs the volume of the water in the brook was increased to four times what it was before. This reduced the average temperature of the water by five degrees so that it never goes above 65° in the summer. The brook is therefore ideal in temperature for the welfare of trout.

Each year in the spring the Outdoor Writers Association of America holds an annual meeting in the Catoktin Mountains. A prominent feature of this conclave is that each member is invited to bring along one or more boys primarily to teach them the elements of sportsmanship and conservation and to instill in them a love for fishing. Some of the members arrive with half a dozen boys or more. No matter how many there are, Prew Savoy invites all of them to his rustic lodge on Otter Valley Run and turns them loose to fish for the trout in his cascade of pools. Boys, many of whom never caught a trout before, catch one after another on flies in his brook. They learn to handle them properly and to release them safely. They are coached in the elements of angling

Otter Valley Run before Improvement Was an Ordinary Mountain Stream

*Otter Valley Run after Improvement Became a Constant
Succession of Deep Pools*

by the authors and columnists who bring them and who also are there to fish them out of the brook when their inexpertness and exuberance cause them to fall in. I have watched these young sportsmen-in-the-making for many years and I have watched Prew Savoy as he saw them having a good time. Although Prew's beautiful trout stream was not built for the entertainment of youngsters I am sure that he believes that in this alone it justifies the expense. As the boys return to the city, filled with his trout, ham and turkey, I am sure that they think so too.

Whether the improvements made in a trout stream are done with minimum cost or on an elaborate scale, if they are done properly they are worth every penny and every hour of effort which is put into them. The trout stream improvements suggested in this book have been made simple purposely. Simple as they are, they are amazingly effective. If more elaborate or more substantial devices are required the United States Forest Service, Division of Wildlife Management in Washington, provides instruction handbooks which are available for the asking.

To build a poor trout stream into a productive and beautiful section of angling water seven requirements must be met before the project can be completely successful. The water must be free from human or industrial waste. Dissolved oxygen is not here considered as a requirement because in trout streams it usually is present in sufficient amount. There must be a favorable range of water temperatures. This range and ways to obtain it (if it is possible to obtain) already have been discussed. The trout must have breeding areas or they will not reproduce. If they cannot reproduce, regular stocking will be necessary. They must have adequate shelter. If the shelter is inadequate it easily can be provided. Shelter means resting places in suitable current flow as well as shaded spots where they may hide. Shelter means protection from fish-eating birds, animals and predatory fish. If shelter is provided it may be assumed that the trout can take care of themselves. Lastly, trout need freedom from the presence of competitive life such as other fish which will consume the same kinds of food as trout do and thus reduce the number of trout that can be supported in the stream. Given these seven attributes of a good trout stream it is obvious that the trout which live in it should grow and prosper. If these seven attributes are contained in proper balance the stream should develop into a self-sustaining biological unit producing the maximum number of trout.

It would seem logical that both anglers and conservation officials in these days of intensive fishing should give more thought to the improvement of trout streams than to stocking fish in improperly developed waters where they can not thrive or where they are too soon caught out. A balance between stream improvement and wise stocking policies is essential. If we anglers are willing to co-operate in making our streams better living places for trout we can enjoy the pleasure of the project and the rich dividends it pays as well.

CHAPTER SEVENTEEN

Trout Ponds

Additional Ways to Improve Angling Near Home

PERHAPS there never was a trout fisherman who did not, at one time or another, have the desire to own a trout pond of his own or to club together with a few other anglers in order to enjoy a part interest in such an enterprise. The project is not difficult of accomplishment even if the partners to it live in a large city. For country or suburban dwellers it is usually amazingly easy.

The trout pond bug bit us about four years before the beginning of the recent war. We did it with a minimum of expense and from it derived a great deal of pleasure although we would have approached the matter quite differently if we had known then what we know now about the requirements which are necessary to the welfare of trout.

In our case it seemed expedient to allow several fishermen friends to participate in the cost and in the work. For the purpose of privacy we formed a club and limited the membership to ten. Topographical maps of the locality we selected indicated that there were several large ponds hidden away in farmers' woodlands. We obtained permission to visit several of these and eventually selected one three or four acres in size nestled in a secluded valley in which there was considerable wild game. The pond was fed by a little brook which had been dammed in years gone by to provide, in addition to the pond itself, a beautiful little waterfall near which we planned to erect a log cabin. We leased the pond for twenty-five dollars a year with renewal privileges. The lease included the right to post and hunt the surrounding property and to make whatever improvements we desired. An important consideration in our choice of the place was that the only road to the pond led through the farmer's yard. He agreed to act as warden while we were away to prevent the raids of small boys and adult poachers who otherwise might have removed the trout nearly as fast as we could have planted them. Brook trout then cost sixty cents a pound. They are a lot more expensive today so the means of keeping a pond out of the reach of unwanted visitors is a consideration of prime importance.

When the New England snows began to melt and the sugar maples give forth their sap for the future glorification of breakfast pancakes the hatchery truck arrived one Saturday with the first load of trout. In anticipation of its coming we had screened the dam so that the fish could not run downstream. Since the brook inlet began on the farmer's property it was not necessary to screen it also. We left it open so that the trout could go up the brook to spawn and to escape the summer heat.

We put five hundred lusty one-pound brook trout into the pond and gave them two weeks to acclimate themselves to their new surroundings before beginning to fish for them. During the first week most of the fish remained near our little dock, hopefully waiting to be fed. Finally they became resigned to their pioneering existence and roamed the pond to seek their food. One day I was encouraged to see one of them chase a little minnow into the shallows and late that afternoon another arched out of the water to catch a fly. The little fellows seemed to be fitting into their changed manner of living admirably. We fished for them with artificial flies only, pinching off the barbs so that the trout could be released without injury.

Soon the fishing at the pond took on the aspects of a game. We considered it less important to record a large number of fish caught and released than to use the lightest possible tackle to catch them. Rods of over three ounces in weight were frowned upon as being in the class of heavy hardware. My little two-and-one-eighth-ounce Thomas was exceeded by a few others which tipped the postal scales at even less, so in self-defense I had to insist that these lighter rods were in the nature of toys and that they were not practical sticks for fishing. The light rod competition became so pronounced that an angler who exhibited a rod in the neighborhood of two ounces had to demonstrate a cast of fifty feet or more to prove that it was in fact a fishing rod and not a candidate for the Queen's Doll House. No one would use leaders tapered to anything but the very finest gut and many of the anglers refused to use flies which they had not tied themselves. While this does not pertain to the development of fish ponds it does have a bearing on the fun which can be derived from fishing them. A one-pound trout on tiny tackle is a much more satisfactory adversary than the same fish handled with heavier gear. I am firmly convinced that the maximum of angling sport goes to the angler who uses tackle so light that the element of suspense is magnified until it is doubtful whether or not the fisherman can land the fish at all. Then the size of the fish becomes less important than the manner of his taking. If his taking is made as difficult as possible it matters little whether he be a great sailfish handled on three-thread line, a big bonefish or salmon on a three-pound test leader or a one-pound trout landed on tiny tackle with the most delicate gut obtainable. Even if light tackle is carried to absurd extremes it is thrilling sport. The record to date was witnessed by those who saw Reginald Ellis of the Du Pont Company's nylon sales department take a six-and-one-half inch snapper Bluefish on a leader which was a single strand of nylon filament from which dolls' eyelashes are made. This leader was two one-thousandths of an inch in diameter, with a breaking strength of two-tenths of a pound. No leader as fine as this ever before was used by a fisherman. It is not sold commercially for fishing leaders. He gave me a piece of it but I laid it down for a minute and it was so nearly invisible that I never did find it again! A human hair would have seemed bulky in comparison!

All during the spring the trout in our pond grew and prospered but then our troubles began. In the course of their nomadic travels a pair of otters came upon the pond. Trout at sixty cents a pound seemed to them to be agreeable fare so they built a home in a high bank along the shore and shared our fish with us. They made a slide down the bank and enjoyed lying there in the sun until they acquired enough energy to swim out and catch another trout or two for dinner. I saw one on the bank one day and went back to the car for my gun. When I returned he was gone. One came to the surface near me when I was fishing from my canoe. I raced back to shore for the gun but then could not find the otter. After a few such occurrences we carried guns everywhere we went. As a result, the otters did not appear any more except one day when we happened to have no firearms available. Evidently they decided to co-operate with a compromise. They would fish while we slept and vice versa. In that manner they seemed to feel that their presence would be more agreeable and that they would get just as many trout. We tried to trap them and to dig them out but were unsuccessful. It seemed that they would roam off for a vacation once in a while but just as we began to hope they were gone for good we would arrive one day and find their slide freshly polished and everything ready for business again.

Then came summer and the pond lilies. They were of the yellow variety of cow lilies and were not pretty at all. They made up in quantity for what they lacked in quality. Whenever we happened to hook into a trout that had evaded one of the otters he would take the greatest delight in circling one or more of the lily stems. Since I have stressed the fact that we enjoyed using light tackle I do not need to relate the result. Someone sold us a cutter bar which was made to tow with ropes back of a boat. In theory this worked very well but with the thing trailing through all those stems no one could row the boat. Eventually we bowed to the inevitable and while the lilies increased in quantity the otters increased in size.

Another trouble was the pond scum which clouded the surface of the water in ugly, gooey masses early in the summer. The pond scum occupied most of the surface which the lily pads did not and left few places which were suitable for fishing. Canoeing on the pond became more and more difficult and our interest in fishing diminished in proportion.

All this time the water became warmer while the brook decreased in flow as the summer advanced. Our bookkeeping indicated that we had killed less than a hundred trout so, disregarding the otters for a moment, there should have been four hundred left in the pond. Of course the otters did not get all of them but they served as an admirable excuse when our wives ordered two trout for breakfast and we returned home with none. During the early summer there were only two places where we could catch any trout at all. One was in an oasis-in-reverse where the encroachments of the lily pads had left a bit of open water near the dam. We found that if we would sink a fly there we would catch an occasional trout. One day I dove off the boat to see why they were there. As might be supposed, I found a spring hole where, in the warmth of the pond, the water was refreshingly cold.

The other place was at the far end of the pond where the brook came in. This was a swampy area filled with grassy hummocks and channels where the water was not over a foot deep. By careful maneuvering one could get a canoe into the channels. There were two little places where we usually could catch a trout. On inspecting these spots we found that they also were spring holes where the water was cold as it bubbled up from the earth. The trout must have had great difficulty in finding such places when the water in the pond was so warm that it was totally unsuited for them anywhere else.

That year, just before the frost came, I went up the brook to see if any trout were spawning there. The place seemed suitable but no large fish were in evidence.

All this seemed rather discouraging; so much so that we debated seriously whether or not we should renew our lease. There were several redeeming features. Once in a while someone would catch a trout in the pond which by size and color could be identified as a native and not as a stocked fish. From this it seemed evident that the few spring holes compensated in part for the warmth of the water and that it was possible for trout to exist all year round in the pond. In the brook in the spring one noticed several tiny trout which furnished the heartening proof that spawning took place there. When we leased this pond we gave no thought to whether or not pickerel, carp or other trash fish were in residence so we were most fortunate in finding none. There were many small forage fish which were of a species that never grew large and the pond abounded in frogs, snails and other aquatic life.

These encouraging features induced us to renew our lease and to plant more trout each spring. Very few of the previously stocked fish were in evidence. Whether they had been victims of predators or had died during the warm summer months I do not know but I assume that both causes of their loss may have been partially responsible. Then came the war and each of the members of the little club had too much to do to warrant continuing the project. We gave up our lease and have not yet renewed it.

This illustrates several facts relating to trout pond management of which we were ignorant during the club's active years. If we had known about them earlier our little enterprise would have been much more successful. Since the war I have studied other trout pond projects with which glowing results have been accomplished at a minimum of expense. There are several simple rules to follow which make all the difference in the world.

The pond which may be an ideal habitat for bass and bluegills may not be suitable for trout. Trout must have cold water temperatures ranging below 70° F. in some part of the pond all year round. Trout require more oxygen than most other species of fish and means must be found to give it to them. If one is considering the possibilities of a small body of water for the raising of trout it is well to study the water temperatures during the warmest part of the summer. If adequate cold water areas can not be found the pond should be discarded insofar as trout raising is concerned. At this time it is well to have a biologist ascertain the oxygen content of the water. It should contain more than five parts per million of dissolved oxygen. If the pond is a dammed-up brook, particularly where there is a waterfall, this bit of research may not be necessary but in any case all means should be taken to aerate the water as much as is possible. In doing this, springs should be found and cleaned out so that they will contribute their maximum flow,

Given sufficient oxygen and cold water we may assume that the pond is good for trout. Without these two vital elements we should use the place only for pond fish or search for a more suitable location.

Means must now be found to keep the trout within the pond or within the boundaries of the waters we own or lease. If an inflowing brook is part of the property the trout should have access to it. Usually they will not spawn in the pond itself but they may use the brook for this purpose and for sanctuary during the hot weather. The brook will provide additional fishing and will enhance the source of food. If part of the brook is not on our own land it may be screened to keep the fish within proper confines. If the pond is part of a trout brook it will be retained by a dam at the lower end. The overflow of the dam must be screened to keep the fish within bounds. The screen must be sufficiently high and sturdy for safety during spring freshets so that fish will not be lost in periods of high water. The screen must be kept clear of leaves and other floating objects which would clog it excessively.

Many a good trout brook has been dammed to make a trout pond, thus providing a beauty spot as well as a source of good fishing. All that is needed is a natural basin wherein the water may be confined on three sides and where the fourth or downstream side narrows sufficiently to make the building of a dam practical. In these days of bulldozers and other mechanized equipment this is not as expensive as might at first be supposed.

In building a dam the land should be surveyed so that an accurate plan may be drawn of the area in which water is to be impounded. The plan should include drawings of the dam itself. Various books and scientific papers are available describing the several types of dams and how they should be constructed. Some of these are listed in the reference material at the end of this book. Before the area is filled with water care should be taken to remove all trees, bushes and other woody growth from the basin of the pond up to the high-water mark at least. It may be well to leave trees and bushes close to the high-water line in certain places around the edge because these will shade and protect the water and will serve as a source of terrestrial food. In other places it may be desirable to clear the underbrush well back from the bank so that anglers will have sufficient room to handle their fly rods. If there are a few large rocks in the basin of the pond they should be left there to provide hiding places for the fish. If the geography of the land permits, a small dam can be built at the upper end of the pond to furnish an added beauty spot and to provide more aeration of the incoming water. A rock dam such as was described in the preceding chapter may be sufficient.

Even though we found it so in the little trout pond project I have described, the control of pond lilies and other aquatic plants should not present a serious problem. We gave up cutting the lily pads because we assumed they always would grow in again and that the work of cutting them would never end. This is not so. The lilies must be cut ruthlessly and completely as often as the leaves appear. This can be done with a scythe, from a boat if necessary. The first complete cutting is the hardest one. Each recutting will find fewer and fewer pads. After four or five cuttings all of the lily plants should be dead and from then on should no longer be troublesome.

In many ponds the spreading of rushes and cattails will present a problem which can be overcome in advance if the banks of the new trout pond are made sufficiently steep so that little or no marshy areas exist around the pond. If plants of this kind are thought to be undesirable they can be pulled up, taken ashore and disposed of. Usually they are so loosely rooted that they can be removed without difficulty. If the pond area infested with these plants is so large that pulling them by hand is impractical they can be poisoned.

The pond scum which gradually made its appearance on our pond late in the spring and which did so much to ruin our fishing could have been eliminated if we had known how to do it at the time. This is done by fertilization of the water. Fertilization encourages the growth of the minute animal and vegetable organisms called plankton because the plankton use the phosphorus, potassium, nitrogen, and other minerals and mineral salts in the fertilizer as food. Thus encouraged, the plankton grow in such numbers that they make the water turbid and prevent sunlight from getting deep down into it. Pond scum is a filamentous algae which depends upon sunlight for its growth. Without the sunlight the pond scum will die and will decompose to increase the fertility of the water.

With or without the presence of pond scum it may be wise to fertilize the pond in order to encourage the growth of plankton which are food for crustaceans, mollusks and small fishes on which the trout depend for their subsistence. If fertilization is to be done it should be done in the early spring before pond scum has had a chance to develop to any appreciable extent. Quite obviously a trout pond made by damming a brook should have a fast flow of water which will eliminate the growth of pond scum and which would also make fruitless the fertilization of the pond.

Fertilizing a pond seems to have good and bad points insofar as the raising of trout is concerned. If the pond is in as poor condition as ours was it would be well to fertilize it, cut the weeds and do everything else necessary to put it into condition to receive the trout before the trout are planted rather than afterward. When fertilization causes such a tremendous growth of plankton as to cloud the water to the extent that pond scum will die this material will fall to the bottom of the pond and decompose. The decomposing organic material may absorb so much oxygen that there will be insufficient remaining for trout. In extreme cases this might cause the trout to die. If they did not die the clouding of the water might still be so intense that the fish could not see an artificial fly; thus for a time spoiling the water for fishing. Fertilizing a pond may be as necessary as fertilizing a garden. If it should be done the pond should be brought into a semblance of proper balance before it is stocked with trout. If the pond is in reasonable balance so that no scum exists a certain amount of periodic fertilization will encourage the growth of food and will do no harm to the trout which may be in the pond at the time.

In the earlier days of fish pond management organic fertilizers such as manure were used. Today results are more economical and more dependable when inorganic commercial fertilizers are employed. The combination generally considered best for plankton culture is eight pounds of nitrogen, eight pounds of phosphate and four pounds of potash per one hundred pounds of fertilizer. The balance is usually calcium or some similar suitable filler.

The amount of fertilizer needed by a pond will vary widely depending upon how fast it is used and how much is already there. Five hundred pounds per acre may be considered as an average requirement but more may be needed at the outset to bring the pond into proper balance. This should not be applied all at once but apportioned once a month in four or five applications during the early spring and summer. It should not be put into extremely deep water or close along the shore. Best results are accomplished by sifting it into the water from a moving boat at a depth of from two to ten feet. Water currents will distribute it evenly.

When a pond is so clear that the bottom can be seen in several feet of water the fertilization of it may be said to be incomplete and more fertilizer will be needed to encourage an added growth of plankton. A white disk lowered into the water is a standard method of testing its turbidity. An easier way is to lower one's arm into the water with the fingers of the hand at a right angle to the arm. If the fingers can be seen when the arm is lowered to the elbow this indicates that added fertilization may be advisable. It should be repeated that fertilization is wasteful in trout ponds having a rapid flow of water through them. In such ponds the fertility of the water must depend upon that of the soil upstream. If the brook entering the pond emanates from a marsh the water may be extremely fertile as has been noted in the instance of the Klamath River. In any case the advisability of fertilization should be considered because it develops the chain of organisms which are consumed by the higher forms of life which trout use for food.

If a pond already in existence is to be used for trout one of the first important steps is to ascertain what species of fish already are in it. This can be done by dredging along the edge of the pond with a minnow sieve. If it is found that large trash fish such as carp, suckers or chubs are in residence, or if predatory fish such as pickerel or bass are there, means should be taken to eliminate them before stocking the pond with trout. Remember what happened at Diamond Lake because there were too many chubs in it! Every trash fish consumes as much food as a trout so for every one there will be one less trout, or each trout will have a little less to eat and will not grow as large in consequence. Every predatory fish presents a similar liability and in addition will feed on the little trout, thus reducing the yield of the pond. Undesirable fish must be eliminated at all costs before a trout pond can become as successful as possible.

To remove undesirable fish from a pond they should be poisoned if the pond's water cannot be drawn off. If it can be drawn off it is well to let it dry up for a few weeks to be sure that eggs of undesirable fish are killed. When the water is drawn off all remaining pools should be netted to be sure that the fish are eliminated entirely.

Poisoning a pond is done by spreading rotenone in it, usually allowing about ten pounds to the acre. It may be placed in a burlap bag and towed through the water by a boat until the poison is entirely dissolved. As the poison takes effect the fish will rise to the top. The poison does not affect them as food. When the fish are entirely removed from the pond no trout should be stocked for several weeks to be sure that none of the poison remains in the water. In many states it is illegal for landowners to poison their waters because of the danger of the poison harming fish farther downstream. For this reason it is advisable to enlist the aid and permission of the state Department of Fisheries and Game to be sure that the poisoning will be carried out properly and legally. Since the purpose of the poisoning is to improve the waters this permission and aid should be given readily.

The poisoning will remove the little forage fish as well as the big ones. Before trout are added small forage fish should be re-introduced to aid in maintaining the balance of the pond and to provide added food for the trout. A forage fish, insofar as this book is concerned, is a fish which subsists mainly on vegetation and which never grows so large that it cannot furnish food for trout. Many species of minnows fall into this category. At certain times they swarm in brook mouths and in parts of ponds and usually can be netted and transplanted with little difficulty. There are hundreds of varieties of fish which fall under the general classification of minnows. Some are ideal as food for trout while others are trash fish which should not be introduced to a trout pond under any circumstances. To insure obtaining suitable species it would be well to ask the co-operation of a state fisheries expert who also should know where they can be obtained most easily. Since desirable minnows feed on plankton and vegetable matter around the pond they convert food which large trout do not eat into food they do eat and which greatly increases their growth.

All of the steps mentioned above need not be taken in the conversion of every pond into a trout pond but all of them are important in one case or another and all of them should be considered carefully to insure giving the pond its proper start. They illustrate that there is more to building a good trout pond than merely buying a few hundred trout and dumping them into whatever bit of water is available. When the average suitable trout pond is started properly it is not difficult to keep it in efficient operation. It should then provide an abundance of good fishing for many years to come. The pond we started before the war was relatively unsuccessful because we did not understand fully the various steps which should have been taken to bring it to its proper state of efficiency. In looking back upon it I am sure that the pond was reasonably suitable for trout and would have proven successful if these necessary steps had been taken.

Not long ago I spent a week end with a gentleman in Connecticut who had built such a pond by damming a small mountain stream. The dam formed a pond about two acres in size which provided a vista of exceptional beauty, especially when I remember how nondescript the ravine looked before his little pond was put there. We sat on the porch before breakfast and watched the happy little trout dimpling its surface in search of flies. Several migratory ducks swam peacefully where the pond narrowed into woodland at its upstream end. Deer occasionally came from the woods to the pond to drink and scores of colorful birds made their homes near by. My host went into the cabin and returned with two fly rods. We played with the trout for half an hour or so and killed two of them for breakfast. When I remarked upon the landscaped woodland beauty of the place my host said, "This pond and the trout in it cost me less than a thousand dollars. It has increased the value of my property by much more than that. Regardless of expense or profit it has added ten years to my life and has provided recreation the value of which it would be impossible to estimate. If you ever write an article about trout ponds," he added, "tell your readers by all means to build one if they have places which are suitable. If they do not, recommend to them that they find such places because the pleasures they can derive from a little pond are beyond comprehension."

CHAPTER EIGHTEEN

Conclusion

Tomorrow's Trout Waters Are What We Make Them

IT WAS NOT so very many years ago that nearly all of our northern coastal rivers and inland streams teemed with trout and salmon. They swept in from the ocean in countless migrating hordes, up the forested rivers, beyond the log cabin settlements of the colonists, onward into the tributary streams of their choice and up the little brooks where they were born, there to lay their eggs in the gravel of the cold, clear water that their kind might be perpetuated in the abundance so lavishly planned by God for the use of man. So great were their numbers that they choked the streams in their annual spawning journeys. Both Indians and white settlers speared or netted them by the cartload to bury them in the fields that the corn might grow tall and green. Conservation was a word unknown. The myriads of leaping, fighting fish would last forever. Their vast numbers palled the palate; they stupefied the imagination.

Much of this can be remembered by men now alive. Yet even in the Klamath, the Eel, the Rogue and in other famous trout and salmon streams of the Pacific Northwest the startling decrease in game fish is a subject of growing alarm. In the East, were it not for hatcheries, bag limits, closed seasons and the valiant fight of sportsmen's organizations, the feeble fishing in those few trout waters which still remain to us would be nearly extinct. The salmon and seatrout runs in New England's broad Connecticut River, so fabulous a few generations ago, have passed from us for all time. Expensive and well-directed efforts to restore migratory runs of game fish in some of the coastal streams of Maine have so far resulted only in the superficial return of an insignificant number of fish. Yet certain of these far northern rivers still boast of small runs of migratory trout. They will continue to do so; even to increase their yield, or they, too, will pass into oblivion as trout waters, depending upon the amount of care and attention which sportsmen's clubs and government officials devote to them. So it is with all Eastern rivers. The streams emptying into the Great Lakes and the Pacific are not far behind.

What has been done to our trout waters that their yields of game fish should be so greatly curtailed or eliminated in so short a time? The destruction still goes on. It is happening to the Beaverkill and the Neversink; to the Penobscot and the Brule; to the Columbia, the Klamath and countless other famous streams. It has been happening for many years. The ruination of the priceless birthright of the American angler still progresses with ever-increasing speed. Much of it can be stopped and many of our trout waters can be restored, but it must be done by the fishermen and conservationists of this generation. It must be done now because tomorrow will be too late.

Let us think back to the days not long gone when all of our streams were banked and shaded by cool, damp forests. Let us remember the many gallons of water stored in the bulging root systems of each live tree, to be released gradually, cold and clear, in times of need when snows are gone and drought threatens. Trees are the saviors of trout streams. Without them there is no storage of water to balance the even flow of the brooks and rivers; there are fewer springs to cool the waters in the summer heat; no shade, no leafy branches to give protection to trout and to harbor insects which provide food for fishes.

Wherever towns sprang from the wilderness the trees were cut to build homes and factories, to provide fields and gardens. They were cut ruthlessly and without planning, laying bare the watersheds and parching the soil. When heavy rains came the few remaining trees had insufficient root systems to hold back the water. It tore down in a flood, eroding the soil, disturbing the food-bearing stream bottoms and even changing the courses of the streams themselves. With the trees gone, man built dams to hold back the floods he had made possible and to provide power for his cities. The dams also held back the fish, preventing them from continuing their migratory journeys to the source waters. The fish grew fewer and fewer. With the trees gone there was no shade to keep the sun from the waters. The waters grew warm; so much so that trout were forced to leave them or die. In some of the headwaters still cold there are trout which remain, but they cannot go to sea as their forefathers did because of the dams and the intolerable warmth or pollution of the water through which they must pass. Thus they remain underdeveloped on their scarcity of food, bearing but faint resemblance to their savage five- and ten-pound progenitors who fattened on the bounty of the sea.

A relatively few selfish men, goaded by the lust for money have been, and still are, tearing down our forests with no thought for tomorrow; ruining our timberlands for years to come. This cannot be said for many of the larger lumber organizations who treat timber as a crop, cutting it scientifically and leaving immature trees to grow, but can be said of the wildcat operators who sweep everything before them, leaving only broken underbrush and piles of rotting branches. Even anglers realize that trees must be cut, but they subscribe to the proven advantages of the more sensible type of cutting which removes only those trees large enough for the harvest and which plants others to take their places.

The cutting of the trees is one reason for the despoiling of our trout waters and the building of dams is another. Stream pollution is the third major reason and is the most culpable because it is the most unnecessary. When we dump into our once beautiful rivers the offal from our homes and the refuse from our factories we ruin the last chance for trout to live in them. We ruin them for boating or for swimming as well. We change them from beauty spots to running sores which spread death and disease. It is true that some rivers in our manufacturing areas must be sacrificed to industry but by the same token others must be held in sacred trust for fishing and for the many other forms of recreation which they can provide and which are equally important to the public welfare. Some of our municipalities, recognizing this, are legislating against factory pollution and in favor of sewage-disposal plants and other means of keeping our rivers clean. Too much of the present pollution is the shameful fault of independent industrialists who should be made to remedy it because it is neither necessary nor for the common good.

All this is most unfortunate for the angler. If it stopped there it might be solved to an extent by influencing the fisherman to throw away his rods and to take up golf. What is not realized by many is that the abuse of our trout streams costs us as a nation far more than the money it would take to end our pollution, to harvest our timberlands scientifically and to insure the means of allowing trout free access to their source waters to spawn. There are several million fishermen who like to fish for trout. There would be many more if good trout waters were more abundant and more accessible. The trouble, time and expense to which an angler will go to catch a trout are an amazing revelation, even to some of the anglers themselves. Those who can afford it will pay, at current prices, at least a hundred dollars for a fishing outfit, another hundred or so for transportation to the stream or lake wherein the "big ones" lie, seven dollars or more a day for sporting camp accommodations and even more for guides' fees, canoe and motor rental plus the many other incidental expenses which are called for on a fishing trip. This often adds up to the substantial total of a few hundred dollars per man per week. The fisherman may return from ten days in the woods with a sprained ankle, excess sunburn, numerous black fly bites, a severe cold and photos to prove that he caught a three-pound trout or two, but he is supremely happy and perfectly satisfied that the large amount of money it all cost was most wisely invested.

This adds up to greater than a sixty-million-dollar fishing tackle industry and nearly one hundred times that large figure for clothes, accommodations, transportation, board, fees and incidentals of many sorts. Angling, whether it be done in the grand manner or in accordance with a radically restricted budget, totals at present an annual expenditure of about four billion dollars, which is big business for all who have anything to sell to those who like to go fishing.

If a good trout stream flows near by, cabins and hotel accommodations usually are at a premium. The local hardware store is filled with impedimenta for the angler. The butcher, the baker and the dairyman have something to sell him to bring in business they would not otherwise get. The carpenter will fix his lodgings and the local garage will take care of his car. The laundry will wash his clothes and the local citizens will guide him for a substantial fee. Everybody profits. The trout are as valuable to the town on the trout stream as if they were made of gold. States and regions recognize this to the extent that they invest many millions of dollars in national advertising in expensive magazines and newspapers to tempt the angler to fish in their streams and lakes. At the same time they drive him away by dumping refuse along these same streams, by allowing a single mill owner or two to pollute them for miles, and by dumping into them the offal from their homes. It is a penny-wise and pound-foolish procedure which is as illogical as constantly putting money into a pocket with a hole in it.

The State of Maine has recognized the value of angling and has profited by it to the extent that it is today an industry of paramount importance. Good management by competent officials has brought in many million dollars and has cost the state virtually nothing. The building of hatcheries, the stocking and analysis of streams and lakes and the salaries of the wardens and of the managing officials themselves are covered entirely by the money paid in for fishing licenses; the majority being purchased by out-of-state anglers who spend added millions of dollars in the state annually. The same is true of other states to a greater or lesser degree. Usually it is lesser. The Commissioner of Fisheries and Game, or whatever he is called, and many of his officials are political appointees who serve at the pleasure of the party currently in power. In one state with which I am well acquainted the Commissioner's vitally important office is filled by patronage. In my memory, I doubt if any commissioner could have told a

trout from a carp when he took office. Yet this country boasts of
many learned aquatic biologists and conservationists who would
have filled the position admirably and at a fee entirely too small
for their knowledge and value. If the new commissioner is in-
dustrious, which is not always the case, he may learn his job in
time, but when he has enjoyed sufficient experience to handle it
to a barely satisfactory extent a new political party takes command and the sad and expensive cycle begins all over again.

In such states ample money usually is appropriated to stock
the waters with fish. Despite the frantic efforts of the Isaak
Walton League and other sportsmen's clubs, this money is oftentimes either misspent or misdirected. Baby trout, raised at ex-
orbitant prices, are dumped into unimproved or inadequate
streams at the wrong time of year, to be promptly jerked out by
fishermen, young and old, who have followed the hatchery truck
to the spot. It takes time for artificially raised trout to acclimate
themselves to their surroundings and to give the angler the sport
which should be expected of them.

Feeder brooks are the nurseries of little trout. If they were left
as such, and not used for fishing, there would be less need for
hatcheries. As the little trout grow large they work down into
the major streams and rivers to give the anglers constant replen-
ishment of fish worthy of the catching. While I must admit that
seven- and eight-inch trout are very delicious when properly
fried in bacon and breadcrumbs for breakfast, it seems much
better economy to fish for the bigger ones somewhere else and to
leave the babies alone to grow up. I still fail to see anything to
be proud of in exhibiting a creelful of undersized fish which have
been jerked out of a feeder brook with a hook and a worm. Live
bait fishing has its place. When properly employed, it is a considerable art. The present lack of abundance of trout in most
trout waters makes it rather shortsighted, however, to fish feeder
brooks by this method. Few baby trout live under such treatment,
even if care is used in removing the hook, because, unlike a fly,
live bait is taken deep into their gullets. Little fish which would
live otherwise are often killed by rough handling. A fish to be

released should be placed in the water gently and held in an upright position until he has recovered enough to remain so of his own accord.

In a few remote sections of this country one occasionally finds a lake or stream so filled with trout that their competition for the relatively insufficient food available prevents them from the normal growth they would enjoy if their numbers were fewer or the food supply greater. Unfortunately, such waters are few and far between, but the taking of trout in them may be actually an advantage to the fishing. In most cases this is not so. Every fish killed means one less to provide sport for anglers and to reproduce his kind. In spite of the scarcity of trout, daily creel limits on many streams are so high that, if all anglers killed the number of trout allowed, the stream quickly would be depleted of game fish, as is often the case. Most of the fish are killed by relatively few anglers who labor under the misconception that a bulging creel somehow establishes their ability. Their excuse, as in the instance mentioned on the Gunnison River, usually is that their actions must be ethical since they are tolerated by the law. Using the twenty fish per day bag limit of the Gunnison as an example, most farsighted anglers will agree that this is too high, both for the good of the stream and for the needs of the fishermen. Five good fish per day should be sufficient for any person in any water. One or two large-sized trout would seem better to establish his ability as an angler and his integrity as a sportsman than a creel full of smaller ones. In many localities where the merits of conservation have been established concentrated scorn is directed against fishermen who kill too many fish; scorn not only from other anglers but from non-angling friends as well. If this scorn and contempt were the reward of an angler exhibiting a creel too full or containing undersized trout, it would seem that this harmful rape of our trout streams must gradually stop. In some states the legal limit for a trout is six inches, obviously much too small for the true sportsman and acceptable only to the type of man who finds pleasure in robbing the cradle.

I know of a stretch of posted water screened from the rest of the stream and stocked with six hundred half-pound trout. This water is fished by a dozen anglers who keep careful records of trout taken and the conditions and type of fly with which they were caught. All are released unless they are hooked so badly that they would die. Records indicate that each of these tagged trout has been caught on an average of four times. While they have been in the stream they have grown amazingly, until each one is now nearly of trophy size. I am sure that every one of these anglers has enjoyed far better sport than if he had killed each fish when first hooked. Quite obviously the stream is better than it ever was, instead of being fished out, as so many of our trout waters are today.

Where there were once more than ten fair-sized fish for each angler there are now, in many streams, more than ten anglers for each fair-sized fish. To insure good fishing in seasons to come, what shall be done to remedy this increasingly disadvantageous condition? Anglers are coming to realize that they must fish more for sport than ever before, and less for meat. We must learn to be content to enjoy fishing yet not to kill too many fish. The practice of bringing home trout to give to the neighbors may satisfy the misdirected egotism of the fisherman but it is quite obvious that it does not improve the fishing. Except in rare cases, the neighbors do not appreciate the gift anyway. They would be fully as content with a pound or two of filet of sole from the corner fish market and happy if the dead fish people wish upon them had been left alive and growing in the streams for other anglers to enjoy.

Why fishermen persist in using too heavy tackle is something else that good anglers can not understand. How much sport is there in handling a trout with gear so strong that he cannot possibly get away? Many fishermen who now thrill to the joys of handling a fine fish on the lightest sort of tackle never realized the fun they were missing until some initiated angler introduced the method to them. Now, the enlightened fishermen use rods so light and leaders so fine that their greatest skill is called upon to bring their prizes safely to the net. Then, whether he be a ten-inch trout taken on tiny tackle or an old buster of several pounds handled on heavier gear, the fish is a prize worthy of the taking and a true compliment to the ability of the angler. I wish that every reader of these lines would try the method and compare it for thrills and satisfaction with the relatively unsatisfactory alternative of never giving the fish an even chance. A good golfer will give an ample handicap to a poorer one. A boxer will not fight a man in a lower weight class. A stable owner will not match a race horse with a draft horse. A hunter will not shoot a fawn or a partridge chick. Then why do not these same men apply the same sportsmanship to fishing?

Tomorrow's trout waters are what we make them. Our efforts to date are nothing to be proud of. The noble and time-honored sport of angling has been badly mistreated by selfish men with neither knowledge of conservation nor appreciation of sportsmanship. Through the increasingly intelligent and concerted efforts of sportsmen's organizations and the developing realization of the remunerative importance of sport fishing by state governments and regional groups this unfortunate trend now is being reversed. The initiative for its continuance must be taken largely by the anglers themselves; by every person who enjoys fishing with a hook and line, regardless of the method employed. If such is done, our trout waters will prosper increasingly. Gradually freed from the pollution man has caused, helped over the dams man has had to build, shaded by the trees man has replaced to cool and steady the waters, and increased in abundance by the anglers who have learned not to kill more than they actually need, big, fighting trout may again teem in our waters that new and succeeding generations of fishermen forever will have them to enjoy.

In 1940 a group of sportsmen in the Outdoor Writers Association of America successfully started a rapidly blossoming movement to instill the principles of conservation and sportsmanship into all who love the out-of-doors and more particularly into the young people to whom the future of sport fishing is of major importance. This organization is called "The Brotherhood of the Junglecock." Anyone who will support its creed may join. There are no dues, no membership rolls, no assessments. It holds annual Campfires in many states to further its worthy purposes which are best illustrated by quoting its creed. With this creed it seems fitting that this book be ended.

CREED OF "THE BROTHERHOOD OF THE JUNGLECOCK"

We who love angling, in order that it may enjoy practice and reward in the later generations, mutually move together towards a common goal — the conservation and restoration of American game fishes.

Towards this end we pledge that our creel limits shall always be less than the legal restrictions and always within the bounty of nature herself.

Enjoying, as we do, only a life estate in the out-of-doors, and morally charged in our time with the responsibility of handing it down unspoiled to tomorrow's inheritors, we individually undertake annually to take at least one boy a-fishing, instructing him, as best we know, in the responsibilities that are soon to be wholly his.

Holding that moral law transcends the legal statutes, always beyond the needs of any one man, and holding that example alone is the one certain teacher, we pledge always to conduct ourselves in such fashion on the stream as to make safe for others the heritage which is ours and theirs.

References

CHAPTER ONE: *Family Traits*

"The Growth Rate of Rainbow Trout From Some Michigan Waters," John R. Greeley, Trans. Am. Fisheries Soc., Vol. 63.

"Standard Check List of Common Names for Principal American Sport Fishes," Outdoor Writers Association of America.

"A List of Common and Scientific Names of the Better Known Fishes of the United States and Canada," Am. Fisheries Soc., Special Publication No. 1.

"Taxonomy and Habits of the Charrs, Salvelinus Malma and Salvelinus Alpinus, of the Karluk Drainage System," De Lacy and Morton, Trans. Am. Fisheries Soc., Vol. 72.

"Growth and Heredity in Trout," H. S. Davis, Trans. Am. Fisheries Soc., Vol. 64.

"The Origin and Relations of the Rainbow Trout," C. McC. Mottley, Trans. Am. Fisheries Soc., Vol. 64.

"Fishes of the Great Lakes Region," Hubbs and Lagler, Cranbrook Institute of Science, 1947.

A Guide to the Study of Fishes, D. S. Jordan, Henry Holt and Co., 1905.

North American Game Fishes, Francesca La Monte, Doubleday and Co., Inc., 1946.

The Western Angler, R. L. Haig-Brown, William Morrow and Co., 1947.

"The Fishes of New England, Part I," Mem. Bos. Soc. of Natural Hist., 1935.

American Food and Game Fishes, D. S. Jordan and B. W. Evermann, Doubleday, Page and Co., 1923.

CHAPTER TWO: *The Travels of Trout*

"Some Observations on the Eastern Brook Trout of Prince Edward Island," H. C. White, Trans. Am. Fisheries Soc., Vol. 60.

"The Influence of Heredity on the Spawning Season of Trout,"
H. S. Davis, Trans. Am. Fisheries Soc., Vol. 61.

"The Spawning Habits of Brook, Brown and Rainbow Trout, and
the Problem of Egg Predators," John R. Greeley, Trans. Am.
Fisheries Soc., Vol. 62.

"Some Phases of the Life History of the Eastern Brook Trout,"
A. S. Hazzard, Trans. Am. Fisheries Soc., Vol. 62.

"The Spawning Migration of Rainbow Trout," C. McC. Mottley,
Trans. Am. Fisheries Soc., Vol. 63.

"When Do the Rainbow Trout Spawn?" H. P. K. Agersborg,
Trans. Am. Fisheries Soc., Vol. 64.

"The Spawning Period of Brook Trout, S. Fontinalis," H. C.
White, Trans. Am. Fisheries Soc., Vol. 64.

"Migration, Growth Rate, and Population Density of Brook Trout
in the North Branch of the Au Sable River, Michigan," D. S.
Shetter, Trans. Am. Fisheries Soc., 1936.

The Migrations of Fish, A. Meek, E. Arnold, London, 1916.

CHAPTER THREE: *Weather and Water Conditions*

The Life of Inland Waters, Needham and Lloyd, Comstock
Publishing Co., Inc., 1937.

Practical Fly Fishing, C. M. Wetzel, The Christopher Publishing
House, 1943.

Streamside Guide to Naturals and Their Imitations, Art Flick,
G. P. Putnam's Sons, 1947.

A Guide to the Study of Fresh-Water Biology, Needham and
Needham, Comstock Publishing Co., Inc., 1941.

"Feeding Habits of Speckled Trout in Ontario Waters," W. E.
Ricker, Trans. Am. Fisheries Soc., Vol. 60.

"Studies on the Seasonal Food of Brook Trout," P. R. Needham,
Trans. Am. Fisheries Soc., Vol. 60.

"Mayflies — A Staple Food of Fishes in Hill Streams," J. G. Needham, Trans. Am. Fisheries Soc., Vol. 63.

"Type of Food Taken Throughout the Year by Brook Trout in a
Single Vermont Stream, with Special Reference to Winter
Feeding," R. F. Lord, Trans. Am. Fisheries Soc., Vol. 63.

"Studies of the Food of the Cutthroat Trout," Hazzard and
Madsen, Trans. Am. Fisheries Soc., Vol. 63.

"A Quantitative Study of Rainbow Trout Production in One Mile
of Stream," E. W. Surber, Trans. Am. Fisheries Soc., Vol. 63.

"A Problem in Trout Stream Management," Moore, Greeley, Greene, Faigenbaum, Nevins and Townes, Trans. Am. Fisheries Soc., Vol. 64.

"A Preliminary Study of an Exceptionally Productive Trout Water, Fish Lake, Utah," A. S. Hazzard, Trans. Am. Fisheries Soc., Vol. 65.

"The Effect of Temperature on the Weight of Fasting Rainbow Trout Fingerlings," W. M. Lawrence, Trans. Am. Fisheries Soc., Vol. 70.

"The Effect of Moonlight on Fishing Success in Fish Lake, Utah," S. Wright, Trans. Am. Fisheries Soc., Vol. 73.

"The Effect of the Full Moon on Trout Fishing," Mottley and Embody, Jour. Am. Statistical Asso., Vol. 37.

Moon up-Moon Down, J. A. Knight, Charles Scribner's Sons, 1942.

CHAPTER FOUR: *Why Lakes Turn Over*

Limnology, Paul S. Welch, McGraw-Hill Book Co., Inc., 1935.

Maine Dept. of Inland Fisheries and Game Fish Survey Reports (I to VII inclusive), Cooper and Fuller, 1939 to 1947.

"A Fishery Survey of Important Connecticut Lakes," State Board of Fisheries and Game, Bulletin No. 63.

CHAPTER FIVE: *More About Lakes*

Northern Fishes, Eddy and Surber, The University of Minnesota Press, 1943.

"Some Observations on the Interrelationships of Sunlight, Aquatic Plant Life and Fishes," T. A. Olson, Trans. Am. Fisheries Soc., Vol. 62.

"Observations on the Effects of Dams on Lakes and Streams," L. R. Richardson, Trans. Am. Fisheries Soc., Vol. 64.

"The Production of Rainbow Trout at Paul Lake, British Columbia," C. McC. Mottley, Trans. Am. Fisheries Soc., Vol. 69.

"The Migration of Fish from a Shallow to a Deep Lake in Spring and Early Summer," W. A. Kennedy, Trans. Am. Fisheries Soc., Vol. 70.

"The Effect of Increasing the Stock in a Lake on the Size and Condition of Rainbow Trout," C. McC. Mottley, Trans. Am. Fisheries Soc., Vol. 70.

"Fish Management Problems of High Western Lakes with Returns from Marked Trout Planted in Upper Angora Lake,

California," Needham and Sumner, Trans. Am. Fisheries Soc., Vol. 71.

CHAPTER SEVEN: *Streams and Rivers*

"Artificial Propagation and the Management of Trout Waters," H. S. Davis, Trans. Am. Fisheries Soc., Vol. 69.

"The Results of Planting Brook Trout of Legal Length in the Salmon Trout River, Northern Michigan," L. L. Smith, Jr., Trans. Am. Fisheries Soc., Vol. 70.

"The 1935 Trout Harvest from Furnace Brook, Vermont's 'Test Stream,'" R. F. Lord, Trans. Am. Fisheries Soc., Vol. 65.

"Research in Stream Management in the Pisgah National Forest," T. K. Chamberlain, Trans. Am. Fisheries Soc., Vol. 72.

"Further Results from Spring and Fall Plantings of Legal-Sized, Hatchery-Reared Trout in Streams and Lakes of Michigan," D. S. Shetter, Trans. Am. Fisheries Soc., Vol. 74.

"Population Depletion in Brook, Brown and Rainbow Trout Stocked in the Blackledge River, Connecticut, in 1942," Thorpe, Rayner and Webster, Trans. Am. Fisheries Soc., Vol. 74.

Trout Streams, P. R. Needham, Comstock Publishing Company, Inc., 1938.

CHAPTER EIGHT: *Return from the Ocean*

"California Steelhead Experiments," A. C. Taft, Trans. Am. Fisheries Soc., Vol. 64.

"Observations on the Spawning of Steelhead Trout," Needham and Taft, Trans. Am. Fisheries Soc., Vol. 64.

"Studies on the Life History of the Puget Sound Steelhead Trout," Pantzke and Meigs, Trans. Am. Fisheries Soc., Vol. 70.

CHAPTER NINE: *Big Trout in Wilderness Waters*

"Michigan's Beaver-Trout Management Program," G. W. Bradt, Trans. Am. Fisheries Soc., Vol. 65.

CHAPTER TEN: *Fishing Famous Gravel Streams*

The Complete Fly Fisherman (Notes and Letters of Theodore Gordon), John McDonald, Charles Scribner's Sons, 1947.

Trout Fishing, E. V. Connett, III, Garden City Publishing Co., Inc., 1933.

CHAPTER ELEVEN: *Big Trout of the Deep Lakes*

"The Effect of Temperature During Development on the Number of Scales in the Kamloops Trout," C. McC. Mottley, Biol. Bd. Canada.

"The Food of the Kamloops Trout," Mottley and Mottley, Biol. Bd. Canada, 1932.

"Productivity Studies in Lakes of the Kamloops Region, British Columbia," D. S. Rawson, Biol. Bd. Canada, 1934.

CHAPTER THIRTEEN: *Riffles and Fast Water Fishing*

Steelhead, C. M. Kreider, G. P. Putnam's Sons, 1948.

The Umpqua River Study, Oregon State Game Commission, 1946.

A Preliminary Report on Fishery Resources of the Rogue River, Oregon State Game Commission, 1947.

CHAPTER FOURTEEN: *Typical Mountain Lakes and Streams*

"The Eastern Brook Trout in the Maligne River System, Jasper National Park," D. S. Rawson, Trans. Am. Fisheries Soc., Vol. 70.

A Preliminary Report on the Diamond Lake Study, F. E. Locke, Oregon State Game Commission, 1947.

CHAPTER SIXTEEN: *Brook Improvement and Stream Conservation*

Fish Stream Improvement Handbook, U. S. Forest Service, Div. of Wildlife Management, 1936.

"Experimental Evidence on the Value of Trout Streams Improvement in Michigan," C. M. Tarzwell, Trans. Am. Fisheries Soc., 1936.

"The Purpose and Value of Stream Improvement," H. S. Davis, Trans. Am. Fisheries Soc., Vol. 64.

"Progress of Stream Improvement in New York State," J. R. Greeley, Trans. Am. Fisheries Soc., Vol. 65.

CHAPTER SEVENTEEN: *Trout Ponds*

Fish Ponds for the Farm, F. C. Edminster, Charles Scribner's Sons, 1947.

"Effect of Organic and Inorganic Fertilizers on Plankton Production," Smith and Swingle, Trans. Am. Fisheries Soc., Vol. 69.

"An Experiment in Removing Coarse Fish from a Lake," Ricker and Gottschalk, Trans. Am. Fisheries Soc., Vol. 70.

"Selective Poisoning of Fish," J. Greenbank, Trans. Am. Fisheries Soc., Vol. 70.

Fish Culture in Ponds and Other Inland Waters, W. E. Meehan, Sturgis and Walton, 1913.